EXILE

EXILE

The Sense of Alienation
in Modern Russian Letters

DAVID PATTERSON

THE UNIVERSITY PRESS OF KENTUCKY

Publication of this book has been assisted
by a grant from Oklahoma State University.

Library of Congress Cataloging-in-Publication Data

Patterson, David, 1948–
    Exile : the sense of alienation in modern Russian letters / David
Patterson.
        p.   cm.
    Includes bibliographical references and index.
    ISBN 0-8131-1888-3 (alk. paper) :
    1. Exiles' writings, Russian—History and criticism.
2. Alienation (Social psychology) in literature. 3. Russian
literature—20th century—History and criticism.   I. Title.
PG3515.P38   1994
891.709'920694—dc20   94-16230

For Luis

Contents

Prefatory Remarks

One of the distinguishing features of Russian thought over the last century and a half is the motif of exile. Indeed, the use of exile as a form of punishment in Russia can be traced back to the Middle Ages, when "undesirables" were sent to the monasteries on the Solovetsky Islands in the White Sea; soon after the Revolution of 1917, these monasteries were turned into the first systematic labor camps. From a political standpoint this motif in Russian letters is addressed in terms of geographic exile, both within and beyond the borders of the motherland; in the social realm it manifests itself as an estrangement of one class from another or an alienation of certain individuals from their own class. But, as is often the case, these external manifestations of exile have their internal implications, and the pursuit of these implications has been a major preoccupation of modern Russian letters. In addition to the authors to be examined here, many others immediately come to mind: the novelists Evgeny Zamyatin, Boris Pasternak, and Andrei Platonov; the poets Anna Akhmatova, Osip Mandelshtam, and Marina Tsvetaeva; the philosophers Nikolai Berdyaev, Sergei Bulgakov, and Semyon Frank.

These authors, as well as many others, demonstrate that for the Russian, exile is not only a social problem or a form of punishment for political crimes. Beyond these categories, it is an expression of that Russian condition that most of all announces the homelessness of the modern human condition in its existential and metaphysical aspects. It is the condition of the castaway that Walker Percy, for example, describes in *The Message in the Bottle* when he says, "In his heart of hearts there is not a moment of his life when the castaway does not know that life on the island, being 'at home' on the island, is something of a charade. At that very moment when he should feel most at home on the island, when needs are satisfied, knowledge arrived at, family raised, business attended to, at that very moment when by every criterion of island at-homeness he should feel most at home, he feels most homeless" (143).

One does not have to look far in Russian letters to find an illustration of what Percy is talking about. Think of Leo Tolstoy's comment on his life when he describes a time of profound personal despair in his *Confession*: "This was happening to me when, from all indications, I should have been considered a completely happy man; this was when I was not yet fifty years old. I had a good, loving, and beloved wife, fine children, and a large estate that was growing and expanding without any effort on my part. More than ever before I was respected by friends and acquaintances, praised by strangers, and I could claim a certain renown. . . . And in such a state of affairs I came to a point where I could not live" (29). What the Russian here says of himself might well be said by much of modern humanity. The problem does not lie in being without a house; rather, it is being without a center that might make life meaningful.

When Tolstoy declares, "I could not live," it is a way of saying, "I did not belong," that a sense of belonging was no longer possible for the man. Edmond Jabès articulates the condition very well in *From the Desert to the Book,* when he writes, "I feel that I exist only outside of any belonging. That non-belonging is my very substance. Maybe I have nothing else to say but that painful contradiction: like everyone else, I aspire to a place, a dwelling-place, while being at the same time unable to accept what offers itself" (29). What is given is never what is needful; the truth is something sought, not something found. The result of the continual miscarriage of this aspiration for a place to dwell, Jabès goes on to show, is that "we all suffer from an absence of identity which we desperately try to fill. It is in this despair that identity really resides" (67). This absence of identity is born of a breach between word and meaning, between the name and the man, between the truth sought in the text and the fact encountered in the world. From out of this rupture Russian letters unfold to ask the question, Who am I? "It is thanks to this rupture," says Jabès, "that the questioning acquires its true freedom and its deep meaning. Truth is always at the end of the questioning, on the other shore, behind the last horizon" (59). And the place where truth resides is precisely that place that we call home.

The question of who I am, therefore, is tied to the question of where I am. Indeed, the first question put to the first man, the question that decides who he is thereafter, is, Where are you? (Genesis 3:9). And his evasive reply of "I hid myself" (Genesis 3:10) is the prelude to his exile from Eden to an alien and alienating place, where he must find some means of dwelling and thus recover himself through some process of redemption. To take on an identity, then, is to take up a residence, to establish a home where one may dwell rather than take to a fortress where we merely survive; it is to have a place and a presence from which one human being may step before the face of another and declare, "Here I am." Since dwelling is tied to such a capacity for response, the linkage to a dwelling place is determined by a linkage between word and meaning, between self and other. Thus the structure of language and the other whom it seeks are tied to the structure of human life. As Jacques Lacan puts it in *The Language of the Self,* "The form alone in which Language is expressed defines subjectivity" (61). And it defines the dwelling place—or the absence of it—for the living subject.

The purpose of this book is to demonstrate through a study of selected Russian texts that the fundamental problem of meaning in human life is a problem of homelessness; that the effort to emerge from exile is an effort to return meaning to the word and thus the self to the other; and that the exile of the word is an exile of human being. The aim, therefore, is not only to make a point about Russian letters but to draw on these Russian texts in an effort to arrive at a deeper understanding of a much larger, more pervasive problem. Indeed, a glance at the many non-Russian works that appear in the bibliography will confirm this point: in addition to more than a hundred Russian and Russian-related sources cited in this study, I have incorporated nearly eighty sources from outside of Russian studies. In an essay that appears in Alexander Solzhenitsyn's collection *From under the Rubble* Igor Shafarevich suggests the kind of connection between Russia and the rest of humanity that we will be seeking here. He writes, "The whole of mankind has now entered a blind alley. It has become clear that a civilization founded on the ideology of 'progress' gives rise to contradictions that that civilization cannot resolve. And it seems to me that the path to Russia's rebirth is the same as the path that will enable man to find a way out of his blind alley, to find salvation from the senseless race of industrial society, the cult of power and the darkness of unbelief" ("Russia" 293–94). Perhaps with the help of these Russians, then, we may find a way out of the blind alley of our own exile.

I have chosen to begin this exploration of exile with an investigation of the superfluous man, because there we have an initial and explicit manifestation of the alienation that creeps into human life. This initial displacement leads to the search for a place that we find in Fyodor Dostoevsky's *Winter Notes on Summer Impressions,* and in both instances we find the word in collision with alien (and often European) forms of discourse. From there I move to a consideration of the connection between external and internal forms of exile in Tolstoy's *The Death of Ivan Il'ich.* (English titles will be used to refer to works in Russian.) Once the interest in an inner life is established, the door is opened to the metaphysical or theological dimensions of exile; moving to the inside of the human being, one cannot deal with the problem of the soul in its exile without dealing with God. "The rupture," Jabès points out, "is primarily due to God who wanted to be absent, who fell silent" (59). After an examination of the theological aspects of Tolstoy's *Resurrection*, therefore, I go next to the theologian Pavel Florensky and then to the religious thinker Lev Shestov. With this metaphysical dimension of exile established, two men of letters who were punished for political crimes are then examined with an eye toward a religious point of reference that they both invoke: Solzhenitsyn, who is an admirer of Pavel Florensky, and Andrei Sinyavsky (also known as Abram Terts). Finally, since the difficulty of emerging from exile is largely a problem of saying the unsayable, I end with an investigation of two poets whose poetry addresses the relation between the exile of the word and the exile of the human being. The first is Joseph Brodsky, a poet heavily influenced by Shestov, and the second is the Russian-Israeli poet Mikhail Gendelev.

Because this study of Russian letters endeavors to make a larger point about the meaning of exile, its intended audience is not confined to Slavicists but includes students and scholars in a variety of areas who are generally concerned with language, life, and meaning. Addressing this more extensive readership, this book undertakes a movement from the realm of exile to the threshold of return, where the encounter with these thinkers becomes an encounter with ourselves. Thus the method I have adopted is existential, proceeding as it does from the premise that (1) in deciding something about these texts, we decide something about ourselves and that (2) our response to these voices entails a response to a voice arising from beyond them. For from the depths of the questions here raised echoes the question that cuts into the depths of each of us: Where are you?

PART ONE
The Word in Collision

1. The Loss of the Word in the Superfluous Man

Modern Russian letters arise through an encounter with Western European letters, and a figure who soon makes his appearance in the wake of that encounter is the superfluous man. He appears, moreover, not just as another literary type but as a paradigm of a person who has lost a point, a place, and a presence in life: the superfluous man is the homeless man. As a literary figure the superfluous man shows up as early as Chatsky in Alexander Griboedov's *Gore ot yma* (*Woe from Wit*, 1824), but he does not acquire his official literary designation until 1850, with the publication of Ivan Turgenev's *Dnevnik lishnego cheloveka* (*Diary of a Superfluous Man*).

The most prevalent shortcoming among existing approaches to this literary figure as he appears in the nineteenth-century Russian novel lies in their almost exclusive focus on the character's reflection of social and political history or on his social-psychological traits. Descriptions of the superfluous man found in the encyclopedias and dictionaries, in fact, encourage such a view. The *Literaturnaya entsiklopediya* (*Literary Encyclopedia*), for example, notes that the primary feature of the superfluous man is his "alienation from his environment" (514), which results from an unsuitable Western European education (518) and the Russian class struggle (530). Echoing this position, the *Kratkaya literaturnaya entsiklopediya* (*Short Literary Encyclopedia*) notes that the superfluous man is distinguished by "an alienation from the official life of Russia," which leads to "profound skepticism, a breakdown between word and deed, and general passivity" (401). And in William Harkins's *Dictionary of Russian Literature* the superfluous man is described as "a hero who is sensitive to social and ethical problems but who fails to act, partly because of personal weakness, partly because of political and social restraints" (373). The accent on the superfluous man's alienation from society is also found in Rufus Mathewson's treatment of the character in *The Positive Hero in Russian Literature* (16), while Frank Seeley translates the social alienation of the man into the social isolation of the Russian intelligentsia. "The drama of the intelligentsia," he claims, "lies in its struggle to break out of its isolation, which means to achieve organic reunion with its own people" (94). And the superfluous man, the argument goes, embodies this drama. Following a similar line, V.V.

Vorovsky sees the main interest in the superfluous man in terms of what the character might reveal about the development of self-awareness in Russian society (103).

Two book-length investigations of the superfluous man as he appears in nineteenth-century Russian literature have come out in English, but neither of them moves very far beyond that mold that regards the character as a figure reflecting a social phenomenon. The more recent volume is *The Superfluous Man in Russian Letters* (1980), by Jesse Clardy and Betty Clardy. These authors argue that "the superfluous man emerged as a result of too much affluence, too much leisure, too much idle time for the children of the privileged class in Tsarist Russian society" (160). The resulting characteristics of the superfluous man, say Clardy and Clardy, are "weariness, boredom, indolence, self-orientation, self-pity, and fear" (19). Like many before them, however, these critics make no distinction between the character in the novel and the man in society. The novel, in their view, is simply a mirror held up to the world rather than a creative voice or network of voices interacting with the world. Hence they make the common error of assuming that what lies behind the superfluous man in the so-called real world is precisely what characterizes the figure in his literary texts and contexts.

The same misconception overshadows the other book on the superfluous man, *Conformity's Children: An Approach to the Superfluous Man in Russian Literature* (1978) by Ellen Chances. Although Chances attempts a new approach by thinking of the superfluous man in terms of conformity, her treatment is still anchored in a social-historical, social-psychological perspective. Her general claim is that "these men are not victors *because* of their nonconformity. What links Eugene Onegin, Pechorin, Rudin, Bazarov, Dostoevsky's underground man, Raskolnikov, Ivan Karamazov, Anna Karenina, Andrey Bolkonsky, many Chekhov protagonists, and certain post-Chekhov is their unconventionality when juxtaposed with society or some order" (19–20). First of all, the implication that superfluity means lack of victory is questionable: the difficulty here surrounds relation, not domination. Second, Chances lumps together nonconformity with society, with God, and with the natural order (whatever that may be) in a manner that would define superfluity with reference to any authority, as if the ways of God and the ways of the world amounted to the same thing. Such an approach might lead us to suppose that any nonconformist in Russian literature is a superfluous man—Dostoevsky's Father Zosima, for instance, who does not see as the world sees or speak as it demands; yet, given his sense of meaning and direction in life, he surely could not be included in the gallery of superfluous men. Further, it must be noted once again that the critic in this case makes no distinction between the man in the novel and the man in the world.

Among the most insightful remarks on the problem of the superfluous man are those found in a work that does not primarily deal with him, in V.N. Voloshinov's *Marksizm i filosofiya yazyka* (*Marxism and the Philosophy of Language*). Voloshinov offers only a few words on the superfluous man, but those few words point the way to a greater understanding of the literary figure and the rupture he represents. Aware of the common explanation of the superfluous man as a person who "arises from the degeneration of the gentry class," Voloshinov notes that this approach "misses the essence of the ideological phenomenon" (21), where the term *ideological phenomenon* refers to the character's word or discourse, to his *slovo*. Voloshinov goes on to state correctly that any treatment of the superfluous man remains incomplete until we bring to light "the specific role of the 'superfluous man' in the artistic structure of the novel. . . . It is clear that the 'superfluous man' did not appear in the novel independently or without some connection with other elements of the novel" (21–22). The other elements of the novel are its dialogical dimensions as they evolved in nineteenth-century Russian literature. These dimensions include the novel's articulation of a multitude of worldviews and ways of speaking, where a given outlook derives its life from its encounter with and response to the outlook of another. And yet with the superfluous man it is not simply a question of one view encountering another. The character's difficulty lies in the failure of encounter; the word is offered but is not received. Thus it dies in the mouth of the one who seeks a place or a presence in the midst of encounter. And when the word expires, so does the soul. In what follows, therefore, we must bear in mind that we are dealing not just with a peculiarity of nineteenth-century Russian literature but with the life of the soul.

Along with the social and political conditions of nineteenth-century Russia, the dialogical discourse of the novel, as it developed during that period, made it possible to introduce a character marked by his contrasting monological discourse. The dialogical element essential to the novel's structure is expressive of the human relation essential to having a place in the world. "Two voices," as Mikhail Bakhtin has said, "is the minimum for life, the minimum for existence" (*Problems* 252). Therefore, it is not just a social or a political condition that situates the superfluous man in a position of exile from life; more than that, underlying that, it is a monological word that fails because it is incapable of evoking a reply that would give it meaning. As a character in the novel, the superfluous man must be understood not only in terms of his relation to society but also in terms of his manner of speaking within the novel. What Bakhtin has said of the novel may be true: "Discourse in the novel is structured on an uninterrupted mutual interaction with the discourse of life" (*Dialogic* 383). But in the case of the superfluous man the discourse that interacts with life proclaims an exile from life. It is a discourse of exile from discourse, a word expressive of the loss of the word. And it has its echo among many of us who long to be part of the clique or the club, a member of the circle or the association, and who are thus void of any other sense of meaning or relation in life. Let us begin, then, with the superfluous man's monological discourse as we consider a few examples of this literary figure.

Monological Discourse

The superfluous man is very often an idle man. He does not eat his bread in the sweat of his brow, and he labors even less in the utterance of his word. Ivan Goncharov's title character Oblomov is a good example. He designates all those who work to support themselves as *others* (79–80), and his words are so idle that he no sooner calls his servant Zakhar than he forgets why he called the man (8). In his monological discourse the superfluous man speaks automatically, out of habit, so that habit becomes "a substitute for happiness," as we read in Alexander Pushkin's *Evgeny Onegin* (65). He talks as he ought to talk, says what a man of his station is supposed to say, and therefore never says anything. "The word becomes one's own," Bakhtin has pointed out, "only when the speaker populates it with his own intention" (*Dialogic* 293); but the superfluous man has no intention, no intensity, through which his word might become his own and thus take on meaning. He has no stake in what he says, and so there is nothing of himself in what he says. Reduced to habit, he is turned over to the vacuity of "a long series of dinners," as it is expressed in *Evgeny Onegin*, condemned "to view life as a ritual / . . . in the wake of the decorous crowd" (202). His speech moves only over the surface of things, keeping to the comfort and complacency of the social script. His word is a mimicking word, and mimicry, which is the opposite of response, is one distinguishing feature of monological discourse.

It is also noted in *Evgeny Onegin*, however, that such a situation is unbearable (202), and so it is. It is unbearable because it is locked into idle talk that has no effect on anything beyond the folded napkin and that is therefore impotent. The sound and the fury of the decisive word are not there, so that the man, like Onegin, grows "utterly cold toward life" (33). Indeed, we find the language of icy impotence associated with other superfluous men. In Turgenev's *Rudin*, for example, Lezhnev asserts that the title character is "as cold as ice" (293), and Rudin himself bemoans his powerlessness to overcome his cold idleness (338). Oblomov too declares that there has never been a flame of his life, either to save him or to destroy him (159), and this has rendered him impotent, the victim of his dressing gown. Thus the monological discourse of the superfluous man is the impotence of the superfluous man; it is void of resolve or decisiveness, empty of anything that might enable the superfluous man to become something other than what he is. "I shall remain the same unfinished creature I have always been," laments Rudin (338). The superfluous man is invariably the same man—or the same non-man—at the end of the novel that he was at its outset, for his discourse is the same, monological discourse. Making no movement, he makes no movement of return that might bring him to a dwelling place.

Because the superfluous man's monological discourse stands outside of any process of becoming, his discourse is confining. Living outside any word that would open up a relation to another human being, he is shut up; imprisoned in his monological word, he is the opposite of the free man. Freedom means being free to become something other than what we are through a capacity for response, a responsibility, toward another. It is the freedom to utter the dialogical word that characterizes the process of hearing and response; it is the freedom to move. Thus the question arises for Oblomov: "What should he do now? Move forward or stay where he was? This Oblomov question was, for him, deeper than Hamlet's question. To go forward meant to suddenly throw the loose dressing gown not only off his shoulders but off his mind, off his soul" (161). Oblomov's question is, in fact, the same as Hamlet's question, which is one that we all confront; "to be or not to be" is the same as "to be free or not to be free." Life or isolation? It will be recalled that in the first part of *Oblomov* the main character has trouble even moving from his bed; Chulkaturin in Turgenev's *Diary of a Superfluous Man* also presents himself in terms of confinement, writing his diary from his sickbed and gazing upon a world whose spring is out of sync with his own winter season. As for those characters who take up some movement through space—Onegin, Rudin, and Mikhail Lermontov's hero Pechorin, for example—their wanderings are merely escape attempts, failed efforts to free themselves from idle chat and loose gowns.

The superfluous man's imprisonment in his monological discourse often leads to a vain effort to become the master of his situation; here, however, he only increases his enslavement and labors himself into no self. Such discourse typically assumes a position of authority or superiority and therefore entails a distance from the other person; but since the superfluous man is unable to act on his word and make it into flesh, his monological discourse invariably reduces him to being a slave to the other. Chulkaturin, for instance, manipulates the Prince in Turgenev's *Diary* into fighting a duel and admits, "I took some pleasure in supposing that I, an obscure man from the country, had forced such an important figure to fight a duel with me" (56). But the Prince would not be manipulated; instead of shooting Chulkaturin, he fires into the air. "I all but wept with resentment and rage," says the superfluous Chulkaturin. "That man had trampled me into the mud once and for all with his generosity" (59). In the case of Golyadkin from Dostoevsky's *Dvoinik* (*The Double*), we see the would-be master as a slave even to his own servant (144), a reversal in relation that also turns up in *Oblomov*, as Nikolai Dobrolyubov has observed (513). Similarly, we find that Pechorin in Lermontov's *Geroi nashego vremeni* (*A Hero of Our Time*) regards even friendship as a master/slave relation (76), and so he strives to subjugate everyone around him to his will and to his word, insisting, "I shall never sell my freedom" (121). But this insistence only increases his enslavement; he loses his freedom and with it himself to the stasis and the impotence of his insistent word. In Turgenev's *Rudin*, to take another example, the character's effort to be a master takes the more subtle form of geniality, "that special geniality which fills people who feel superior to others" (272). Instead of a dialogical relation to others, the superfluous man tries to establish a master/slave relation. But, as we have seen, he ends not by mastering the other but by enslaving himself in the confines of his discourse, which becomes the place of his exile. As a definitive feature of his exile, the superfluous man's loss of the word is thus manifested by his loss of freedom. Left only with himself and his monologue, he is capable of loving only himself; his is a discourse before the mirror.

Narcissistic Discourse

Here we should recall a few details from the tale of Narcissus as related in Ovid's *Metamorphoses*. We discover first of all that Narcissus is "so cold that no youth, no maiden touched his heart." He therefore rejects the love of the nymph Echo and is condemned to "love himself, and not gain the thing he loves." Thus condemned, he approaches a pool one day to quench his thirst only to be overcome by a greater thirst: "He loves an unsubstantial hope and thinks that is substance which is only shadow. He looks in speechless wonder at himself and hangs there motionless." Realizing that he has fallen to loving only himself and only for himself, he cries, "I burn with love of my own self; I both kindle the flames and suffer them. . . . What I desire, I have; the very abundance of my riches beggars me." Finally, pining for himself alone, Narcissus dies of physical and spiritual starvation; he too dies from a loss of the word (see Vinge 7–11). Like all myths, be it noted, the myth of Narcissus addresses a universal aspect of human being, and its application to the superfluous man underscores his universal significance with respect to the problem of exile.

In the tale of Narcissus we can see reflections of what has already been noted about the superfluous man: his coldness, his impotence, his enslavement. But there is more. The inability to offer himself and his love to a woman signifies a loss of the word, since the word is one's own only inasmuch as it is offered to another; my word is the word I give. This inability to offer a woman a word of love is a feature of almost every superfluous man; think of Pechorin and Rudin, for instance. Scholars such as Thomas Rogers, in fact, have noted that the superfluous man is "cowardly and inferior when it comes to women" (30), but, again, these scholars have failed to connect this loss of a capacity for responsive relation with the superfluous man's loss of the word. His inability to offer himself and his love is an inability to speak the vow that would bind him to the woman and free him from himself; thus the intensity that would make the word one's own and lend it meaning is in this instance the intensity of love. If Oblomov, for example, has Olga's love but does not know what to do with it (284), it is because he does not know how to respond to it. And in the *Diary of a Superfluous Man* Chulkaturin confesses, "The unhappiness of people who are shy—shy out of egoism—lies precisely in the fact that even though they have eyes which stare wide open, they either see nothing or see everything in a false light, as if they were looking through tinted glasses. Their observations, indeed their very thoughts, get in their way with every step they take" (35). Their observations, like their discourse, paralyze them because they are trapped in the confines of self-observation. Hence, as with Narcissus, the language of the superfluous man is one that clings to the self and refuses the other, it is a language couched in the dative case of "to me" and "for me." The superfluous man's failure to gain himself by offering himself lies in the narcissistic aspect of his discourse, in the word spoken of, by, and for himself alone.

The superfluous man's love, then, is self-love, the love of Narcissus; it is the paralyzed love of what is merely a shadow, a self-infatuation beggared by its own abundance. The word spoken is uttered only to the mirror, for the sake of vain self-justification. "I suddenly became engrossed in the contemplation of my own face," notes Chulkaturin (37). It is not surprising, then, to find that the superfluous man's preoccupation with himself often takes the form of a diary or a first-person account, as in the case of Lermontov's character Pechorin; and in the *Diary of a Superfluous Man* Chulkaturin begins by saying, "I'll just relate to myself the story of my life," since "to sit around and do nothing is boring; to read is sheer idleness" (11). In these instances the discourse itself is the mirror into which the superfluous man gazes and that holds him captive. In Pechorin's case the narcissistic discourse for himself underscores his confession that "I have loved myself for myself, for my own pleasure" (129). Rudin is also characterized as a man who is entrenched in his self-love (247), but perhaps the most pitiful expression of this narcissism is found in Goncharov's *Oblomov*; while Tarant'ev and other guests were visiting him, Oblomov "did not notice what was being done or listen to what was being said. He simply gazed at his small, white hands and caressed them with love" (38). The loss of the word here announces itself in just such a gazing upon and caressing of oneself. Gazing upon himself, the superfluous man loses his word to the gaze; the sign loses its referent, signifying only itself and therefore signifying nothing.

As in the case of Narcissus, the superfluous man's self-love becomes self-alienation; the word spoken only to the self and for the self becomes the word spoken against the self. Why? Because it meets with no reply other than its own echo. In his narcissism, as in all narcissism, he loves himself but cannot gain the thing he loves, and this frustration results in a division of the self. The superfluous man's narcissistic discourse is what lies behind the "schism in the soul" (Seeley 96) and the "deep inner conflict" (Budanova 111) that the critics often emphasize in their comments on this figure. Quite frequently the superfluous man's inner division takes the form of a duel; here, as ever, violence denotes the collapse of the word and the appearance of the distance that cuts one person off from another, Onegin, Pechorin, and Chulkaturin all fight duels. In *The Double* Dostoevsky gives this division graphic expression through the two Golyadkins. To be sure, in most instances the superfluous man has his alter ego with whom his life and his discourse are at odds; Onegin has his Lensky, Rudin his Lezhnev, and Chulkaturin his Biz'menkov, who, significantly, acts as the Prince's second in their duel.

Upon a closer examination we find Pechorin asserting, "For a long time I have been living not by the heart but by the head" (148); here he refers to two voices, two views, in conflict within him, echoing his earlier statement that his "whole life has been but a chain of sad and fruitless contradictions to the heart and to reason" (74). It will also be noted that the frustration of the discourse before the mirror often leads to contempt for what is in the mirror; self-love ends in self-hatred. Such self-contempt is prominent in Chulkaturin and Oblomov, and in each case it is rooted in a contempt for one's own discourse, or rather in the failure of that discourse: the awkward speech, the idle talk, the lies told, the promises unkept—all the aspects of a word spoken only for the sake of the self and ultimately lost to the self.

Because narcissistic language begins with self-love and ends in self-contempt, it starts with an assertion of independence unto oneself and results in an isolation from oneself. Golyadkin's insistence in *The Double* that he is his "own man" (115) indicates his exclusion from the company of men. One will also recall the awkward manner in which Chulkaturin's so-called friends invariably receive him: "They would become very uneasy; the way they would smile when they came up to me was not entirely natural; they would not look me in the eye . . . but would rather look mainly at my cheeks . . . and then immediately step aside and just stand there for a while without moving" (22). Here the eyes of the other become the mirror through which the self gazes upon itself. And so along with the superfluous man's confinement in his discourse we have his exile in his discourse, the isolation of Narcissus at the pool; in his refusal to offer his word to the other, he is left to the forlornness of his narcissistic word. It must be pointed out, however, that the narcissistic word in this case is not a word of his own making. Rather, it is a word that he has borrowed from a ready-made discourse and that he allows to speak for him. He receives the word of the crowd, but he instills it with no intention or intensity, with no responsibility, of his own. Instead, he follows a script by which he may gain the recognition of others only to lose his word and with it himself to the script. This brings us to a third point in our consideration of the loss of the word in the superfluous man.

Discourse Spoken Rather than Speaking

The superfluous man's loss of the dialogical word isolates him from himself as well as from others, and the manifestation of that loss often takes the form of the written word; this is one instance of discourse spoken rather than speaking. Unable to endure the dangers and the vulnerability of generating a speaking presence before the face of another, the superfluous man prefers the safe confines of the imprint on the page. The written word provides him with a distance to the point of absence, so that he need not place himself in a position of vulnerability, especially in the presence of women. The ink and paper speak for him; hence he does not speak but is spoken. Examples of the importance of the written word to the superfluous man are found at every turn; Rogers has already cited the pursuit of writing on the part of Onegin, Rudin, and Oblomov (30). To his remarks it should be added that Onegin and Rudin are never so open with the women in their lives as in the letters they write to them; indeed, in these letters they come as close as they ever do to offering their word, their confession, to another. Nevertheless, it is the letter that the woman has before her, not the man; once the scrawl is on the page, his living voice is superfluous. Along with these cases we might also mention Golyadkin's lament over the fact that the Double has imposed on him the need to put everything into writing (175–76). And then, of course, we have the diaries of Pechorin and Chulkaturin. As is often the case with confession writers, the superfluous man here writes his confession in order to avoid confessing, that is, to avoid facing another.

In addition to the superfluous man's need for the written word, there is his preoccupation with the word of the other, so that he fashions his speech according to his anticipation of how it will be received. Here too one discovers a link between the loss of the word and the loss of self; forever anticipating the judgment that may issue from the other, the superfluous man is never here but is scattered "out there," torn from himself in an assessment of himself from the standpoint of the judgmental eye of the other. Thus we see another sense in which his discourse is spoken rather than speaking; it is programmed by the other's anticipated reaction, shaped by the fear of judgment. One finds it, for example, in Golyadkin's repetition of phrases such as "so they say" and "as the saying goes" in his effort to become part of a social circle that is always beyond his reach (119, 120, 160, 178). In Chulkaturin too we observe a man whose superfluous discourse is geared to the discourse of the other. "I compared myself to others," he writes, "and recalled the slightest glances, the words people had spoken, people whom I wanted to impress" (20). Even as he is about to fight the duel with the Prince, Chulkaturin is obsessed with how the other might view him. "Oh, God!" he thinks. "If only this sneering gentleman does not take my nervousness for timidity!" (58). It may be noted that Chulkaturin's ultimate failure to gain the recognition of the other comes out in the Prince's mutilation of his name, as he calls him "Shtukaturin" instead of Chulkaturin (55). The self that is foundering on the loss of the word here loses itself in the loss of the name.

Related to the superfluous man's fixation on the other's perception of him is his mimicry of the other's word. This too makes his discourse spoken rather than speaking, a discourse of echo and imitation. Pechorin, for instance, declares that "the world has warped" his soul (38), and in a remark to Princess Mary he explains why: "Everyone has seen in my face signs of evil characteristics that were not there; but they were expected to be there, so they were born" (104). Although this statement is part of Pechorin's manipulation of Princess Mary, it also contains a revealing element: Pechorin is incapable of being anything except what others make of him, either in a positive or in a negative sense; even in his rebellion, he remains in the power of the social code and is determined by it. In his own way, Rudin is also fashioned from borrowed expressions and mimicked phrases. We find out from Lezhnev, for example, that despite Rudin's eloquence and memorable bits of wisdom, the words were never his own but were taken from Pokrovsky (297). Hence it is not Rudin who speaks but another; Rudin's discourse—and therefore Rudin himself—is spoken rather than speaking. In the end we hear his mournful cry, one that indeed characterizes the superfluous man: "The phrase ruined me, ate into me, until I could not free myself from it" (365). The phrase ruined him because it was not of his own making and had nothing of his own intensity about it. As it ate into him, he starved from his attachment to it, just as Narcissus starved at the side of the pool.

"Thus," to borrow an insight from Jacques Lacan, "the subject, too, if he can appear to be the slave of language is all the more so of a discourse in the universal movement in which his place is already inscribed at birth, if only by virtue of his proper name" (*Écrits* 148). Applying Lacan's insight to the superfluous man, we are able to extend further the context of our concern with this figure from the confines of Russian literature to a general concern for modern man. In the discourse that is spoken rather than speaking the superfluous man seeks a reflection of himself, of his name, in the word of the other. But whatever he finds, it is only an image, only a shadow, empty and void; whatever the word he may borrow, a word not one's own is a word that empties the self of itself. This is what makes the discourse of the superfluous man an empty discourse. There is nothing of himself in his utterance; at best, there is merely an echo of himself in the word he has borrowed. The superfluous discourse, the discourse of the loss of the word, is a hollow discourse, and the superfluous man is a hollow man. He seeks no truth that might give his word substance and depth, for that would mean taking up a dialogical response to the other in place of his monological mimicry of the other; it would mean letting go of the handrails of fixed phrases and ready answers that imprison him; it would mean turning away from the mirror. And that he cannot do.

The void that haunts the superfluous man's discourse comes out in a variety of ways. We see it, for instance, in the superfluous man's inability to offer anything but emptiness to the other; thus Lermontov's hero Pechorin asserts, "My love has brought happiness to no one because I have never sacrificed anything for those whom I have loved" (129)—which is to say, I have never offered myself in my word, never been one with my word, and so I have no self, no word. In *The Double* we find that Golyadkin has trouble speaking because he has nothing to say (114); although he identifies himself as a man who wears no masks and plays no games (124), his words demonstrate that he does just what he denies. Indeed, the mask is the opposite of the face from which the word issues; the mask that eclipses the face eclipses the word. "The face speaks," as Emmanuel Levinas has pointed out. "It speaks, it is in this that it renders possible and begins all discourse" (*Ethics* 87–88). Speaking through the mask, the superfluous man adds nothing to the discourse of the other; he is but an echo chamber, a hollowness, where the word is reduced to a sound void of sense. Thus each of these superfluous men we have considered, without exception, is left only with his lamentation. In that lamentation we discover not only the superfluous man's emptiness but something more: his inability to offer or receive, to summon or respond, in a stepping before the countenance. This important point brings us to the fourth indication of the loss of the word in the superfluous man.

Discourse Void of Summons and Response

We began this chapter with a few remarks on the superfluous man's idleness and idle talk; having moved from there to his emptiness and empty word, let us now consider the sense in which the superfluous man is mute and paralyzed. For these are the first signs of a discourse void of summons and response. Nor are they simply the signs that distinguish the superfluous man; rather they are symptoms that might render any man superfluous and therefore homeless.

The superfluous man is paralyzed in that he cannot move beyond himself; as long as he remains in the stasis of what he is, he remains paralyzed. And because he cannot speak for himself, he is mute. Recall, for example, Chulkaturin's comment that between his thoughts and his feelings and "the expression of those thoughts and feelings—there has always been some senseless, incomprehensible, and unsurmountable obstacle" (20). And: "Since I am a superfluous man who is locked up inside himself, I am terrified of expressing my thoughts, especially when I know beforehand that they will come out all wrong. Sometimes it even seems strange to me that people can speak so simply, so freely" (22). Here the superfluous man's loss of the word and the immobility into which it casts him are quite clearly stated. His paralysis and muteness go together because in order to move, he must be able to speak and free himself from the straitjacket of being spoken. Indeed, the lines just cited from Turgenev's *Diary of a Superfluous Man* prefigure the subsequent events surrounding the character, as soon as the Prince complicates Chulkaturin's attempt to win Liza, the superfluous man falls into the rigidity of "a stubborn silence" and, he says, "sometimes for days on end I would never utter a sound" (44). In *The Double* Golyadkin's inability to speak and thus move into a relation with the other is described precisely as a paralysis (133–34) and as a muteness (226). Further, in his comments on Oblomov, Dobrolyubov cites the character's "complete inertness resulting from his apathy toward everything that happened in the world" as his distinguishing feature (508). Freely translated, this is an expression of the superfluous man's paralysis resulting from that loss of the word that is revealed through an utter lack of response to the discourse of the other.

The failure to act is part of the failure to respond, and this is what lies behind the breakdown between word and deed so often mentioned in regard to the superfluous man. It will be recalled, for example, that the *Kratkaya literaturnaya entsiklopediya* emphasizes this gap between word and deed as a fundamental characteristic of the superfluous man (401); and in an article on the superfluous man B. Brusov reminds us that Nikolai Chernyshevsky and Dobrolyubov viewed this collapse as the chief aspect of the character (110). The rift between word and deed arises because the superfluous word is the lost word, the word cut off from any act that might engender its meaning. It is neither responsive nor calls for a response; as we have seen, it is monological, narcissistic, and imitative, and therefore it is enslaving, isolating, and paralyzing. Looking among the superfluous men before us, we may note Golyadkin's insistence that he is a "man of action" (116) opposite the fact that he never acts on anything he says. The most explicit example of the word/deed breakdown is found in Rudin. There we hear his friend Lezhnev predicting that

"Rudin's words will remain only words and will never become deeds" (294); in the end Rudin himself cries out in despair, "Words, all words! There were never any deeds!" (364). The superfluous man's word is an empty word because there is no deed, no active response or responsive action, to instill it with substance. And to the extent that he brings no substance to his discourse, he beckons no response to it.

Alexandre Bourmeyster uses the term *belle âme* to describe the superfluous man (263), and it will prove helpful to examine that term at this point, especially if we consider it in the light of Anthony Wilden's remarks on the *belle âme* in his commentary on Lacan's *The Language of the Self*. "The *belle âme*," says Wilden,

is a consciousness which judges others but which refuses action. In his vanity, the *belle âme* values his ineffective discourse above the facts of the world and expects it to be taken as the highest reality. . . . Thus the *belle âme* refuses the world and attains, not being, but nonbeing, 'an empty nothingness.' . . . But he fears the loss of the very void he discovers he is. His relationship to being-in-the-world and to being-with-others can very aptly be characterized as the 'splitting of the ego.' . . . The *belle âme* fears the other because he wants so much to be the other, but being the other means losing himself. The whole paradox of identification is involved: seeking to be identical with the other . . . is to lose one's own identity. [289–90]

This search for identity is a search for a place where the man may emerge from his exile. To be in exile is, among other things, to be where one does not want to be and hence to be who one does not want to be; and the longing to assume a different position here manifests itself as a longing for another identity *in order to be oneself*. There lies the paradox of identity and the predicament of its loss through the loss of the word, not only for the superfluous man but for anyone.

Viewing the superfluous man as a *belle âme*, we observe first of all that the superfluous man's judgment of others comes in an evasion of response to others. What some critics have regarded as his "moral superiority" (see, for example Chances 18 and Rogers 49) turns out to be a lack of response capability; the distance implied by "superiority" consists of that absence of self that accompanies the loss of the word. The superfluous man's discourse is ineffective because, again, it neither answers nor calls. That he expects his discourse to be taken as the highest reality is especially well illustrated in the language of Chulkaturin, Golyadkin, and Rudin at their social gatherings; commenting on the dance in the *Diary of a Superfluous Man*, for instance, Chulkaturin notes, "I suddenly felt remarkably malicious, and I remember taking an unusual delight in this new sensation; it even produced in me a certain respect for myself" (50). Here we see a judgmental, monological discourse void of any calling out or calling forth. Insofar as the superfluous man mimics the other and is concerned with the other's opinion of him, his discourse bears a longing for identification with the other rather than a response to the other. As Wilden points out, this is where the splitting of the ego arises in the paradox of identification; recall, for example, the divided self and the "schism in the soul" underscored by Seeley (96). Indeed, Wilden's rendition of the *belle âme* provides us with a thumbnail sketch of the superfluous man's discourse as one that announces the loss of the word; it suggests just how that discourse may be viewed as monological, narcissistic, spoken rather than speaking, and void of summons or response.

Wilden, however, offers us one more point to consider with respect to this last aspect of the loss of the word in the superfluous man; he helps us to see that the man whose discourse is void of summons and response is himself a void, "an empty nothingness." In the opening remarks to this essay reference was made to the dialogical structure of the novel and to the superfluous man's place within that structure; arriving now at the nothingness of the superfluous man, we come full circle, back to his place within novelistic discourse. In its dialogical dimensions the discourse of the novel consists of a process of speaking and hearing; as such, the novel's discourse serves as a backdrop for defining the absence of this process in the superfluous man. Further, because the novel is dialogical, a dialogical concept of truth lies at its foundation. In the words of Bakhtin, truth in the novel "is not born nor is it to be found in the head of an individual person, it is born *between people* collectively searching for truth, in the process of their dialogic interaction" (*Problems* 110). Dialogical interaction, again, consists of summons and response, but the superfluous man's discourse, as a discourse of the loss of the word, is outside of that interaction and is therefore outside of truth, outside of meaning, in the realm of "an empty nothingness." To be sure, Chulkaturin arrives at this point as he nears the end of his diary. "I know these memories are unhappy and insignificant," he writes, "but they are all I have. Emptiness, terrible emptiness!" (76). What is the terrible emptiness he invokes? It is the emptiness of the soul in its loss of the word.

There is more to the nothingness of the superfluous man, however, than the isolation of his discourse from the realm of truth. To get at that "more" we may lend an ear once again to Bakhtin. "Every dialogue," he argues, "proceeds as though against the background of a Third who is invisibly present, standing above all the participants in the dialogue. . . .

The Third referred to here has nothing to do with mysticism or metaphysics . . . but is a constitutive feature of the whole expression" (*Estetika* 306). In *The Language of the Self* Lacan entertains a similar notion
by saying, "The Other with a big 'O' is the scene of the Word insofar as
the scene of the Word is always in third position between two subjects.
This is only in order to introduce the dimension of Truth" (269). Signifying the realm of truth, the Third is present in the process of speaking
and hearing, when that process is undertaken not in manipulation or
negotiation but in the name of the truth; indeed, this Third may be identified with Truth, with the holy or sacred Word that decides the truth of
all words. But since the superfluous man's discourse is a discourse
of the lost word, it has no contact with the truth; the sacred is absent
from his relation to the other. When the sacred is thus lost, so is the
word—so is the man. Ultimately, then, the superfluous man's discourse
is itself superfluous because it is void of anything sacred; his condition
of exile is precisely an exile from what is holy, an exile from the truth.
The more we sense the presence of the holy in the discourse of the novel,
the more we feel its absence from the superfluous discourse. In the voice
of the superfluous man, therefore, there is a double voicing, especially
when the novel, such as Turgenev's *Diary of a Superfluous Man*, is written in the first person. The novel includes an authorial stance indicative
of an interest in the truth in its address to the reader, yet the voice that
arises from the page affirms the truth as that which is absent. Thus the
voice speaks from the core of a rupture.

    As for the question of who the Third or the Holy One might be, a
variety of answers may be offered: the Third is Spirit, Word, God, Father, and the like. All such notions are conspicuous by their absence
from the discourse of the superfluous man; from Onegin to Oblomov,
no superfluous man has a relation to God, for example, and this is what
places figures such as Tolstoy's Levin and Dostoevsky's Ivan Karamazov outside the categories of superfluity. A good illustration of the superfluous man's loss of a relation to the truth of the sacred may be found
in Golyadkin. Near the end of *The Double* he seeks a hearing with His
Excellency, whom he regards as his one source of salvation and whom
he looks upon as a father (213), but he meets only with silence. Russian
literature does, however, offer us a character in whom we find a movement beyond superfluity and into the realm of truth; it is Laevsky in An-
ton Chekhov's *Duel*. Although he begins under the label of "superfluous man" (354, 374), in the end Laevsky is no longer a superfluous man,
for his discourse becomes dialogical, responsive, searching; in short, he
establishes a relation to the realm of truth, which is a realm opposed to

exile. Thus we read his closing thoughts: "In their search for truth people take two steps forward and one step backward. Suffering, error, and weariness of life pull them back, but the thirst for truth and a resolute will push them forward. And who knows? Perhaps one day they will reach the real truth" (455). The pulsating movement that takes us toward the truth? It is the movement of summons and response.

It may be that not all of these indications of the loss of the word in the superfluous man will apply to all superfluous men all the time. But we have defined a tendency, a model, by which the character may be recognized in his condition of exile as it is manifested through a loss of the word. By now we should have some grasp of the elements that go into the superfluous man's loss of the word; by now we should be able to see that this loss is articulated through a discourse and not simply through a social or political environment that might make the man superfluous. Before we leave the subject, however, it must be pointed out that, allowing room for the exception, each aspect of the loss of the word in the superfluous man is related to all the others. The breakdown between word and deed is linked to the superfluous man's lack of freedom; his self-love is connected to his paralysis; the absence of a relation to the holy characterizes his isolation and therefore his own absence. It should also be emphasized once more that the elements that make the character's discourse expressive of a loss of the word receive their definition from their counterposition to the discourse of the novel. While the character neither responds nor summons response, the novel itself does both; while the character is isolated, paralyzed, and seeks no truth, the novel is open-ended, evolving, and struggling to give voice to a truth.

Although the superfluous man may summon no dialogical response, the novel in which he appears does just that. Who is summoned? We are. Or better: I am. The discourse of the novel and, within it, the discourse of the superfluous man call my own discourse into question: suddenly the problem of exile confronted in the superfluous man becomes my problem. If I do not respond to the word I encounter, if I do not answer for myself and with my self, then I too fall prey to a loss of the word. For me, the superfluous man's historical situation is not confined to the past, and approaching the character in strictly social and historical terms constitutes a flight from responsibility; for I am contemporary with the word as it is offered to me through the novel. I cannot put the voice behind me because it is ever before me, calling upon me to answer and calling into question my responsibility, my response capability, by which I seek the word that decides who I am and where I am. This is where the real collisions with the word take place.

2. The Collision of Discourse: Dostoevsky's *Winter Notes*

According to the *Literaturnaya entsiklopediya,* the alienation from self and society that distinguishes the superfluous man arises to a large extent from his Western European education (578). If the "terrible emptiness" suffered by a Chulkaturin is tied to ideas distinguishing Western European education, it is because those ideas repudiate the presence of any higher relation at work in human relation, as discussed in the previous chapter. This conflict between the Russian and the European education, moreover, has a linkage with the development of the dispute between the Westernizers and the Slavophiles. For the Russian, this conflict entails more than the issue of adopting one ideological position over another. Beyond the political question there unfolds a desperate spiritual struggle for identity, one that, for many thinkers of the period, harbors implications for the very salvation of the soul. Here too, then, what concerns the Russians has broader implications for all of humanity. In the collision of one discourse with another one finds the soul endeavoring to generate a presence and thus a word of its own, grounded, as Bakhtin puts it, "in the loving consciousness of another (person, God)" (*Estetika* 98). The conflict between Russia and Europe is a conflict between word and alien word that has life-and-death ramifications for any human being in his or her relation both to humanity and to a higher being. As the alien and alienating discourse invades the familiar, a condition of exile creeps into the homeland. French phrases and German ideas fill the mouths and empty the souls of the Russian intelligentsia; torn from his word, the man is torn from himself. Yet it is in the midst of this absence that issues of substance come to bear. Taking up this conflict, Dostoevsky takes up that text that, says Joseph Frank, has "been sadly neglected by students of his work" (247): it is *Zimnie zapiski o letnikh vpetchatleniyakh (Winter Notes on Summer Impressions).*

About three years after his return from exile, on 7 June 1862, Dostoevsky left Petersburg on his first excursion to Europe, to the "land of holy wonders," as he ironically terms it (ironically, because he lifts the phrase from the poem "Mechta," written in 1834 by Aleksy Khomyakov in a lament over the death of the West). During the next ten weeks he visited a number of cities, including Berlin, Dresden, Paris, London, Geneva, Florence, and Vienna. He recorded his impressions of Europe, particularly those of Paris and London, and they first appeared as *Winter Notes on Summer Impressions* in the February 1863 issue of *Vremya*, the journal published by his brother Mikhail and edited by himself. Although he indicated to his younger brother Andrey that his principal motive for making the trip was to see some specialists about his epilepsy, the roulette tables at Wiesbaden may also have been a lure. In fact, Dostoevsky lost a substantial sum in that city, where he went after spending only a day in Berlin. But, judging from his *Winter Notes*, the most important reason for Dostoevsky's firsthand encounter with European culture was to engage those ideas that, he believed, were destroying the Russian soul, ideas that produced such despairing and divided figures as the underground man and Ivan Karamazov. That place to which a number of Russian intellectuals had been exiled turns out to be the very origin of ideas that create a condition of exile in the heart of Russia itself. To be sure, Frank has pointed out that in *Winter Notes* "Dostoevsky seizes the occasion to explore the whole tangled history of the relationship between educated Russians and European culture. . . . *Winter Notes on Summer Impressions* may thus be viewed as a prelude, or better, as a preliminary draft of *Notes from Underground*" (233).

Bringing us "right to the threshold of his great creative period" (Frank 247), Dostoevsky's *Winter Notes* opens up the conflict of ideas that goes into the making of his subsequent art. Planted in this short work are the seeds of many of the upheavals that characterize the dialogue of ideas in his great novels. Examples include Raskolnikov's notion of the Napoleonic crime in *Crime and Punishment*; Myshkin's implicit rejection of egoism and ambition in *The Idiot*; the critique of revolutionary ruthlessness and conservative stupidity in *The Possessed*; and the theme of self-sacrifice and brotherhood in *The Brothers Karamazov*. The polyphony of voices in interaction with each other, which is a stylistic feature of *Winter Notes*, is also a distinctive feature of the subsequent major works. In this chapter we shall examine that conflict and the interplay of ideas that engenders it. Although the scene of the conflict may be the streets of London and Paris, the collisions that shape it transpire in the soul of the author himself. And he introduces them into the soul of his reader, making his reader into one for whom the world has been made strange. As Frank has noted, the "inverted irony" that runs through the text "turns back on the writer as a means of turning *against* an imagined judge and critic in the person of the reader" (236). Hence the elements of exile at work in *Winter Notes* are more spiritual than geographical, and, as we shall see, they come with implications for anyone who is an heir to the European outlook. Let us proceed, then, to explore the conflict of discourse in the encounter with the alien other, its implications for a relation of brotherhood between the self and the other, and its revelations concerning the nature of the European exile.

The Alien Other

The incongruity of the alien manifests itself in *Winter Notes*, first of all, through an incongruity of discourse within the text itself. Gary Saul Morson has observed in *The Boundaries of Genre*, for instance, that "after three generally playful sketches, there occurs a revelation of such horror and significance that it may be seen to parody and discredit retrospectively the earlier playfulness and parody" (22). And so, says Morson, "the flaneur turns prophet" (25); Dostoevsky assumes an authorial stance that is alien to itself. This stance, which opposes itself to itself, comes out very early in *Winter Notes*, when, for example, he declares, "I would not lie by any means, not even as a traveler. Yet if I begin to depict and describe even a single panorama, then I am bound to lie, not because I am a traveler but simply because in my circumstances it is impossible not to lie" (2). Thus Dostoevsky sets out to engage discourse with discourse by making the truth "perceptible," to borrow a phrase from Lacan, "under the inverted sign of the lie" (*Language* 269). The traveler here is not a tourist, not a curiosity seeker; rather, he seeks a truth from which the lie has exiled him. Assuming the position of an exile who undertakes a penetration of exile, he rejects the role of traveler and all those trappings that condition and thereby occlude the perception of the traveler. Indeed, in the capacity of tourist the traveler is the opposite of the exile. Journeying with the *Reichard Guide* in hand (see *Winter Notes* 5), the text of what the tourist might perceive precedes him and keeps him at a safe distance from any reality that he may encounter. Dostoevsky, however, closes that gap to create a place where word may meet with alien word. Insisting on his own discourse of encounter instead of that which is spoken for him in the *Reichard Guide*, he all but boasts, "I was in London and yet did not see St. Paul's. It's true, I didn't. I did not see St. Paul's Cathedral. There is a difference, of course, between Peter and Paul, but, all the same, it was rather improper for a traveler" (5). It is as an exile that Dostoevsky would confront the otherness that has made him into an exile.

Such an approach collapses the distance not only between the real and the contrived but also between the reader and the text. In *Winter*

Notes, Frank points out, Dostoevsky maintains an "extremely close 'dialogical' relation with the reader ('my friends'), who becomes an implicit and invoked presence *within* the text and is constantly appealed to as an interlocutor" (235–36). In this way Dostoevsky sets up the reader for an encounter with herself or himself as an alien other within the text. Yet, since he begins by addressing the truth under the inverted sign of the lie, he initiates this alienation by presuming a certain familiarity. "Who," he asks, "among all of us Russians (that is, those who at least read the journals) does not know Europe twice as well as he knows Russia? I put 'twice' here out of courtesy, but ten times is more accurate" (1). Who is the alien other? It is precisely the Russian himself, that is, the Russian who reads the journals that instill him with the alien, European word; indeed, it is anyone who is subject to the materialistic ideas that come out of Europe. Opposing discourse to discourse, Dostoevsky opposes truth to lie by raising a question where there is normally a ready answer. The formulas with which his question comes into conflict emerge, for instance, when he writes, "There is no native soil, no people; nationality is merely a system of taxation; the soul is a *tabula rasa,* a piece of wax from which the real man can be immediately molded, the general, universal man, the homunculus—you need only apply the fruits of European civilization and read two or three books. And how serene, how majestically serene we are, since we doubt nothing and have solved and signed everything" (21). But his declarative statements are often interrogative and his interrogative often declarative. This reversal is, of course, indicative of the rupture couched in the question. "To question," as Edmond Jabès has said, "means to break; it means to set up an *inside* and an *outside*" (71). The question, therefore, is gauged to set up a condition of opposition and alienation that defines the state of exile. Here the reader who is inside the text is outside himself or herself. Drawing the reader into a discourse that divides itself against itself, Dostoevsky exacerbates the division that inheres in exile by placing himself and his reader both inside and outside that group he addresses as "my friends," once again making the familiar into a form of estrangement. After all, he too reads the journals.

Yet it is as an exile, in the way that Moses was an exile, that he surveys the European vista, as "a kind of overall panorama. The entire 'land of holy wonders' will unfold before me all at once, from a bird's-eye view, like the Promised Land viewed from the perspective of a mountain top" (2). Already the flaneur, to use Morson's word, is beginning to turn prophet, and this allusion to Moses is more revealing than one might suppose at first glance. For according to the *Midrash Rab-*

bah, "Moses said to God: 'Master of the Universe, the bones of Joseph are entering the Land, and am I not to enter the Land?' The Holy One, blessed be He, answered him: 'He who acknowledged his native land is to be buried in that land but he who did not acknowledge his native land does not merit to be buried in his land' " (37). When Moses fled Egypt as a murderer and went to Midian, he tried to pass himself off as an Egyptian (see Exodus 2:19); but Joseph never hid the fact that he was a Hebrew. As the one who denied his origins, Moses remained the one in exile. To be sure, the *Midrash on Psalms* tells us that the Israelites were returned from exile for four reasons: "they did not change their names; they did not change their language; they did not reveal their secrets; and they were not wanton" (217). In short, they remained who they were despite where they were. The difficulty facing the Russian is similar—the change of language into French, for example, among the upper class— but it also has its important differences. The Russian is unable to remain who he is precisely in the midst of his homeland, a point that Dostoevsky makes by writing, " 'Lord, what kind of Russians are we?' flashed through my mind from time to time while I was on the train. 'Are we in fact really Russians? Why does Europe create such a powerful, magical, alluring impression on us?' " (*Winter Notes* 8). And so Dostoevsky proceeds through the question to return his reader to the homeland, to return from an exile *within* the homeland, by taking the reader *outside* that land and into the soul. The place that he views from the mountain top, then, is not just the land of holy wonders; it is Holy Russia herself.

Jabès maintains that "we have no other reality than the reality books confer upon us" (74); to live in a world of books is to live in a world of voices that shape our own voice. Thus it is through a selective commentary on the book—that is, on Russian literature—that Dostoevsky traces what he ironically calls "the gradual and beneficial influence of Europe on our fatherland" (*Winter Notes* 16). Among those Russian authors whose names appear in *Winter Notes* are Alexander Pushkin, Peter Chaadaev, Vissarion Belinsky, Nikolai Nekrasov, Ivan Turgenev, Mikhail Saltykov-Shchedrin, and others who have a place in the dispute between the Westernizers and the Slavophiles. But the European discourse, which is alien to the Russian soul even when cast in the Cyrillic alphabet, alienates the Russian reader who encounters that discourse and who then attempts to imitate it through books. In *Winter Notes* and elsewhere Dostoevsky objects to the reality conferred upon the Russian by the European book as unreal because it renders the Russian soul unreal to itself. Recall, for instance, the lines that appear near the end of *Zapiski iz podpol'ya* (*Notes from Underground*), words that come from the mouth of a character who has been made alien to himself by his conflict with the European discourse couched in rationality and social science. "Leave us to ourselves," he says, "without a book, and immediately we become confused and lose our way—we shall not know where to turn, what to cling to, what to love and hate, what to respect and despise. We even feel that to be men is too heavy a burden—men with real bodies and blood of our own; we are ashamed of this, we consider it a disgrace, and, out of habit, we long to be some sort of unprecedented 'universal men' " (178–79). This text does not simply follow soon after *Winter Notes*; it inhabits those notes like a word held back, in conflict with the words that appear in black and white. The conflict of discourse, therefore, includes an outlook that goes beyond the confines of what is said; the tension established in the opening chapters of *Winter Notes* comes out in a conflict between the said and the unsaid, between the self and itself.

The following passage from *Winter Notes* provides a good illustration of this: "Oh, good heavens, do not think, my friends, that I am suddenly setting out to argue that civilization is not progress, but, on the contrary, in recent times in Europe it has stood over all progress with the whip and with prison! Do not think that I am about to demonstrate that among us civilization and the laws of true, normal development are barbarically mixed, to demonstrate that civilization has long since been condemned in the West itself and that there only the property owner stands up for it in order to save himself some money" (23). Here one is reminded of the author's warning, "I am bound to lie" (2). For what is stated here is a truth placed under the inverted sign of the lie, and in this way the conflict of discourse is both posited and sustained. In these lines the truth reverberates in the hollowness of the lie suggested by such terms as "whip," "prison," and "barbarically mixed." Those terms derive their power to alienate from the conflict between the passage just cited and passages that precede them, such as: "We put on silk stockings and wigs, hung little swords on ourselves—and behold, we were Europeans. Not only was there nothing disturbing in all this, but it was even pleasant" (18). And: "So what if not everything around us now is still not very beautiful; we ourselves are so wonderful, so civilized, so European that even the people are ready to vomit from looking at us. The people now regard us as complete foreigners; they do not understand a single word, a single book, a single thought of ours—but, as you will, that is progress" (21). One is reminded of Kierkegaard's remark in *The Sickness unto Death* that the immediate man "recognizes himself only by his dress, . . . he recognizes that he has a self only by externals. There is no more ludicrous confusion, for a self is just infinitely different from externals" (187). Making use of the ludicrous, Dostoevsky makes visible to the Russians the exiles they have become by holding up to them the mirror of their native people from whom they are isolated. As the people look at the intellectuals, they see themselves, not as debonair Europeans but as the phonies whose image makes the people vomit. Thus the accent on the outside, on clothing and image, is calculated to engage readers in a consideration of what may inhabit their inside; the question of what they signify in their European dress leads them to the question of their significance.

Invoking the people who regurgitate their inside in the face of those who are all outside, all surface, Dostoevsky once again seeks the truth under the inverted sign of the lie. Just as winter is turned against summer, so is the sign turned inside out. Hence the answer, "solved and signed," that "there is no native soil, no people" (21), is called into question by turning the reader toward those who do not read and whose vision, because they do not read, is free of the contamination of the European outlook. This turning about and tearing away, which is a mode of return, is effected by means of a question: "Can it be that there is in fact some kind of chemical bond between the human spirit and its native soil, so that you cannot tear yourself away from it and, even if you do tear yourself away, you nonetheless return?" (9). Invoking the soil, of course, Dostoevsky invokes a sign that signifies a spiritual center that may provide the basis of community and brotherhood and that is absent from the European discourse. As Martin Buber expresses it in *I and Thou*, "True community does not come into being because people have feelings for each other (though that is required, too), but rather on two accounts: all of them have to stand in a living, reciprocal relation to a single, living center, and they have to stand in a living reciprocal relation to one another" (94). For Dostoevsky, the soil is just such a living center; it signifies one earth, one bread, and one body, the source from which we arise and to which we return. This is what is absent from the European discourse, and it introduces to the Russian soul an absence or a nothingness with which the author here is in constant communication. As the basis of community, the soil is the basis for brotherhood. And the insertion of the word *soil* into his discourse makes the conflict of discourse in *Winter Notes* into a conflict between the discourse of the crowd and the discourse of the community. Opposite the alien other, then, we have the other as brother.

The Other as Brother

In his notebooks from 1876–1877 Dostoevsky writes, "Let us embrace strongly, let us kiss and begin as brothers. . . . You see, I know that there is nothing higher than this thought of *embracing*. What will you, with your positivism, give me in exchange?" (*Neizdannyi* 529). Why is the act of embrace so significant to Dostoevsky? Because the substance we assume within ourselves lies in the embrace we give to another, because in the embrace we experience a nearness to the life, to the heartbeat, of another that reveals to us the dearness of the life of all. This nearness, in the words of Levinas, "is quite distinct from every other relationship, and has to be conceived as a responsibility for the other, it might be called humanity, subjectivity, or self" (*Otherwise* 46). The European ideologies seek freedom, equality, and fraternity for every individual, yet they omit the one thing necessary to the life and meaning of the individual, namely a capacity to be present for the sake of another. European discourse, then, does not generate proximity to one's neighbor but distance from him or her; it is not about responsibility but about privilege. There, Dostoevsky points out in *Winter Notes,* freedom, as well as the equality and fraternity associated with it, means "equal liberty for everyone to do anything he wants within the limits of the law. When may you do anything you want to? When you have millions" (48). An important insight is to be found in these few words. Dostoevsky understands that freedom lies not in doing anything I want to do for myself but in realizing what I must do for the other. It is distinguished, therefore, by a capacity for response, by a responsibility to the other and for the other. When liberty is tied to property, to things that one may manipulate to one's own ends, it reduces both self and other to the same status; here liberty is defined in terms of power, that is, as a capability on the part of the self to dominate the other. Conceived in terms of responsibility, liberty is definitively linked to that equality of self and other that unfolds on a single level in an I-Thou relation. Embrace is impossible when one person is lying at the feet of another. The I of the European discourse, both alienated and alienating, means "I who am opposed to you"; the I of true brotherhood means "I who am with you, who am here for you." In the case of the former the law is viewed as a limitation placed on the self; in the latter it signifies a living center from which the community derives its life and thus sanctifies the dearness of the other. The former is a version of a rationalistic materialism that reduces the living soul to lifeless dust; the latter is expressive of a humanistic spirituality that takes on only as much life as it imparts to the other.

The counterfeit version—or perversion—of liberty, equality, and fraternity that comes out of the European discourse is characteristic of the utopian socialism of men like Etienne Cabet and Robert Owen. Dostoevsky admired these thinkers prior to his exile to Siberia, but by the time he made his journey to Europe he recognized that the socialists all fail because, as Morson notes, they base "love on law and brotherhood on rational self-interest" (*Boundaries* 25). If such a notion of brotherhood is false, then we must ask what true brotherhood might be. In *Winter Notes* Dostoevsky has a lengthy but noteworthy reply:

Brotherhood must be created no matter what. But it turns out that brotherhood cannot be created because it creates itself, is given and found in nature. But in the French nature—to be sure, in the Western nature in general—it has not shown up; what has shown up is a principle of individuality, a principle of isolation, of urgent self-preservation, self-interest, and self-determination of one's own *I*, a principle of opposition of this *I* to all of nature and all other people as a separate and autonomous entity. . . . In true brotherhood, it is not the separate personality, not the *I*, that must plead for the right to its own equality and equal value with *everyone else*, but rather this *everyone else* must *on its own* come to the one demanding his right to individuality, to this separate *I*, and on its own, without his asking, must recognize his equality and equal value to itself. . . . This very rebellious and demanding individual, moreover, must above all sacrifice all of his *I*, his entire self, to society, and not only without demanding his rights but, on the contrary, giving them up to society unconditionally. [48–49]

Opposed to the talk about rights we find here an invocation of sacrifice, of making sacred. The sanctity of one human being lies in a capacity to affirm the sanctity of another, the individual takes on substance and significance precisely to the extent that she or he attests to the depth and the dearness of the other.

Levinas helps us to see this point when he asserts, "All my inwardness is invested in the form of a despite-me, for-another. Despite-me, for-another, is signification par excellence. And it is in the sense of the 'oneself,' that accusative that derives from no nominative; it is the very fact of finding oneself while losing oneself" (*Otherwise* 11). The epigraph to *The Brothers Karamazov* comes to mind: "Truly, truly, I say unto you, unless a grain of wheat falls to the earth and dies, it remains alone; but if it dies, it bears much fruit" (John 12:24). In the Russian outlook that Dostoevsky brings into conflict with the European view the soil to which a grain of wheat may fall is the sign of the community of human beings. And in *Winter Notes* he offers us an example of how the dialogue of brotherhood might unfold within a human community. "What would brotherhood consist of," he asks, "if it were put into rational, conscious language? Of this: each separate individual, without any compulsion, without any benefit to himself, would say to society, ' . . . This is my highest happiness: to sacrifice everything to you and to do you no harm in doing so. I shall annihilate myself. . . . ' The brotherhood, on the other hand, must say, 'You offer us too much. . . . Take everything that is ours too. Every minute and with all our strength we shall try to increase your personal freedom and self-revelation as much as possible' " (50). And the author adds, "Now there is Utopia indeed, gentlemen! Everything is grounded in feeling, in nature, not in reason. To be sure, this is even a kind of humiliation of reason" (50). Thus the wheat speaks to the soil and the soil to the wheat in a contravention of the sterility of European reason. Reason is only half the man, as it is said in *Notes from Underground* (115). And the other half? It is the soil, the living center, of the community, which is the very thing from which the European ideologies would divorce themselves. As the discourse of reason, the European discourse is the discourse of only half the man; dividing the human being in half, it cuts him off not only from national origins but from the very source of life. In short, it is the discourse of an exile of the soul from itself and therefore from the other as brother.

Although Dostoevsky uses the word *Utopia* to describe a condition of brotherhood, Joseph Frank points out that he believed it "actually *existed*—though in forms that were often imperfect and distorted—at the heart of Russian peasant life" (243). Frank goes on to explain, "The Russian, for whom brotherhood is a vital instinct, experiences no inner conflict as the result of the self-sacrifice demanded by life in his village" (245). And only where brotherhood thrives does the self find its highest realization and revelation of itself through the sacrifice of itself for the sake of another. In *Winter Notes* Dostoevsky makes this point by saying, "Voluntary, completely conscious self-sacrifice imposed by no one, sacrifice of the self for the sake of all, is, in my opinion, a sign of the very highest development of the personality, of the very height of its power, the highest form of self-mastery, the greatest freedom of one's own will" (49). Here the language of development and the will to power that characterizes the European discourse is appropriated to bring out the lie of that discourse. The inverted sign of the lie is itself overturned to make the language of privilege into a language of responsibility as one encounters it, for example, in Levinas's *Ethics and Infinity*. "It is precisely insofar as the relationship between the Other and me is not reciprocal," he argues, that I am subject to the Other; and I am "subject" essentially in this sense. It is I who support all. You know the sentence in Dostoevsky: "We are all guilty of all and for all men before all, and I more than the others." This is not owing to such or such a guilt which is really mine, or to offenses that I would have committed; but because I am responsible for a total responsibility, which answers for all the others and for all in the others, even for their responsibility. The I always has one responsibility *more* than all the others. [98–99]

What Levinas enables us to see about the conflict of discourse in *Winter Notes* is that it is a conflict of conceptions of the self, of the I that inhabits one discourse over against another. That which speaks in the midst of all discourse, then, is not only the word itself but the word of the self, that is, the word that engenders the self. The problem of the other as brother, therefore, is a problem that calls into question the truth of the soul in its relation to the other.

In the text and contexts of *Winter Notes*, to go abroad is to move from truth to falsehood and therefore from the true self to a false self. As Lizaveta Prokofevna expresses it in the closing lines of *The Idiot*, "all this going abroad, all this Europe of yours, all of it is but a fantasy, and all of us, when we are abroad, are a mere fantasy" (589). But, again, it is by moving into the lie that Dostoevsky makes the truth visible. The question that arises at this juncture, then, concerns the matter of what constitutes the truth of the person who stands in a relation to the other as brother, over against rational self-interest. Or: what is it that *makes sacred* in the sacrifice of the self for the other? In *Winter Notes* Dostoevsky replies to this question by affirming that the sacrifice "*must happen of itself; it must be present in one's nature,* . . . in a word: in order for there to be a principle of brotherly love there must be love" (49). The personality that has developed the highest is the one in which love runs the deepest. In the discourse that views the other as brother the self *is* the love that it offers. Thus we may have a better sense of what underlies Stepan Verkhovensky's statement in *The Possessed*, when he cries, "What is more precious than love? Love is higher than existence—love is the crown of existence, so how can existence not be subordinate to love?" (679). As for the conflict of discourse under consideration, the two views of love and its relation to life expressed by Ivan and Alyosha Karamazov are worth noting. In an exchange illustrative of the European outlook in conflict with the Russian view, the European-educated Ivan asks Alyosha how a man is supposed to love life without knowing the meaning of it. Alyosha replies, "It must be just so; one must love it in spite of logic, as you say, and above all prior to any logic, for only then shall I ever come to understand its meaning" (253). Yet love, as Dostoevsky conceives it—the love that must *be there*—is not so much a feeling locked away inside the self as it is a presence that arises *between* self and other. "Feelings dwell in man," Buber states it in *I and Thou*, "but man dwells in his love. This is no metaphor but actuality: love does not cling to an I, as if the You were merely its 'content' or object; it is between I and You" (66). Love is a living presence, "higher than existence," as Verkhovensky says; it dwells both within and beyond the soul of the individual. And since the self is essentially the love it offers, there is no I in isolation but only the I of a polarity; the *between* space is where the soul comes to life and emerges from its isolation and exile. The truth that Dostoevsky seeks is neither a datum nor an ideology but a way of being; it is the truth of love, the truth that lies not in what we know but in what we are.

Through love, then, the human being arrives at himself or herself by way of the other, that is, by way of the brother or sister. This is the revelation of which Ippolit speaks in *The Idiot* when he says, "Casting your seeds about, your 'kindness,' your good deed in whatever form it may take, you offer up a part of your personality and you receive into yourself a part of the other's; you are in communion with one another, . . . and already you are rewarded with a knowledge, with a most unexpected revelation" (390). What is revealed is that love that is the origin of both self and other and that makes each a brother or sister to the other; what is revealed in the communion or counion of two is the light of love as a third, living presence. The condition of the European exile is just the opposite of this relation. It is the hell of selfhood, in which the self consumes itself in a longing to be as God. The effort to become as God, of course, signifies the Fall; and the European exile is a condition indicative of the human being's fallen condition. Embracing the omniscience of reason and the omnipotence of science, humanity loses itself to the kingdom of Moloch that has risen up east of Eden.

The European Exile

The discourse of the It-world that makes the human being into a commodity is a discourse couched in the worship of things; as such, it is a discourse of idolatry. Both in London and in Paris—indeed, throughout Europe—Dostoevsky meets with "the same desperate struggle to maintain the status quo out of despair, to tear from oneself all desires and hopes, to curse one's future, and to bow down to Baal" (*Winter Notes* 36). The hopelessness of this condition is rooted in the fact that the idol breeds the very despair that draws the human being toward it. To be sure, the state of despair—a state in which the soul is scattered over the surface of externals, at odds with itself and longing to be what it is not—is the condition of the exile of the human being from himself. Infinitely different from externals, the person who bows down to Baal, the god of externals, is infinitely distant from himself or herself. Here we may note that the Hebrew word *baal* not only signifies the ancient idol but also means "owner" or "possessor." In the European exile he who would own much is much owned; those who bow down to Baal are possessed by the idol in every sense of that terrible word. Invoking the idol of the Scriptures, moreover, Dostoevsky inserts into his text a scriptural discourse that is contrary to the European discourse. The truth that he opposes to the lie, therefore, is more than a Russian truth; it is the truth of that higher being who brings into judgment all the contingent truths of humanity, European, Russian, and otherwise. Thus when he notes that "Anglican priests and bishops are proud and wealthy, live in rich parishes, and grow fat with their conscience completely at peace" (42), those men are implicated not by the Russian word but by the Holy Word whom they betray in their betrayal of humanity. Suddenly one realizes why St. Paul's Cathedral and the Cathedral of Cologne held little attraction for Dostoevsky: what is worshiped in those places is not the one invisible God but the surface features of the architectural and cultural achievement. What is worshiped, in short, is the idol.

In *Winter Notes* one of the primary temples in which the idol is worshiped is the Crystal Palace of London, that huge glass and steel exhibition hall where the scientific and technological accomplishments of humankind are displayed. There too, there especially, the discourses of the exile and the kingdom come into conflict. In a description that bespeaks the collisions silently taking place in this temple, Dostoevsky writes,

You feel a terrible force has united all these people here, who come from all over the world, into a single herd; you become aware of a gigantic idea; you feel that here something has already been achieved, that here there is victory and triumph. You even begin to be afraid of something. No matter how independent you might be, for some reason you become terrified. . . . It is a kind of biblical scene, something about Babylon, a kind of prophecy from the Apocalypse fulfilled before your very eyes. You feel that it would require a great deal of spiritual resistance and denial not to succumb, not to surrender to the impression, not to bow down to fact, and not to idolize Baal. [37]

The scriptural text that Dostoevsky makes heard in the midst of his own text is found in the Revelation to John:

And I saw a beast rising out of the sea, with ten horns and seven heads, with ten diadems upon its horns and a blasphemous name upon its heads. And the beast that I saw was like a leopard, its feet were like a bear's, and its mouth was like a lion's mouth. And to it the dragon gave its power, and his throne and great authority, . . . and the whole earth followed the beast of wonder. Men worshiped the dragon, for he had given his authority to the beast, and they worshiped the beast, saying, "Who is like the beast, and who can fight against it?" [13:1–4]

Though it is bathed in light, the Crystal Palace houses a terrible darkness. And Dostoevsky enables us to glimpse that darkness through the conflict of discourse that transpires in a space between the text and its subtext, between what he says and what he leaves unsaid.

Thus, as Frank has noted, the Crystal Palace "became for Dostoevsky an image of the unholy spirit of modernity that brooded malevolently over London; and in his imagination this spirit takes the form of the monstrous Beast whose coming was prophesied in the Apocalypse" (239). Again, the conflict of discourse at work in *Winter Notes* goes beyond the confines of political or ideological encounter to assume a metaphysical dimension, as the passages just cited suggest, and that dimension makes the conflict of discourse into a battle between spiritual life and death. Dostoevsky's comment on the turmoil he finds in London comes to mind, where he says, "There is a stubborn, blind, already inveterate struggle here, a struggle to the death between the general individualistic basis of the West and the necessity of somehow getting along with each other, of somehow putting together a community and settling into a single anthill" (36). It should be pointed out, however, that within the framework of London itself the struggle is not so much between life and death as between one form of death and another. In this connection Frank explains, "English (Western) society was thus dominated by the war of all against all, which at best, since some form of social order had to be created, would lead only to the 'ant-heap'—to the total, unthinking compliance of human volition with the commands of the social Moloch" (241). The principle by which the Exilarch Moloch rules is "twice two equals four," and, as the underground man declares, " 'twice two equals four' is the beginning of death" (*Zapiski* 119). Because London is one of the centers of the European exile, life there is no longer an option; exile is itself that living death that is manifested through the various forms of spiritual death. Life becomes an option not in what Dostoevsky encounters but in the discourse that he introduces to his encounter, particularly that discourse that contains the allusions to the Holy Word. For life thrives only in the soil of the holy, of the hale and the whole, as it is revealed in the heart of the homeland. And the homeland, the opposite of the land of exile, lies wherever brother embraces brother.

One of the forms of exilic death that Dostoevsky discovers in London is the death of sleep, the death of drunkenness. In London, he tells us, "everyone is drunk, not with cheer but dismally, miserably, and, in a rather strange way, silently. . . . Here you do not see the people but a loss of consciousness, systematic, submissive, encouraged" (38–39). The death that inhabits the European discourse of exile announces itself in a loss of the word, in a drunken slurring of the word to the point of silence. In his reference to the *silent* drunkenness Dostoevsky makes use of an opposing discourse to make heard the silence of the isolation and desperation in which humanity is exiled. The European exile is, in short, the exile of the word, since the word lies at the heart of human relation; the absence of the word is just what distinguishes the silence of the anthill. As a condition of sleep, moreover, the exilic condition is the fallen condition that Lev Shestov describes when he says, "Knowledge and the ability to distinguish good from evil, that is, what the fruit of the forbidden tree brought man, did not awaken his mind but put it to sleep" (*Kierkegaard* 104). The fruit of the forbidden tree is the fruit of the European Enlightenment, particularly in its French form, where reason and virtue are presented as the high court of truth in life. In that Enlightenment Dostoevsky perceives a darkness inhabited not by people but by a loss of consciousness, that is, by a blindness or a muteness of the self in its relation—or nonrelation—to the other. "These millions of people," he cries out in *Winter Notes,* "abandoned and driven away from the human feast, shoving and crushing each other in the underground darkness into which they have been thrown by their elder brothers, gropingly knock at any gate whatsoever and seek entrance so they won't suffocate in the dark cellar. It is a final, desperate attempt to separate themselves from everything, even from the human image, if only to be something of their own, if only to avoid being with us" (39). The underground man, who "not only can but must exist in our society" (*Zapiski* 99), is, of course, the embodiment of these millions. His cellar is the site of the European exile that has eaten its way into the Russian soul, and in this lies an important link between Dostoevsky's *Winter Notes* and his *Notes from Underground.*

Moving from London to Paris, Dostoevsky moves from the nocturnal gloom and depravity of the Haymarket to the sunlit gardens and boulevards along the Seine. Yet here, at the very center of the bourgeois gaiety, the despair that characterizes the European exile is more insidious because it is more subtle. Stricken by the "calm of order" (36) that abounds there, Dostoevsky portrays the French capital by saying, "This is the most moral and most virtuous city in the whole world. What order! What prudence, what well defined and solidly established relationships; how secure and sharply delineated everything is; how content everyone is; how they struggle to convince themselves that they are content and completely happy, and . . . and . . . they have stopped at that" (35). Once again, just as one discourse underlies and belies another in Dostoevsky's text, so does one condition haunt another in the condition of exile that he encounters in the City of Lights. Heirs to Diderot, Voltaire, and Rousseau, the bourgeois Parisians cling to a clearly defined and solidly established virtue that itself has no ground, or rather is rooted in the false and sterile ground of a rationalist materialism. The bourgeois, as Dostoevsky puts it, "has a frightful supply of ready-made ideas, like firewood for the winter" (56); but because those ideas are ready-made, they eclipse the voice, the presence, and the response capability of the human being. Like the superfluous man, the bourgeois is spoken rather than speaking. Void of a capacity for response, the bourgeois leads a life void of human relation and therefore empty of human being. In his exile from the other as Thou he is exiled from himself as I, as well as from that higher being who can be the only ground of truth in human relation. Buber has maintained that "there is nothing that can so hide the face of our fellow-man as morality can" (*Between* 18). Why? Because when it is cast in the code of fixed formulas and ready answers, morality is turned over to those externals that efface the soul. In its Parisian mode the European exile is distinguished by just such an effacement of the human being. The bourgeois stops at virtue and contentment because he does not speak the word that might break the code and bring him face to face with another human being, where he might recognize his or her own humanity.

Robbed of the face and therefore of the word, the human being is robbed of his divine image and becomes one more object in a landscape of things. Like all objects, his or her value as a human being is determined by a market of exchange, and the worship of mammon takes over. In Paris, as in London, the god is Baal, as Dostoevsky implies when he proclaims, "To amass a fortune and possess as many things as possible has become the primary code of morality, a catechism, of the Parisian" (45). Here too the careful selection of a word, *catechism*, brings discourse into conflict with discourse. For *catechism* comes from the Greek term *katekhismos*, which means "to teach by word of mouth." But in the case of the bourgeois the catechism that fills his mouth drains his soul of the dialogical word of human relation. Living in a world of superiors and subordinates, the bourgeois never meets another face to face; instead, he is turned over to the cringing servility Dostoevsky describes when he writes, "Cringing servility is eating away more and more into the bourgeois nature, and more and more it is considered a virtue. . . . The Frenchman passionately loves to get ahead, to look good in the eyes of those in power and cringe before them" (53). Torn from himself and lost in the look of those in power, the bourgeois is cast into that exile that has taken over the West, both then and now: it is the exile of social standing, professional distinction, and monetary success—all those things that are pleasing to the eye and that we clamber to hold up to the eyes of others. Jean-Paul Sartre's comments on the look of the other may help us to see that we are dealing not only with a nineteenth-century Russian condition but with the fundamentals of the human condition. "This self which I am," he explains, "this I am in a world which the Other has made alien to me, for the Other's look embraces my being and correlatively the walls, the door, the keyhole. All these instrumental-things, in the midst of which I am, now turn toward the Other a face which on principle escapes me" (350). Who is the exile? It is he who is rendered faceless by the look of the other whom he would seduce into recognition.

Although in his exile the bourgeois may have lost his humanity, he is nonetheless a human being. In the light of the foregoing, then, one can understand why "the bourgeois is still afraid of something, in spite of his self-confidence," as Dostoevsky states it (37), why "he is still in terrible dread of something" (45). Having consumed those fruits that open his eyes to reason and virtue, he looks around to discover that he is not as God and that what he had thought to be the firm ground is in fact the brink of an abyss. In the words of Shestov, "It turns out that knowledge cannot rest on itself and must demand trust; and not only does it fail to allay terror but actually provokes it" (*Afiny* 85). Thus the rupture is felt in the dread that invades the soul; thus the exile is made manifest. And no one knows better than Dostoevsky that the European exile arises not only east of Eden but east of Europe itself, in the heart of Petersburg, where the underground man pens his notes from the depths of his cellar.

By now it should be clear that Dostoevsky's *Winter Notes on Summer Impressions* goes well beyond the categories of those Russian travelogues that precede his text. Consisting of a multitude of texts, of voices in conflict with voices, *Winter Notes* bespeaks not only what is present in Europe but also what is absent from Russia; more than that, it reveals the problematic condition of anyone who seeks a presence in the world through a presence in language. The conflict of discourse, indeed, bears the features of language that Michel Foucault, for example, describes when he says, "Language always seems to be inhabited by the other, the elsewhere, the distant; it is hollowed by absence. Is it not the locus in which something other than itself appears?" (*Archaeology* 111). In Dostoevsky's text what is made present by its absence is the contrary of exile, that is, a condition of human relation that is expressive of a higher relation; such a relation is just what characterizes the dwelling that enables a person to be at home in the world. And the place where such a relation assumes its most profound form is, ideally, marriage. "Marriage can never be renewed," Buber tells us, "except by that which is always the source of all true marriage: that two human beings reveal the You to one another" (*I and Thou* 95). In the final chapter of *Winter Notes*, "*Bribri* and *Ma Biche*," Dostoevsky drives home in a deceptively playful fashion the death of human relation and higher relation within the European exile. Indeed, the epithets themselves—*bribri*, meaning "little bird," and *ma biche*, meaning "my little nanny goat"—efface the human image. As for the nature of their marriage, Dostoevsky notes, "Since marriage for the most part is marriage of capital and there is very little concern for mutual inclination, *bribri* has no problem with dropping in somewhere away from *ma biche* on the side" (66). The worshipers of mammon come to resemble the thing they worship; marriage is not the marriage of souls that would reveal the living presence of the eternal Thou—it is the marriage of money. And while money may not be able to buy everything, in the end it is used to justify anything.

Thus the conflict of discourse in Dostoevsky's *Winter Notes* is a conflict between God and mammon, spirit and matter, life and death. The stake in coming to terms with that struggle, therefore, lies not just in understanding a text but in penetrating the substance of one's own life as it is engendered by one's own word. For we cannot engage this text without engaging the discourse of our own lives in the midst of the conflict we encounter. "There exists an unbridgeable gap," Jabès has argued, "between the writer and the book which the reader is called upon to fill" (85). The rupture that Dostoevsky addresses is felt both between the lines of the text and in that space between reader and text. As we move on to Part 2, we move into this breach between life and word.

PART TWO
The Breach between
Life and Word

3. Monological Death and Dialogical Life: The Case of Ivan Il'ich

In Part 1 we examined the problem of exile as it enters life from the outside, so to speak, in the collisions of the word that transpire between the superfluous man and his society, between Dostoevsky's view of the Russian soul and the discourse of Europe. We also found that these collisions with what is both alien and alienating have certain implications for the inner life of any human being. The soul itself is externalized, turned inside out, in its relation to the world, to other souls, and ultimately to God. The conflict of discourse thus leads to a breach between the world and the inner life that it would either foster or threaten. Turning now to Leo Tolstoy, we take a turn to the inner depths of exile that open like a wound in the collision with the discourse of the outer world.

Like Dostoevsky, Tolstoy was versed in the phrases and formulas of the European discourse, and in his *Ispoved'* (*Confession*) he describes this doctrine to which he once subscribed: "Everything that exists is rational. Further, everything that exists is evolving. And it is evolving by means of an enlightenment. The enlightenment in turn undergoes change through the distribution of books and periodicals. We are paid and respected for writing books and periodicals, and therefore we are the most useful and the best of people" (21). He goes on to explain that this self-satisfaction rooted in the outward signs of distinction was undone at the sight of an execution in Paris on 25 March 1857. "When I saw how the head was severed from the body," he confesses, "and heard the thud of each part as it fell into the box, I understood, not with my intellect but with my whole being, that no theories of the rationality of existence or of progress could justify such an act" (23). Thus the encounter with death brings into play another faculty: the whole being, the depth dimension of the person's inner being. In an effort to convey the nature of this shift to the inside, Tolstoy uses the analogy of a sick man. "It happened with me," he writes in the *Confession*, "as it happens with everyone who contracts a fatal internal disease. At first there were the insignificant symptoms of an ailment, which the patient ignores; then these symptoms recur more and more frequently, until they merge into one continuous duration of suffering. The suffering increases, and before he can turn around the patient discovers what he already knew: the thing he had taken for a mere disposition is in fact the most important thing on earth to him, is in fact death" (26). One will easily recognize here the scenario for a piece written nearly seven years after the *Confession*, in 1886. For this inner realm of illness is the setting for the tale *Smert' Ivana Il'icha* (*The Death of Ivan Il'ich*), where we see a man cut from the cloth of the French bourgeoisie now placed in the midst of Russian society. There the character follows all the recipes for the "good life" only to plunge into the breach between life and word that announces from within his condition of exile. There he enters into a dialogue with himself that finally opens up a life that had been eclipsed by the monological discourse of death.

These, of course, are not the terms in which this piece is usually understood. Before we go into a detailed examination of the tale, then, some difficulties with existing approaches should be pointed out. In one article, for example, Gary Jahn says of *The Death of Ivan Il'ich* that "there are, in fact, few stories whose intended meaning is so abundantly clear" (237). But, judging from the varied reactions to this story, such a sweeping claim is at best questionable. Indeed, Jahn's article itself rests on a fundamental misunderstanding of the work. Mistakenly supposing that Tolstoy sets out first to frighten and then to reconcile the reader with death, Jahn's chief concern is whether or not the piece is artistically successful. And yet any response to this text on a strictly aesthetic level constitutes a flight from its collisions that is consistent with Ivan Il'ich's own flight from life. "An aesthetic position," Karl Jaspers has pointed out, "wills 'form.' It turns against the infinite relationships of things, against what is in the background, the nebulous, the fluctuating. In it there is the urge towards objectivity in form, . . . towards the changeless over against the becoming" (*Truth* 27). The immutability that Jaspers associates with the aesthetic position is characteristic of what we refer to here as a monological outlook. Seeking the immutability of the changeless, the aesthetic position is ruled by a longing for the surface calm and the external order that Dostoevsky describes in his comments on the French bourgeois in *Winter Notes* (36) and that characterizes the mode of death found in Ivan Il'ich.

Jahn's false assumption that the problem facing Ivan Il'ich is the acceptance of death, however, is fairly common among the critics. Such a view is shared, for example, by Edward Wasiolek (177), Robert Russell (629), and Michael V. Williams (229). Even Boris Sorokin, who has written one of the better studies of Tolstoy's piece, asserts that its theme is "the confrontation and eventual reconciliation of the individual with death" (487). The erroneous view that Tolstoy is writing about the difficulty of giving death a nod has led further to perhaps the most misleading of the critical approaches to *The Death of Ivan Il'ich*, namely the psychology-of-death or the death-and-dying treatments (see, for example, the analyses by Hollis L. Cate, James J. Napier, and Walter Smyrniw). Like the articles that focus on the acceptance of death , these investigations fall prey to the very confusion—to the very death—from which Ivan Il'ich himself struggles to extricate himself. Here too one succumbs to a will to the form, that is, to the fixed formulas and ineluctable categories that isolate and insulate the thinker from life's dialogical collisions.

Some critics, however, have the insight to see that Ivan Il'ich's difficulty lies not in saying yes to death but in distinguishing between life and death and thus perceiving the substance of spiritual life. Rima Salys, for instance, acknowledges the intensification of Ivan Il'ich's spiritual life as he engages himself in a dialogue about his life (23), yet this study amounts to little more than a summary of Tolstoy's tale. In a more thorough analysis John Donnelly argues that "a person is dead when stripped of his autonomy regardless of how operative his cerebral functions. . . . Death is viewed as alienation from virtue" (117). But, as we shall see, the difficulty facing the person is not an autonomy of the self, which is a form of monologism, but a dialogical relation to the other, and the person's alienation is not from morality but from humanity. Also taking up the virtue or value argument but from a different standpoint, the Soviet critics B. Tarasov (156) and N.K. Gei (361–62) claim that the character's death comes as a result of his misguided adoption of bourgeois values. The Soviets' objection, it must be noted, does not fall into the same category as Dostoevsky's indictment of the bourgeois in *Winter Notes*. While Dostoevsky seeks some kind of spirituality that may be expressed in loving human relation, the Soviets oppose a Marxist materialism to a bourgeois materialism, setting up one monological stance over against another. Ivan Il'ich's exilic condition does not consist of failing to be virtuous or subscribing to the wrong ideology. Indeed, he is not a liar, a thief, or an adulterer but is generally virtuous and follows all the rules for right living prescribed by his elder counselors and college advisors. Nor is it a matter of replacing one ideology with another, since all ideologies rest on the externals of preconceived codes and ready answers, ending, as Jaspers states it, in "an automation which is emptied to the point of heedlessness" (*Truth* 27). As we shall soon discover, it is a certain inward movement manifested in human relation that distinguishes spiritual life in Tolstoy's tale. It is a life, therefore, that is revealed and established in this world, and not a hereafter "beyond time and space," as William Edgerton has claimed (300). God is not inaccessible to the world, Tolstoy would later express it, but is "in the world and in the interactions among people" (*Soedinenie* 113), and that is where Ivan Il'ich must seek the kingdom: in the dialogical interaction with human beings.

It was indicated above that Sorokin's article on *Ivan Il'ich* is one of the better treatments of the work, despite his mistaken rendition of its theme. He has astutely observed, for example, that Tolstoy's "statement, though hardly clear and unequivocal, amounts to saying that any man who chooses a life of 'ease,' 'pleasure,' 'comfort,' and 'propriety' chooses spiritual death" (487). He also correctly notes that "in the end, this cocoon of protective things and routines which he views as a comfortable 'womb' . . . becomes his spiritual 'tomb' to which he finds himself confined without ever having 'lived' " (500); in other words, instead of creating for himself a place in the world, the self-centered stance of I-for-myself has exiled Ivan Il'ich from the world. The question to be addressed here is the question of how and why the state of exile is couched in a monological discourse, while the movement into spiritual life is a movement into the dialogical word. The weakness of Sorokin's investigation, then, is rooted not so much in his assessment of Ivan Il'ich's death as in his failure to assess the work's message concerning spiritual life and the relations that foster it. He suggests something about that message when he concludes, "The answer to the puzzle of death is love and compassion" (502), but he offers very little analysis or explanation of the "answer." To be sure, the puzzle or the question that torments Ivan Il'ich and that we confront here is the puzzle of life. "What is 'it'?" he asks (228). What is the one thing needful? In answering, "Love and compassion," as Sorokin does, we have answered, but perhaps we have not yet understood. Let us see, then, what we are to understand.

The Monological Death of Ivan Il'ich

Nicolas Berdyaev has said, "The last achievement of the rationalized herd mind is to try to forget about death altogether, to conceal it, to bury the dead as unobtrusively as possible" (252–53). No statement better sums up the opening pages of *The Death of Ivan Il'ich*, for immediately we encounter the veil of distance from the other that characterizes monological discourse. Shvarts, for example, a man described as Ivan Il'ich's "true friend," will not allow the dead man's passing to intrude on his card game (180); and Petr Ivanovich, who had known the deceased from childhood, flees to conventional gesticulations in the face of the image of death that renders him mute (178). In such actions and failures to act Ivan Il'ich's friends prove themselves to be among the dead burying the dead, and one is suddenly stricken by the irony of the thought that passes through the minds of these men at the outset of the tale: "He is the one who has died, not I" (177). The acknowledged death is the death of the other, while the veiled death is *my* death. To declare that the other is dead is to insist that I am safe. Yet this abrogation of the other for the security of the self is just what places the self in the power of death. Death is the way of the herd-mind that would cover up death, the way of the crowd, the path charted by what They say. It lies in the monologism of officialdom that effaces the human being with marks of identification that occlude his or her humanity; it lurks in the customs and in the surface fixations of decorum and propriety— *prilichie*, as Tolstoy calls it, a word that turns up as a noun and an adjective throughout this portrait of life's struggle with death (for example, 177, 185, 189, 190, 191, 194, 196, 220, 225). The primary concern on the part of Ivan Il'ich's associates, we are told, is the significance of his demise for their promotions and changes in rank (176–77), which underscores their orientation toward death. For the preoccupation of officialdom and society with the outward trappings of rank points up an entrapment in the It world, the world of what is pleasing to the eye. It is no coincidence that Ivan Il'ich repeatedly refers to death as *it* (for example, 210–11), for death is the It, the reduction of oneself and others to marks of distinction, power, and property. In the It world of death the human being is never face to face with the other in an I-Thou relation but always above or below, hence always nowhere.

Thus, contrary to the dialogical word of relation, which forever seeks a reply, the monological word of the It world seeks only the elimination of any reply. Relegated to the marketplace of negotiation where a person learns to sell himself or herself, the monological word seeks not another word but the last word, until finally it may declare, "He is the one who has died, not I." This discourse of death that underlies the monological discourse of the crowd is the thing "most ordinary and most terrible" (184) that Ivan Il'ich, like so many of us who struggle for survival in the marketplace, has mistaken for life. His fall into the It world of monological officialdom—his fall into death—begins with his completion of law school. There he becomes versed in the fixed formulas of the law and in the rigor mortis of the letter, the first of the building blocks that go into the construction of his self-styled tomb. In a revealing description of the initial stages of this spiritual death we get a clear picture of how the worm of monological death begins to eat its way into life: "At the School of Law he was just what he remained throughout all his life: a capable man, cheerful, good-natured, and sociable, but strictly carrying out what he considered his duty. He considered his duty to be what was so considered by the most highly placed people. He was not one to curry favor, either as a boy or as a man, but from his earliest years he was drawn, like a fly toward light, to the world's most highly placed people, making their ways and their views of life his own and establishing friendly relations with them" (185). Imitating the monological discourse and the myopic outlook held by people of rank and authority, Ivan Il'ich fails to establish a voice and therefore a presence of his own. He does not speak but rather is spoken by the scripts and formulas of the fashionable. His duty, the *ought* that determines his direction in life, is dictated by those in authority, so that the path he follows is chosen for him; that is to say, it is not chosen at all, and therefore it is not lived. Void of any inner resolve that might impart to him an active, living substance, Ivan Il'ich is not what he speaks but what he is told to speak. Unable to generate a decisive word of his own, he succumbs to a deadly mimicry of the "right" crowd, like a fly drawn to a darkness that passes for light and that ultimately consumes him. To be sure, mimicry is the earmark of monologism; it is the imitated reaction that Tolstoy opposes to responsive interaction.

Hence we find that Ivan Il'ich's first steps toward death come with his parroting of the They, which occludes any response to the Thou. The death of the man is the death of his word. An early indication that the loss of the word accompanies the loss of life appears in the passage on the man's promiscuity. "All this," we read, "fell under the rubric of the French saying, *il faut que jeunesse se passe*. Everything was done with clean hands, in clean undershirts, with French phrases, and most important, in the highest society, consequently with the approval of people of high standing" (186). The use of the French formulas to justify his actions accentuates the absence of the word. "Teach French," as Levin states it in *Anna Karenina*, "and unteach sincerity" (253). There is no being oneself in the language of the alien, and for Tolstoy the French language represents the very calm of order and absence of soul that it does in Dostoevsky's *Winter Notes*. The French word is not the Russian word, not the word of Ivan Il'ich. It is uttered to give lies the appearance of truth and to create an illusion of solidity about sheer wind. The man seeks approval because he is incapable of response; he speaks French because he cannot speak himself. Indeed, he has no self, no life, apart from the fashionable forgery justified by people of rank; even his wife addresses him as "Jean," the French variant of his name, in an undoing of his name and therefore of his essence. All of this underlies the deadly desire that Tolstoy describes in the *Confession* as "a desire to be better not in my own eyes or in the eyes of God, but rather a desire to be better in the eyes of other people. And this effort to be better in the eyes of other people was very quickly displaced by a longing to be stronger than other people, that is, more renowned, more important, wealthier than others" (17). And so among the first manifestations of monological death we find an aesthetic of seduction. Reduced to an inwardness that does not go beyond clean underclothes, Ivan Il'ich is not a living soul but a dead object who dies all the more in his treatment of others as objects, using them to his own ends and his own satisfaction, as always happens in promiscuity.

The seduction of the other amounts to a reduction of the self; the soul invariably suffers what it inflicts. Ivan Il'ich reduces himself and others to a voiceless It not only in his youthful temptation to use women as objects but also in his taste for power. Like the empty French phrases that accompany the former, a corruption of the word is concurrent with the latter. Now, as an examining magistrate, Ivan Il'ich felt that "everyone, everyone without exception—the most important, self-satisfied people—everyone was in his power and that all he had to do was to write certain words on a piece of paper with a heading, and this important, self-satisfied person would be brought before him as an accused man or as a witness" (187). Here the sign of death is the written word that eclipses the voice, the word of judgment that displaces relation. Flesh and blood become paper and ink, and logos is made into a logo, so that even the law degenerates into a tool to serve the person rather than a truth that he or she may serve. As an examining magistrate he is the bearer not of the law but of the monological code by which examination overtakes embrace and declaration subverts response. Finding the main satisfaction of his position to be the power it provides him, Ivan Il'ich subordinates the human being to his own insignia and places him under a printed heading, just as he subordinates himself. Again, he dies in his treatment of others as dead objects, condemned by the judgment he hands down, one It above another instead of an I face to face with a Thou. His taste for power, which is "the main interest and attraction of his new office" (187), is a taste for death.

Tolstoy helps us to see this point more clearly by reiterating it just after Ivan Il'ich has his fatal accident. In a passage that outlines quite ex-

plicitly the contrast between monological isolation and dialogical relation, he writes, "A man may come and want to find out something. As
a person, outside the official realm, Ivan Il'ich would be unable to have
any kind of relation to such a man; but if his relation to this man were
official, something that could be expressed on a piece of paper with a
heading, then within the limits of these relations Ivan Il'ich would do
everything, absolutely everything possible and thus observe the sem-
blance of friendly human relations, that is, he would be courteous. As
soon as the official relation ended, so would every other relation" (196).
If at times he let the "human" and the official relations mingle, he did
so because "he always felt he had the power, when needed, to again
choose the official and cast aside the human relation" (196). The man assumes a facade, and nothing but a facade, of human relation only when
the official seal on the page directs him to do so. Just as he is no more
than his official title, the person before him is no more than the information on a piece of paper. And the purpose of information is to serve
the power of manipulation for the one into whose hands it may fall.
Here, however, the man who is informed is soon deformed, emptied of
all presence as he is drained of a capacity for dialogical response. Having no voice of his own, Ivan Il'ich cannot respond to the human voice
that summons him, which is the voice of life. Every time a human voice
appeals to him, he has the opportunity to come to life; every time he
turns to the official document, he turns away from life and inters himself ever deeper within the sepulchre of the code. As we are told, when
his official relation comes to an end, so does every other relation. So
does his illusory life.

Just as the written word on the official document is external to the
spoken word within the human voice, so is death external to life, or better: death is precisely the external. While the dialogical word lives in its
transfer from mouth to mouth and thus in the penetration of one soul
by another, the monological word is confined to the exterior, monologism, as the breeder of spiritual death, is the -ism of exteriority. Looking to Tolstoy's text, therefore, it should not be surprising to discover
that the term *external—vneshnii—*is a watchword in the monological
death of Ivan Il'ich. The realm of power, to be sure, is the realm of the
external, and in *The Death of Ivan Il'ich* we find the two linked as signs
of death: "The awareness of his power, of the ability to destroy any person he might want to destroy, the importance, entirely external, attached to his entry into the court and the meetings with his subordinates, his success before superiors and subordinates, and, the main
thing, the expertise he felt in handling cases—all of it delighted him"

(191). But the man's external importance comes at the expense of internal substance; his power, once again, comes at the expense of presence. Situated between superiors and subordinates, he is neither here nor there, never standing on the same level with the other in a dialogical relation. Distinguishing himself by his ability to destroy rather than nurture life, he destroys all life of his own. Even in his marriage—ostensibly the vessel of life and the place where the deepest relation of an I to a Thou unfolds, where the self generates its most profound presence by offering up itself to the other and for the sake of the other in an affirmation of that holiness that sanctifies marriage—even there Ivan Il'ich is transfixed by the external. "Of family life," we are told, "he demanded only those comforts of a domestic meal, a housewife, and a bed, which family life could give him, and, the main thing, the propriety of external forms required by public opinion" (190). Why, indeed, did he marry? For two reasons: "He found it pleasing to himself to take such a wife, and he was doing what was considered correct by the most highly placed people" (188–89). Marriage in this case has nothing to do with the higher relation and revelation of the Thou; rather, it is an affirmation of the rule of the They. Before the couple can utter "until death do us part . . . ," death has already preceded them. Like the realm of power, the realm of public opinion represents the world of surfaces, of externals, of what captures the eye and with it the soul—in short, it is the kingdom of death.

In death Ivan Il'ich is exiled from the openness and the freedom that signify being *here* and is cast out *there*, scattered over the surface proprieties of social position and official rank. Imprisoned in a place outside of himself, he soon sets about constructing the prison, the fortress, the tomb that he mistakes for a home, just as he had mistaken death for life. Thus it is in the midst of his home that Ivan Il'ich is most homeless and least present; the place where he ought to be at home is in fact a place of exile, for here we find him most dispersed over the exteriors of those fixtures that firmly affix him to the void. Isn't "alienation," Emmanuel Levinas reminds us, "primarily the fact of having no home? Not to have a place [or a voice] of one's own, not to have an interior, is not truly to communicate with another and thus to be a stranger to oneself and to the other" (*Nine* 107). Hence the man's failure at human communication and communion deprives him of that interior that distinguishes the home. Upon finding the "perfect place" in Petersburg, for instance, he undertakes the task of making his new stronghold assume the aspect of a home, like a man digging his own grave and loving it. He "supervised the construction himself," the author relates, "selected the wallpaper, added to the furniture, especially antiques, which he regarded as particularly fashionable in style, and handled the upholstery; everything grew and approached the ideal that he had set for himself. . . . Looking at the yet unfinished drawing room, he could already see the fireplace, the screen, the bookstand and the little chairs, and over there the dishes and plates along the walls and the bronze pieces, as they would be when everything was in place" (194). Indeed, everything is in its place—everything except Ivan Il'ich. Everything, every detail, has the proper look, the look that blinds the man who looks upon it. He has drawn the veil over the memento mori. One will recall, in fact, that the accident that leads to his demise occurs when he is adjusting a veil, a curtain: "Once he climbed a ladder to show an upholsterer who did not understand how he wanted the drapes to hang, and he slipped and fell" (195). In this statement we can see that death consists of drawing the curtain over the light. One meaning of the Russian verb "to fall," *upast'*, it should be noted, is "to perish" or "to die"; in his concern with the drapes, Ivan Il'ich slipped and died, though he was dead even as he ascended the ladder. Death here is not so much the end or absence of life as the thing that hides life. The fall of the first man comes to mind: on the day that he surely dies, his first act is to hide himself. Thus Ivan Il'ich falls and dies in the act of hiding.

The Angel of Death, the Angel with a Thousand Eyes, lurks in the drawing room. Yet the angel comes not simply to take the man but to leave him with a new set of eyes, through which he may ultimately see the light he has veiled. Penetrating the veil, however, is no easy matter. Ivan Il'ich must engage the angel and wrestle the new eyes from him. In order to live, he must confront the death he has mistaken for life; in order to return from his exile among externals, he must wrestle his way to the interior. Here, as everywhere throughout this tale, anyone who must confront the Angel of Death will recognize traces of himself or herself in the character of Ivan Il'ich.

Wrestling with the Angel

The struggle with the angel begins with the realization of the utterly alien and incongruent. It begins with the tearing away of a deception. "There was no deceiving himself," we read. "Something terrible, new, and highly significant, more significant than anything that had ever been in Ivan Il'ich's life, was taking place within him" (203). An interior is opening up within the man who had been lost to externals, and suddenly he hears something, new and terrible. Here death, in the words of Jabès, "is the white space that separates the vocables and makes them intelligible, it is the silence which makes the spoken word audible" (105). What is the sound of the interior? It is the sound of silence. For at this juncture the vocables are not quite audible, at best making themselves heard in a gasping "Can it be?" The terrible thing referred to in this passage is often taken to be the clinical death announced in the obituaries. By now, however, it should be clear that this is not the case. Ivan Il'ich collides not with the oblivion of a death that awaits him but with the nothingness of a death that has passed for life, with the nothingness or the empty "white space" of his inner self. It is true that he laments, "There was light, and now darkness. I was here, and now I am over there!" And then he asks, "I shall be no more, but what will be? Nothing will be. Where shall I be when I shall be no more?" (207). But these lamentations, these questions, are those of a man who has never known the light, who has always been absent from life, never *here* but dispersed along the dead material surface of drawing rooms and official documents. It will be noted, for instance, that immediately after putting these questions to himself, he tries unsuccessfully to light a candle (207): the darkness is upon him, not approaching him, revealed as the darkness of the interior to the man who knew no inwardness. The real question for Ivan Il'ich, the terrible question is not "Where will you be?" but "Where are you now?" The real problem he confronts in his confrontation with the Angel of Death is not that he is yet to be *there* but that he is yet to be *here*.

It is important at this point to bear in mind the inversions that occur as Ivan Il'ich is thrown back on himself, turned inside out in the process of assuming an interior. For the turnarounds that take place in his wrestling match with death serve to define the death that he had thought to be life. For example, the man for whom the official relation was the only relation is himself turned over to the monological distance and indifference of officialdom upon his first visit to the doctor. "Everything," he finds,

was done as it was always done. There was the waiting, the doctor's affected air of importance, so familiar to him since it was the same he had known in court, the thumping, the listening, the questions demanding predetermined and clearly unnecessary answers, the knowing look which suggested that if you just submit to us we will take care of everything, we know beyond a doubt how to arrange it, it is all the same for everyone. All of it was precisely as it was in court. The look he had put on for the accused was exactly the look that the famous doctor put on for him. [199]

The predetermined answers, the knowing look, the insistence on sub-mission—all of these are features of the monological death that refuses to engage the human being and that Ivan Il'ich himself engages. Thus the one who had been entrenched in the living death of isolation from human relation is now left to the isolation of himself: "He had to live on the edge of death by himself, without a single human being who might understand him and pity him" (205). When we read that the man is now in a state of constant despair (208), we are reminded that he has always been locked into despair, languishing in that sickness unto death, as Kierkegaard calls it, characterized by the absence of relation and hence by the absence of self. In this despair, as Kierkegaard points out, "death is not the last phase of the sickness, but death is continually the last" (*Sickness* 154). This is what makes death something with which the man must wrestle.

We have seen that a life grounded in externals is a life grounded in that which veils death. Still unable to distinguish between life and death—still, therefore, in the clutches of death—Ivan Il'ich persists in the cover-up: "He tried to return to the initial lines of thought that had previously hidden from him the thought of death" (209). And: "Ivan Il'ich sought consolations, other screens, and other screens appeared" (210). Just as the monological discourse occludes the face of the other, so does it obscure the face of life. For truth abides in a position between two who are dialogically gathered in its name, each offering himself or herself up to the other for the sake of the truth. Hence, doing battle with death, the man does battle with a lie, and here too there is an inversion: he who had lived a lie now has the lie turned back on himself. This point comes out very clearly when we read, "Ivan Il'ich's main torment was the lie. . . . And this lie tortured him; it tortured him that they did not want to acknowledge what they all knew and what he knew, but wanted to lie to him about his terrible condition and even wanted to force him to take part in this lie. The lie—the lie enacted over him on the eve of his death, the lie that must reduce this terrifying, solemn event of his death to the level of all their visits, their curtains, their sturgeon for dinner— . . . was horribly tormenting for Ivan Il'ich" (213–14). The lie—both his own and the one perpetrated by others—is connected to vari-ous aspects of the monological death here described; it is death itself. It is associated with curtains that shut out the light and with the isolation that snuffs out relation. Eclipsing human relation, the lie eclipses also the relation to God, which is expressed in the dialogical truth of the hu-man relation; it underscores the absence of life and finally the absence of God: "He wept over his helplessness, over his terrible loneliness, over the cruelty of people, over the cruelty of God, over the absence of God" (221). Here Ivan Il'ich experiences the ultimate turnabout: having failed to generate any presence in life, he becomes a void that can see God as nothing but a void.

It will be noted that this turnabout is a turning point, for here the voice of his soul first puts the question to him: " 'To live? To live how?' asked the voice of his soul" (222). This question draws Ivan Il'ich into the initial stages of dialogue and takes him to the heart of life, to child-hood, the thing swallowed up by death. As we shall discover below, the figure of the child is a messianic figure, the one who brings about the sick man's resurrection to life. It is with the memory of childhood, therefore, that Ivan Il'ich begins to suspect his confusion about life and death. His change in consciousness, moreover, is accompanied by a change in discourse, so that he now thinks of his past existence in offi-cialdom and society not as something *comme il faut* but as something *deathly*. "And the deathly official office," his thoughts run, "and the worry about money, and a year of it, then ten, then twenty—always the same. And the further it went, the more deathly it was. It is just as if I were going downhill while imagining that I was going up. And that is exactly how it was. I was going up in public opinion, and just to that extent life was slipping out from under me" (222–23). Once the word *mertvyi* (deathly) takes the place of the word *prilichnyi* (proper), the needful question takes the place of the vain lamentation: "Perhaps I have not lived as I should have?" (223). The man who had made a liv-ing by judging others—who had lost his life in making a living—now comes before a last judgment. While death lay in the ready answers and fixed formulas of monologism, life begins to stir in the dialogue that arises through the question. What Tolstoy says in his *Confession* we can hear Ivan Il'ich saying: "I realized that this was not an inciden-tal ailment but something very serious, and that if the same questions should continue to recur, I would have to answer them. And I tried to answer them. The questions seemed to be such foolish, simple, childish questions. But as soon as I laid my hands on them and tried to resolve them, I was immediately convinced, first of all, that they were not childish and foolish questions but the most vital and profound ques-tions in life" (26–27). Opening up a dialogical stance, the question opens up the face of the other, the face of oneself as other to oneself. Wrestling with the angel, Ivan Il'ich wrestles with himself.

But the wrestling match is not yet at an end, for we are told, "Whenever the thought . . . occurred to him that all this had come about because he had not lived as he should, he immediately recalled all the correctness of his life and drove away this strange thought" (223). And: " 'It would be possible to explain if it could be said that I had not lived as was needful. But this is impossible to concede,' he would say to himself, recalling the legality, correctness, and propriety of his life" (225)— recalling, that is, all the facets of his monological death. Notice here the implication that the man did not die from a slip on a ladder but from the monologism, from the code of the social outlook, that had passed itself off for a way of life. The deadly monological word of the crowd, the word with which Ivan Il'ich wrestles, continues to confound any dialogical word of his own. He has indeed followed all the rules and therefore all the lies for living "the good life." Again, life cannot be decided by the monological forms and formulas of the They but must be created through the dialogical response to the Thou. This response is the substance of responsibility to the other and for the other, which in turn is the basis for any dialogical life about the self. The appeal to legality, to correctness and propriety—all the things prescribed by the herd— is precisely what the sick man must free himself of. To be sure, such self-justification, for Ivan Il'ich as for every man, is a major obstacle to life, the thing that enslaves and paralyzes him: "This very justification of his life chained him and would not let him move forward and tormented him more than anything else" (228). The chains of death are the chains of self-justification, which is a distinguishing feature of the monologism that seeks not another word but only the last word. Once he breaks free of those chains, he is finally able to attempt a plea for forgiveness (229) in place of his insistence that he is not guilty (223). Dialogue begins with confession.

Before he dies, then, Ivan Il'ich vanquishes death: "In the place of death there was light" (229). The light that now takes the place of death is the light of life, of dialogical relation, of God, who could hear his utterance of *prosti* (forgive) in what came out as *propusti* (let it pass); unlike the monological word, which is empty, the dialogical word always harbors a word within the word, and God is the one who hears what is unsaid in the spoken. Where dialogue happens, it is He who is addressed through the address to the Thou. And it is He who summons the address. The response to God, then, is of a piece with Ivan Il'ich's last, loving response to his family. The relation that harbors life is a single relation. Having seen the man break through, however, we must press the issue further than most critics have pursued it. We must now ask what Tolstoy reveals to us about dialogical life and living.

Dialogical Life and Living

The figure of life who here stands out in sharpest contrast to the living dead is Gerasim. The life that Ivan Il'ich ultimately finds in a relation to God and to human beings is exemplified in this peasant, whose first words in the tale, pronounced on the occasion of the dead man's funeral, are "It is God's will. We shall all be there too" (183). This assertion is counterposed to the lie of "He is the one who has died, not I" (177), uttered by Ivan Il'ich's colleagues. In addition, Gerasim's liveliness and readiness to do what must be done (181) are set opposite Petr Ivanovich's lethargy and hesitation in the face of the deceased (178). The human proximity that belongs to dialogue lies in this doing for others, in this activity that is contrasted with the distance, indifference, and impotence of the monological mentality. Thus from the start we see that dialogical life over against monological death is rendered in terms of truth versus lie, of response and action opposite confusion and convention. Life, like the truth, is rooted in dialogical response; death, like the lie, is steeped in monological imitation. Note, too, that at the end of the first chapter we see Gerasim "thinking of what he must do" (184), a parallel to the expression on the dead man's face, which said "that what was needed to be done was done, and done rightly. There was also in this expression a reproach and a reminder to the living" (179). Even in death the face of the deceased carries on its dialogue with life. It summons the living to respond to the light of relation that may force them from their deathly isolation. And Gerasim is a beacon of the light that Ivan Il'ich finally glimpsed.

More important than this parallel, however, is the contrast between Gerasim and Ivan Il'ich. Opposite the language of disease and despair surrounding the latter, Gerasim is described as "clean, fresh, . . . always cheerful, serene" (212). We also notice that "the strength and vitality of Gerasim's life alone did not trouble but rather soothed Ivan Il'ich" (213). Why? Because Gerasim's vitality bears witness to the vital and therefore affirms the dearness of that life that unfolds in the offering up of life to the other. In his service to the sick man Gerasim demonstrates that the spiritual need of the self is met by attending to the material need of the other. Suddenly what matters is something more than what meets the eye, something that belongs to the inner life of the human being. And Ivan Il'ich is shown this through Gerasim. With one very important exception that will be noted shortly, Gerasim is the only person who touches Ivan Il'ich, the only one who has a relation and not an aversion to him. The manner of Gerasim's touch is also meaningful: he takes the sick man by the legs and, for a time, thereby comforts him. One is reminded of the age-old significance of the legs, dating at least as far back as the myth of Antaeus, who, so long as his feet were in contact with his mother Earth, had the strength of the Earth herself. As a peasant and a figure of life, Gerasim is a man of the earth, of the source of life; taking Ivan Il'ich by the legs, he helps the man to regain contact with life. In his touch Gerasim reveals the openness necessary to the truth of human relation, and his touch signifies the fact that "only Gerasim did not lie" (214)—which is to say that only the I of Gerasim is the I-for-the-other of dialogue and not the I-for-myself of monologue. The truth of dialogical life and living is always for-the-other. Just as the touch is connected with life, the truth is connected with the touch. Thus in Gerasim we behold the substance of dialogical response and responsibility, the substance of life: it is the touch of the truth and the truth of the touch.

Because Gerasim responds to the sick man, he is able to summon a response from him, one that comes first as a question and then as a confession: "Looking at Gerasim's sleepy, good-natured face with its high cheekbones, it suddenly came into his head: what if my whole life, my conscious life, has not been what 'was needful'?" (226). And then Ivan Il'ich "suddenly saw that none of it had been what was needful, that it had all been a terrible, huge deception that hid both life and death" (227). At this juncture, in the face that beams with life and the face darkened by death, Tolstoy presents perhaps the most significant contrast between Gerasim and Ivan Il'ich; in this opposition of one face to the other we have the revelation of responsibility and the summons to human relation. In contrast to the monological written word on the official document, the face is the source of the spoken word and of dialogical interaction, even though nothing may be said. From the face comes the assignation to respond to the question of life: where are you? Revealing to him that he has lived wrongly, Gerasim's face announces to Ivan Il'ich his absence from life. From the face of the other comes the voice of the self, much like the voice that springs from Olenin in Tolstoy's *Kazaki* (*The Cossacks*): "To live for others, to do good! . . . There is something leading me on which is stronger than I. I am tormented. But I was dead before" (268). Taking note of this, we cannot help but recall once again the message, the reproach and the warning, that speaks from the face of Ivan Il'ich himself as he lay dead: "On the face was the expression that what was needed to be done was done, and done rightly. There was also in this expression a reproach and a reminder to the living" (179). Even from the other side of this life the trace of a revelation speaks from the face and from beyond it, like the echo of a word that can be heard only as an echo.

In the end the revelation of the path to life opens up to the dying man through another face. Here we must recall an important matter mentioned above, namely the messianic significance of the child in this tale. Retracing his life, Ivan Il'ich finds that the closer he had been to childhood, the more alive he had been. "The further back he went," we read, "the more life there had been. And there had been more goodness in life and more of life itself. The one and the other merged" (224–25). In this innocence the child knows nothing of dissemblance or distinction, of propriety or pretense. Open, exposed, and vulnerable, his face is the face of his soul, through which he offers his soul to the other and is ready to receive the offering of the other. As in *Anna Karenina*, the child is the one who, "with his innocent outlook on life, was the compass that showed them how far they had diverged from what they knew was right but did not want to see" (174). Ivan Il'ich's child Vasya, in fact, is the only person other than Gerasim who responds to the dying man, and he responds with his face, with his "frightened and condoling look. Except for Gerasim, it seemed to Ivan Il'ich that Vasya alone understood and pitied him" (220). Except for Gerasim, Vasya is also the only one who touches the man. If the face of Gerasim poses a question and elicits a confession from Ivan Il'ich, the face of the child Vasya opens up to him the way and the light of dialogical life. The revelation of life is the revelation of the child. The child is his savior. Listen:

"Yes, none of it has been what was needful," he said to himself, "but that does not matter. It can, the 'needful' thing can be done. But what is the 'needful' thing?" he asked himself and suddenly fell silent. This was at the end of the third day, an hour before his death. At that moment the schoolboy quietly crept toward his father and went up to his bed. The dying man was still crying out in despair and waving his hands. His hand fell on the schoolboy's head. The schoolboy caught it, pressed it to his lips, and started to weep. At that moment Ivan Il'ich fell through and saw the light, and it was revealed to him that his life had not been what was needful and that it was still possible to correct. He asked himself: "What, indeed, is 'needful'?" And he fell silent, listening intensely. Then he felt someone kissing his hand. He opened his eyes and caught sight of his son. [228–29]

How is the truth of dialogical life and living revealed? Through the touch of the child and the compassion of the face in its exposure to the hand; through the offering of the lips, from which the dialogical word sounds as an echo in the midst of words and resounds in the silence of a kiss. Surprisingly, and almost without exception, critics have failed to comment on this moment in Tolstoy's tale. Yet by now we can see that it is a crucial moment indeed. For just as Ivan Il'ich falls through and sees the light, Tolstoy's message itself comes to light.

The dialogical life that emerges when we read, "There was no death" (229), is spiritual life, the eternal life to which Berdyaev refers when he writes, "Eternal life is revealed in time, it may unfold itself in every instant as an eternal present. Eternal life is not a future life but life in the present, life in the depths of an instant of time. In those depths time is torn asunder. . . . Inwardly, from the point of view of eternity unfolded in the depths of the moment and not projected into time, death does not exist" (261–62). Having lived in anticipation of the future and in nostalgia for the past, Ivan Il'ich never truly lived, never found a presence in the present moment, until his last moment of life. Tolstoy has shown us that for every human being, and not just for this particular character, life is presence and that presence lies in dialogical response; his message is that life is human relation and that dialogical relation is rooted in responsibility. We must seek life not in the monologism of social or professional position but in the face of the one who is now before us. Responding to the summons of the face, we hear the call to life. Thus one may see the misunderstanding behind the claim that in *The Death of Ivan Il'ich* life lies in autonomy and virtue, and one realizes how far we fall short in identifying the "answer to the puzzle of death" simply as "love and compassion" (Sorokin 502). Love? Yes. Compassion? Of course. But Tolstoy unveils the how and the where of life and living, of love and compassion, on a level that transforms such an answer into a question. Coming before the literary work, the reader encounters not a skull amid the wine cups and the roses but the face of a child and in the face a question: where are you? Confined to critical explication, our response is no better than the vain pretense that marks the monological death of Ivan Il'ich. As Bakhtin has argued, "in *explication* there is only one consciousness, one subject; in *understanding* there are two consciousnesses, two subjects; there can be no dialogical relation with an object; therefore explication is void of dialogical features. Understanding is always, to some extent, dialogical" (*Estetika* 289). Bringing us into contact with the human voice that speaks through the text, understanding is more existential than intellectual. Above and beyond our critical reply to Tolstoy, we must respond with our lives to the life of Ivan Il'ich.

And yet, Tolstoy realizes that the response to the character entails a response to something that transcends both the character and the text from which he speaks. The movement from the monological formula that creates a breach between life and word is a movement into a dialogical relation that strives to fill or heal that breach; as such it is a movement from a state of exile into a higher relation. Exile is precisely exile from the Most High. This proposition, of course, introduces to the notion of exile a theological aspect. And Tolstoy pursues that aspect in the last of his major novels, in *Voskresenie* (*Resurrection*).

4. The Theological Aspects of Exile: Tolstoy's *Resurrection*

In 1888, two years after the publication of *The Death of Ivan Il'ich*, Tolstoy began work on *Resurrection*, a project that would occupy him at intervals for the next eleven years. During this period he was also pursuing a number of theological and other religious writings, texts that have a bearing on how one might read the text of *Resurrection*. Implicit to these religious texts is the premise that exile, as a human condition isolating one person from another, can be overcome only through a life lived in such a way that it testifies to a higher relation. It is from a position of exile that the need for redemption manifests itself, and redemption is to be achieved through a return to human relation grounded in divine relation. Such is the premise that shapes Tolstoy's last great novel. Commenting on the novel, he noted in his diary on 15 December 1900 that he wrote it "without any thought of preaching to people" (487). Nonetheless he does bear witness to that relation to a higher truth that decides the truth of human relation—or, as we shall see, to that human relation that reveals the truth of a higher relation. Tolstoy's interest in a higher truth and its theological implications for the notion of exile is a point often ignored by the existing critical assessments of the novel. The strictly aesthetic approach, for example, frequently comes to the conclusion that, as a work of art, *Resurrection* does not measure up very well against *War and Peace* or *Anna Karenina*; in this vein T.G.S. Cain argues that the novel is more important for the studies of human alienation that follow it than for any artistic merits of its own (183–84). Viewing the work in its relation to society, on the other hand, John Bayley takes the novel's value to lie in its severe social criticism, claiming that "the reality of the book is in its presentation of the corpse that a corrupt social order has made of the life and enterprise of the body" (261). R.F. Christian links Tolstoy's assessment of society to a higher relation, declaring that *Resurrection* "is not a search but an analysis of society in the light of revealed truth" (229), but he does not explore the theological implications of such an analysis.

In this chapter we shall examine in detail those theological elements of exile at work in Tolstoy's *Resurrection* as they develop through his main character Nekhlyudov, who undergoes a process of seeking redemption, not only for having wronged the condemned woman

Maslova, but for having generally lived at a distance from the other human being. The concern, therefore, is not with the artistic merits of the book or with its effectiveness as a commentary on Russian society. Rather, drawing on those theological works that Tolstoy was writing around the time when he produced the novel, we shall bring to light certain connections between the work of art and the theological elements of exile that underlie the text. Tied to such an approach, of course, is the question of whether a novel can do very much in the way of expounding a given theology; but how we answer that question depends on the theology expounded. In the case of Tolstoy's *Resurrection* the novel not only expounds a certain theology but is thematically shaped by it, insofar as the novel addresses the notion of exile in terms of an exile from that human relation that derives its truth from a relation to the divine. Because exile is here viewed as a human condition calling for a human response, we shall find that Tolstoy's theology is anthropocentric; that is to say, it is not distinguished by speculation on attributes of God or on points of doctrine but rather unfolds in the midst of human life as it is lived. And, since his novel constitutes an interaction with that life, it lends itself to the inclusion of such a theological dimension. Indeed, the very title of the book suggests what, for Tolstoy, is the ultimate point of any theology: the defeat of death. This subject matter concerns us, then, not as an object of curiosity neatly confined to Russian literature but as a matter of ultimate concern for anyone who must die.

As Tolstoy sees it, the struggle for anything immortal arises only from a context of mortality. Examining the novel in the light of Tolstoy's theological thought, we shall find that at the basis of *Resurrection* lies a theological outlook, according to which the return from exile is born of a higher truth that is to be worked out by human beings in a human realm, and not by a divine institution or a god or even a godman. The first step in this investigation of the theological aspects of exile in the novel, therefore, will be an consideration of the Russian Orthodox theology and the Church represented in the novel.

The Attack on the Church

The truth that Tolstoy expounds in the text of *Resurrection* is, in his view, the truth of the Gospel, which he regards as a holy text. This is the text that serves as a reference point from which the position of exile is defined; it stands above his polemic as the position from which the truth of his own position, over against that of the Church, is determined; thus the image of the Word himself, the image of Jesus, is often seen hanging precisely in those places where he is betrayed—in courtrooms, prisons, and other institutions of officialdom. One place in which Tolstoy sets up this opposition, with the Gospel standing above the implied opponents, is in a church service, which he describes by saying,

To none of the participants, from the priest and the superintendent to Maslova, did it occur that Jesus himself—whose name the priest endlessly repeated in wheezing tones, praising him with all sorts of strange words—had forbidden precisely what was being done here; that he had forbidden not only the meaningless babble and the blasphemous incantation of priests and teachers over bread and wine, but in the most explicit terms had forbidden one group of people to refer to others as their teachers; that he had forbidden prayers in temples and had commanded each person to pray in solitude; that he had forbidden temples themselves, saying that he had come to destroy them and that one must pray not in temples but in spirit and in truth; and that, above all, he had not only forbidden judging people and holding them in confinement, torturing, humiliating, and executing them as it was done here, but he had come to set free those who were captive. [143–44]

One immediately sees at work here a monological discourse of judgment called into question by dialogically engaging it with the discourse of another authority. It is not just any other authority, however, but the authority of the "hagiographic word," as Bakhtin calls it, of a discourse "without a sideward glance, calmly adequate to itself and its referential object" (*Problems* 248). Thus the authority of the word in *Resurrection* is couched in the Word itself (or himself); it is the authority of truth, which Tolstoy sets up over against the authority of power. Drawing on that authority, Tolstoy establishes a relation between the ritual performed in the temple and the actions perpetrated outside of it: the dogmatic theology of the Church is worse than wrong—it is harmful, for it creates the rupture that exiles life from the word and human being from human being.

In his *Kritika dogmaticheskogo bogosloviya* (*Critique of Dogmatic Theology*) Tolstoy makes a statement that characterizes his attitude toward the Church as it is expounded in the novel. "Before I doubted the teaching of the Church and was reading the Gospel," he writes, "I could not at all understand these words: 'Whoever says a word against the Son of Man will be forgiven; but whoever speaks against the Holy Spirit will not be forgiven, either in this age or in the age to come.' Now these words are all too terribly clear to me. This is the word uttered against the Holy Spirit, which will not be forgiven either in this age or in the age to come: it is the teaching of the Church" (314–15). Explaining more specifically what the nature of the offense is, he goes on to say, "The Church's teaching has twisted the spirit of the teaching into a negation of all life: instead of poverty, it fosters luxury; instead of non-judgment, the most cruel judgment; instead of forgiveness for transgressions, hatred and wars; instead of non-resistance to evil, executions" (322). One is reminded of Carl Jung's insight on the function of the institutional, monological creed. "What is usually and generally called 'religion,' " he writes,

is to such an amazing degree a substitute that I ask myself seriously whether this kind of "religion," which I prefer to call a creed, has not an important function in human society. The substitution has the obvious purpose of replacing immediate experience by a choice of suitable symbols invested in a solidly organized dogma or ritual. The Catholic church maintains them by her indisputable authority, the Protestant church (if this term is still applicable) by insistence on faith and the evangelical message. As long as these two principles work, people are effectively defended and shielded against immediate religious experience. [52–53]

And to be shielded from religious experience is to be cut off from life and from truth. Departing from the hagiographic word to impose its own monological authority, the Church imposes a permanent truth in the way that Karl Jaspers describes when he says, "The unfulfillment of communication and the severity of its miscarriage become the revelation of a depth which nothing but transcendence can fill. . . . Detached from this as permanent truth, instead of being itself, truth degenerates into a knowledge of something, to a finished satisfaction, instead of a consuming demand in temporal existence" (*Vernunft* 80). Indeed, this is what the Church represents in *Resurrection*; with its fixed formulas and ready answers it devours the humanity it pretends to serve.

In his novel Tolstoy represents the Church most directly through its human agent, that is, through his portrait of the priest. The attending priest at Maslova's trial, for example, "was very proud of having sworn in several tens of thousands of men and of continuing to serve in his declining years the glory of his Church, fatherland, and family, to which, in addition to a house, he would leave capital amounting to thirty thousand rubles in securities. It never occurred to him that his work in the court, which consisted of having people swear oaths on the Gospel that forbids them, was not good" (33). Once again, the exile characterized by a distance from the holy is expressed through the disparity between hagiographic word and dogmatic discourse; once again, there is a Book beneath this book, and its truth is used to expose the lie. Just as Judas betrays the Word for thirty pieces of silver, so the priest betrays him for thirty thousand. And, like Judas, the priest commits his betrayal under the guise of embrace, with a kiss, as it were. Between these lines, then, one hears Tolstoy echoing Kierkegaard's outcry: "The very existence of these priests is an untruth. Being completely secularized and in the service of the State (royal functionaries, persons of social position, making a career), they obviously could not very well tell the congregation what Christianity is, for to say this would mean resigning their posts" (*Attack* 97). The hidden side of such a priest is, of course, disbelief. Thus, in another description of a priest presiding over a religious service, we are told, "He did not believe that the bread had been made into the body, that pronouncing many words was of any use to the soul, or that he had actually eaten a piece of God—it was impossible to believe such things—but he believed that it was necessary to hold to such a belief. The main thing that confirmed him in this belief was that by fulfilling its demands for eighteen years he received an income on which he could support his family, send his son to the gymnasium, and place his daughter in religious school" (144). Thus the betrayal of the truth of the holy text lies not only in a contradiction of its teaching but in a false mystification of one of its institutions, here the institution of the Eucharist—made false, in fact, by being made into an institution or a point of dogmatic theology.

The point to be noted from the standpoint of Tolstoy's theology is that the meaning of the Church lies in its human manifestations; the teachings of the Church are no better, no worse, than its teachers. What is violated in the betrayal of the truth, moreover, is not just a certain moral sensibility but a sense of human reason as it is incarnated in the Book. This feature of Tolstoy's theology becomes quite clear when we recall that in his translation of the Gospels Tolstoy renders the Greek word *logos* as *razumenie*, which is a cognate of the word for "reason," *razum*, and means "understanding" or "comprehension." But the existential aspects of the religious thought found in *Resurrection*, despite all the similarities, are not akin to the religious existentialism of a Kierkegaard, who viewed faith as a passion and who embraced the notion of an Absolute Paradox at work in Christianity; rather, Tolstoy's theology is existential to the extent that it takes theological substance to lie in human responsibility, as well as in human reason. Thus he holds Toporov—the head of the Church in *Resurrection*, who is modeled after Pobedonostsev, head of the Holy Synod—responsible for what the Church itself represents. "The post held by Toporov," we read, "involved an inner contradiction which only a stupid person void of moral sensibility could fail to see. Toporov possessed both of these negative characteristics" (305). Once more the notion of contradiction implies the distance that distinguishes exile. And the fact that contradiction is a point of criticism tells us that exile entails not only a distance from the holy but also a distance from the logos understood as *razumenie* or rational understanding. Since rational understanding belongs to human being, this contradiction is a contravention of the human image. Precisely stated, the contradiction is that the Church, which, according to its doctrine, was established and upheld by God, requires human intervention, including violence, in order to survive. Further, like the priest mentioned above, Toporov "was not a believer and found such a condition very comfortable and pleasant" (306). Yet the creed promoted by the Church is the very thing that promotes cruelty among its followers. "Were it not for this faith," we read of the prison officials, "it would not only be more difficult but perhaps impossible for them to use all their strength to torment people as they were now doing with a completely easy conscience" (145). Why? Because this "faith" fosters a sense of duty to an ideology made into an idol, which eclipses the responsibility underlying human relation. And so Tolstoy brings under attack a creed disbelieved by its educated proponents, yet justifying the crimes of its uneducated believers.

In the novel, however, there is another position from which the doctrines of the Church are called into question, that of the educated nonbeliever; one representative of that category is Nekhlyudov's friend Selenin, who "could not help knowing that he was right in rejecting the truth of the Church's teaching. But under the stress of his living conditions he, an upright man, entered into a small lie, and . . . it led him into that big lie in which he was now trapped" (291). This description of Selenin calls to mind Tolstoy's description of himself and of the members of his class in the *Confession*: "My break with faith occurred in me as it did and still does among people of our social and cultural type. . . . People live as everyone lives, but they all live according to principles that not only have nothing to do with the teachings of faith but for the most part are contrary to them. . . . The teachings of faith are left to some other realm, separated from life and independent of it. If one should encounter them, then it is only as some superficial phenomenon that has no connection with life" (14). In Selenin's case the "big lie" is the lie of the very teaching that Selenin had rejected, namely that all higher truth is inaccessible to human reason and that revelation is in the keeping of the Church alone. Once again, the rigidity of the letter that distinguishes dogmatic theology veils the face of both human and divine being. From the standpoint of Tolstoy's anthropocentric theology, there is no "higher truth" that is beyond the access of human reason as it unfolds in human life. In his *Soedinenie, perevod i izsledovanie chetyrekh Evangelii* (*Harmony, Translation, and Investigation of the Four Gospels*) Tolstoy insists that, according to Jesus, "God is not the inaccessible God that He was before, but God will be in the world and in the interactions among people" (113). His novel, then, is not simply modeled after life or intended to be a critique of life; rather, it is designed to insert into life that element of the divine that the Church would steal away. For unless the truth is lived in the midst of life and not just expounded from the pulpit, there can be neither life nor truth: what Tolstoy is after is a lived theology. And, just as the defeat of death concerns all who must die, the interest in a lived theology has implications for all who must live.

Toward a Lived Theology

Our examination of the notion of a lived theology begins with an important point that Tolstoy makes in *Tsarstvo Bozhie vnutri vas* (*The Kingdom of God Is within You*), namely that man's freedom does not consist of his ability to do whatever he wants to do, independent of life's flow, of its creatures, and of its influence on him; rather "it lies in his ability to recognize and affirm the truth around him, to act freely and joyfully on what is eternal and infinite, fulfilled by God or the life of the world" (403). Here, indeed, God is the life of the world, the human life that longs to be free in the world—free, that is, not in the sense of doing whatever you want to do but in the consciousness of what you must do. Thus freedom and destiny are tied together, or, as Buber puts it, "Fate is encountered only by him who actualizes freedom. That I discovered the deed that intends me, that, this movement of my freedom, reveals the mystery to me. . . . This free human being encounters fate as the counter-image of his freedom. It is not his limit but his completion; freedom and fate embrace each other to form meaning; and given meaning, fate—with its eyes hitherto severe, suddenly full of light—looks like grace itself" (*I and Thou* 102). Hence Nekhlyudov discovers that his freedom lies not in being the master of himself but in being the servant of God: " 'Yes,' it occurred to him, 'to feel oneself not the master but a servant,' and that thought filled him with joy" (235). And so the character sets out to live the idea expressed by his author in *Mysli o Boge* (*Thoughts on God*), where we read, "People know two Gods: one whom they want to force to serve them through prayers demanding from Him the fulfillment of their desires—and another God, whom we must serve, the fulfillment of whose will must determine the direction of our lives" (35). And how does Nekhlyudov assume the status of God's servant? By serving others: a lived theology is lived in the offering up of one's life for the sake of the other in a realization that the path to God leads through the human being before us. The truth that sets us free is the truth revealed not from on high but from within human relation. And the principle that guides a lived theology, in the words of Nekhlyudov, is "the eternal, immutable, urgent law that God Himself has inscribed upon peoples' hearts" (362): if you want to know God, then look to the heart, both within you and before you. For the heart is God's favorite dwelling place, and it is the one place where the human being may dwell, free from exile.

It is the other, therefore, the human being who stands before him, who announces to Nekhlyudov his exile from God. Coming under the gaze of "a hundred eyes" (187) that peer at him in anguish from prison cells, Nekhlyudov is forced to gaze upon himself through those eyes and thus through the eyes of God. Seeing himself through the eyes of the other, he realizes his responsibility to the other and for the other, who is both God and human being; he offers his love to Maslova, for example, "not for his own sake but for her sake and for the sake of God" (314). To become a servant of God, acting for His sake alone, is to become as nothing before God; and, in Tolstoy's lived theology, to become as nothing before God is to become as nothing before the other. If the return from exile is a return home and if the home signifies an interior, then this becoming as nothing is the means by which the person assumes an inwardness over against what is pleasing to the eye. Only by thus placing the concern for the other infinitely above concern for the self can any clarity of self be achieved. "Now," Tolstoy relates, "everything was simple, because he [Nekhlyudov] was not thinking of what would become of himself—he had no interest in this—but he was thinking only of what he must do. And, surprising as it may seem, although there was no way he could determine what was needful for himself, he knew without a doubt what was needful for others" (234). Once again we see that the spiritual needs of the self are met by meeting the physical needs of the other, this is how matter is transformed into spirit. Thus setting out to act on behalf of the other, Nekhlyudov ultimately returns to himself with a self, one characterized not so much by self knowledge as by being-for-the-other. Signifying the dearness and the depth of the other, he takes on a depth, a significance, of his own; standing before the other, he stands for what is beyond both himself and the other.

"God does His work through us," says Tolstoy in *Thoughts on God* (36), and God is able to work through us only when we become as nothing before Him and thus as an opening through which He may pass into the world. Bakhtin expresses it by saying, "What I must be for the other is what God is for me" (*Estetika* 52). The God of a lived theology is a lived God, and it is through me, in my being-for-the-other, that God is able to enter life; answering to the other and for the life of the other, I answer for the life of the origin of life. God is the shadow of man, as the Hasidic saying goes, and through the love that we offer to the other, God reveals Himself as love. The exile of the other, therefore, is my exile, and the love I offer to the other is the one path to the other side of exile. "God is love," Tolstoy insists, "that is, we know God only in the form of love; and love is God, that is, if we love, then we do not have gods but God. . . . Love is in itself the manifestation (consciousness) of God" (*Mysli* 38–39). A lived theology, then, is a theology that places its accent on love as the human path to the divine, as the intersection of the human and the divine; God must be lived, not theorized, and only in the love between human beings can any single human being recognize himself or herself as one created in God's image. Opposite this lived theology is the dogmatic theology of rules and regulations, a theology of officialdom ruled by officials. To live by regulation is to live at the expense of human relation, since relation is grounded in response; again, living within the regulation, we flee to the code, so that the formula eclipses the voice and therefore the self or soul of the human being. A lived theology, then, is a theology lived in the realm of human relation, that is, in the dynamic interchange of response and responsibility. Wherever exile is an issue, this interchange is an issue; here too what we are dealing with goes far beyond a literary character's struggle with the Russian prison system.

In his struggle Nekhlyudov discovers that the fixed phrases of the dogma prepared beforehand guide the officials who lead others into exile and yet who are themselves the exiled ones. They are exiled in the already said, in the "dead flesh of meaning," as Bakhtin calls it (*Estetika* 117). The presence and responsibility demanded by the living situation, on the other hand, launch the human being into the realm of the yet-to-be. Here the man does not look to the *pre*scription that speaks for him and thus hides the face of the other, rather, he looks to the face that summons him to step before the countenance. This process of becoming present is just what Tolstoy's lived theology requires. And so, eying the prison officials, it strikes Nekhlyudov that "they saw before themselves not people and their obligations toward them but the duties and demands of their office, which they placed above the demands of human relations. That is what it all comes down to," thought Nekhlyudov. "If it can be admitted that there is anything more important than love for a fellow human being—even if for a single hour or in a single instance—then any crime can be committed against people without the slightest feeling of guilt." . . . Perhaps these governors, inspectors, and policemen are needed, but it is terrible to see people void of the primary human attribute—love and compassion for one another. [360–61]

Nothing is more important than love, not as an attribute of God (God is not one thing and the attribute something else) but as the one thing needful in human relation, the portal through which the divine enters the human. Reflecting on the ramifications of this theological point that evolves in the pages of Tolstoy's novel, one is reminded of a startling statement made by Ludwig Feuerbach in *The Essence of Christianity*. "God as God has not saved us, but Love, which transcends the difference between the divine and human personality. As God has renounced himself out of love, so we, out of love, should renounce God; for if we do not sacrifice God to love, we sacrifice love to God, and, in spite of the predicate of love, we have the God—the evil being—of religious fanaticism" (53). Just as Tolstoy's attack on the Church entails this kind of renunciation, so does the lived theology of *Resurrection* entail this kind of affirmation.

Such a position, of course, bears serious implications for how one is to view the Christ. Just as it is not God but love (or love equated with God) that saves us, so, too, is it not the godman that saves us. "To acknowledge Christ as God," Tolstoy declares, "is to reject God" (*O razume* 13), because, as Tolstoy sees it, this amounts to an exclusion of that spark of the divine that makes every person a child of God. Human exile is that condition in which we have nothing but the human. If Christ alone is the son of God, then he is not the godman but the mangod who becomes the object of worship in a displacement of God. And once God is displaced, then nothing is true and everything is permitted. Tolstoy comments on this point in a letter to Hamilton Campbell, a minister of the Free Church of Scotland, dated 27 January–6 February 1891; he writes, "Christ being God is a belief that can be kept only by people who do not accept his teaching, . . . which cannot be accepted by clergy because it destroys at once their position and shows that their vocation is only a pretense to feed at the cost of the people" (*Letters* 475). Nonetheless in *Ponyatie o Boge* (*The Concept of God*) Tolstoy maintains, "I believe in Christ, and I understand quite clearly what he says about the Father; and I am conscious of my own sonhood to God" (11). Tolstoy's accent on human being places his Christ firmly in the realm of human being. Thus subscribing to the Arian heresy, Tolstoy makes Christ into the incarnation of humanity, not the incarnation of God; the declaration of Christ's divinity makes Christianity into a messianism that excludes humanity and, with humanity, God. Thus Tolstoy's Christ and his "Christianity" represent not the dogmatic exclusiveness of the Church's doctrine but the human universality of a theology lived within any human life ruled by love for human beings. "In every person," he believes, "there is a spark of God, the spirit of God; every person is a son of God" (*O razume* 15). The exclusiveness of Christianity as it is expounded through the doctrine of the Church not only excludes one group of human beings from another, but it also isolates the human from the divine. Hence life is detached from life.

Near the end of *Resurrection* Nekhlyudov encounters an old tramp who embodies the lived theology that Tolstoy is attempting to expound, in all its human universality and human spirituality. When, for example, Nekhlyudov asks him why there are different religions, he replies,

There are different religions because people believe in other people and not in themselves. I too have believed in other people and have wandered about, as if I were in the taiga; I went so far astray that I lost all hope of ever finding my way. There are Old Believers and New Believers, Sabbatarians and Khlysty, those who have priests and those who don't, Austrians, Molokans, and Skoptsy. Each creed extols itself alone. And so they all crawl around like blind pups. There are many religions, but the spirit is one. In you, in me, and in him. That means: if each were to believe in the spirit within himself, then all of them would be joined together. Let each be himself, and all will be one. [431]

Only where the universal is thus embodied in the particular can the human being emerge from exile. And only a lived theology can bring about this embodiment: when each is who he or she is, *in spirit*, all are one. For the spirit is that transcendent center that makes possible a community of people, rather than a crowd of the self-interested. Being oneself, each human being may be the truth that God has inscribed on the heart, free of the dogma of one crowd over another. The old tramp goes on to explain to Nekhlyudov that, "like Christ," he has been persecuted (431). And, when the authorities ask for his name, he says that he has no name except Human Being; when they ask his age, he answers that he has none, since he has always been and always will be; when asked about his parents, he claims that they are God the Father and Mother Earth; when asked whether he acknowledges the Tsar, he replies that he is a tsar unto himself (431–32).

The name by which he calls himself, "Human Being," includes all that is said about his age, his parents, and so on. It signifies a gathering together of heaven and earth, of the mortal and the immortal, into a single figure, as it is all gathered into the figure of the Christ. To recognize oneself as a human being is to see oneself as one created in the image of God, a son of God who bows down to no one and yet is a servant to all, for he is a servant to the God who abides in each and in all. In the old tramp, who is a paradigm of one who lives the Tolstoyan theology, we have a theological stance in which unconditional exclusiveness and unconditional inclusiveness are of a piece; no single feature of life is of absolute importance, but all facets of life are contained in the relation to the spirit that is one, that is, to God. Buber articulates this position in *I and Thou* when he says, "Looking away from the world is no help toward God; staring at the world is no help either; but whoever beholds the world in him stands in his presence. . . . Of course, God is 'the wholly other'; but he is also the wholly same: the wholly present. Of course, he is the *mysterium tremendum* that appears and overwhelms; but he is also the mystery of the obvious that is closer to me than my own I" (127). The task of Tolstoy's lived theology, of his anthropic theology? To become who I am, a human being and thus an expression of divine being. For in that dynamic of becoming that draws together the human relation and the divine relation lies the dynamic of redemption from exile.

The Dynamic of Redemption

Richard Gustafson has correctly pointed out that "*Resurrection* is a story of sin and redemption. The sin, as always, is a failure of human relatedness" (162); he goes on to explain that Nekhlyudov "is saved, not because he is more worthy, but because he makes the effort to be saved. He begins with a flawed conception of sin as a past act, a single, individual violation of love he can correct. . . . Through life the sinner learns that in order for his soul to keep on growing, he must participate in the redemption of this unjust world . . . by clearing himself of his judgments so that he can right now help to create human relatedness" (175). There is no redemption for the individual that does not include redemption for all; not just the individual but the world itself is in exile. What Gustafson describes, then, is Nekhlyudov's need to assume responsibility not merely for himself but for all. Indeed, this responsibility that makes the particular into a vessel of the universal is a definitive feature of the self, as Levinas reminds us when he says, "The self, the subjection or subjectivity of the subject, is the very over-emphasis of a responsibility for creation" (*Otherwise* 125). Through life, in this world, right now—and not in an afterlife, in another world, or in the hereafter—the redemption of the human being is worked out in an answerability for human life as it unfolds in the world. "One does not find God if one remains in the world," Buber expresses it. "One does not find God if one leaves the world. Whoever goes forth to his You with his whole being and carries to it all the being of the world, finds him whom one cannot seek" (*I and Thou* 127). To be sure, we find in this remark an elucidation of Nekhlyudov's own confusion. He knows that he cannot remain in the world, since there, the narrator tells us, "when he would think, read, or speak about God, truth, wealth, and poverty, everyone around him would take him to be out of place and somewhat ridiculous" (53). And so Nekhlyudov attempts to take leave of the world by following Maslova to Siberia, replacing one form of exile with another. He fails to realize that, as Gustafson notes above, his sin lies not in a particular act but in a way of being that isolates him from human relation and therefore from higher relation; to approach one is to draw nigh to the other.

Redemption, then, does indeed entail a dynamic, that is, a continual movement of drawing nigh; in the movement of return an infinite interior opens up, so that the one thing needful is ever yet to be achieved. This Tolstoyan view of redemption underlies Nekhlyudov's rejection of the doctrine of a completed redemption as it is espoused by orthodox Christianity, where redemption is a matter that has already been settled, removed from the realm of the yet-to-be. "Salvation has come," Nekhlyudov hears a preacher proclaim. "It is here, easy and joyous. This salvation is the blood shed for us by the one son of God. . . . His suffering, his blood, saves us" (270), as if there were nothing that remained to be done, no working for salvation in fear and trembling. In *O razume, vere i molitve* (*On Reason, Faith, and Prayer*) Tolstoy dismisses this view by arguing that "no one is completely free of sin; no one is completely holy. We can only *strive* to become so" (7). He goes on to insist, "There is no teaching more immoral and harmful than the teaching that man cannot achieve perfection by his own strength, . . . that reason is not sufficient for understanding the truth" (9–10). It is not Christ's blood but his truth that offers us redemption; each person is a child of God, irreplaceable, which means that no other can substitute for him, not even Jesus. "I am I," Levinas states this point, "in the sole measure that I am responsible, a non-interchangeable I. I can substitute myself for everyone, but no one can substitute himself for me. It is in this precise sense that Dostoevsky said: 'We are responsible for all, for all men before all, and I more than all the others' " (*Ethics* 101). According to the reasoning that rules Tolstoy's reading of the Gospel, no other can take my place because it is I who must take the part of the other. Those whom Nekhlyudov sees suffering need *him*, require *his* help, and not the help of the one who was crucified two thousand years ago. If Jesus is to be viewed as the redeemer, then it is not because he has removed our sin but because he has announced our responsibility.

Thus it is through a realization of his responsibility to the other and for the other (to and for Maslova, for example) that Nekhlyudov is able to pray: "He asked God to help him, to settle into him, to cleanse him, and even as he asked it was already fulfilled. The God who lived within him awakened" (109). *Even as he asked*, be it noted. We think we pray to God, but this is not exactly the case, for the prayer is itself divine; in the prayer that comes to our lips we discover the divine image in which we are created. "Prayer," writes Tolstoy in *On Reason, Faith, and Prayer*, "lies in . . . summoning in myself my divine origin. . . . Prayer lies in . . . calling forth within oneself the divine aspect of the soul, in being carried over into it and, through it, entering into intercourse with Him of whom it is a part" (15). God is not the object of worship that the Church would make Him out to be; rather, He is all subject, the I Am who alone is able to speak and to listen at the same time. This brings us to a striking implication: God too is in exile. The redemption of the self entails a redemption of God through the loving relation of the self to the other, that is, to that part of the human other that harbors a spark of the divine. To feed the hungry is to feed God; to comfort the afflicted is to offer God comfort. The awakening of the divine thus underlies the series of awakenings experienced by Nekhlyudov in his struggle for redemption and resurrection; indeed, anyone who has read the novel cannot help but notice the motif of rising from and falling into sleep. In his diary, for instance, he notes, "I have not written in my diary for two years, and I thought I would never return to such childishness. Yet it was not childishness but conversation with my own self, with that true, divine self which lives in every man. All this time I was asleep" (135). Dialogue is as essential to the dynamic of redemption as love is; all dialogue, even the dialogue with the self, entails an encounter with God and with the other, in whom God dwells. And, just as Nekhlyudov returns to his diary and his dialogue, so does the dynamic of redemption entail a movement of return. It is a return to the Word, to prayer, to the self by way of the other, it is a return to that Within that is a synonym for Above.

Nekhlyudov's oscillation from sleep to wakefulness, therefore, is not a movement back and forth but a movement of return, a spiraling upward in an ascent toward the divine through the human, toward himself through others. One manifestation of this process as a movement of return comes when Nekhlyudov "not only remembered but actually felt himself to be as he was then, when he was a boy of fourteen praying to God to reveal to him the truth, when he wept at his mother's knees upon their parting and promised her that he would always be good" (233). Hence the salvific significance of the child that we discovered in *The Death of Ivan Il'ich* may be found in *Resurrection* as well. This aspect of redemption is accentuated even more emphatically in the novel's last chapter, when Nekhlyudov finally turns to that text that has ruled the entire text of the novel. Opening up Matthew 18:3–4, he reads, "Verily I say unto you, Except ye be converted, and become as little children, ye shall not enter the kingdom of heaven. Whosoever therefore shall humble himself as this little child, the same is greatest in the kingdom of heaven." Whereupon Nekhlyudov reflects, "Yes, it is so" (453). And to thus humble oneself is to rid oneself of all judgments of others and to forgive; forgiveness is the offspring of dialogical love and loving dialogue. Our exile lies in the judgment we pronounce; born of forgiveness, redemption is the opposite of judgment. It is the door through which we pass in our return from exile.

Where, then, lies the key to redemption as it is worked out in the midst of human life, and not in the adherence to some specific doctrine? This is Nekhlyudov's answer:

The thought which seemed to him at first so strange, so paradoxical, even laughable, more and more often finding its confirmation in life, suddenly struck him as the most simple, indubitable truth. Thus it became clear to him that the one sure means of salvation from the terrible evil that people suffer lay in the realization that people are forever guilty before God and are thus incapable of punishing or reforming others. . . . The answer he had been unable to find was the same that Christ had given to Peter: it lay in forever forgiving everyone, in forgiving an infinite number of times, because there are no people who are themselves free of guilt. [455]

Guilty before God, I forgive the other; forgiving the other, I seek God's forgiveness. And what, we ask, makes such forgiveness, such redemption, possible? Love: it is neither God nor a godman who has saved us, one is reminded of Feuerbach's remark cited above, but love. Thus, writes Tolstoy, "we know that we pass from death to life if we love our brother. He who does not love his brother has no eternal life" (*O razume* 19). The dynamic of redemption from exile is a dynamic of love. If exile is an issue for all who must live and die, return and redemption open up for all who can love. This is the portal through which the divine enters the human; this is the one thing needful, which no doctrine can provide.

In his final comments on *Resurrection* Gustafson explains that the repeated "action of awakening, uncovering, and forward movement into the world is the action of resurrection, the redemption which is the eternal process of growth in life through the restoration of love" (206). Love, as Tolstoy notes above, opens up the eternal, and the eternal is made manifest in repetition. "Exclusive love for God (with *all* your heart)," Buber expresses it, "is, *because he is God*, inclusive love, ready to accept and include all love" (*Between* 51–52). This is the antinomy by which Tolstoy equates the infinite and the finite, and only such antinomy can bring an end to exile; the place of exile is the place where the infinite equals the infinite and the finite the finite, as Tolstoy himself indicates in the *Confession*. Describing the thought process that had kept him locked into despair, he writes, "Throughout my reasoning I was constantly comparing the finite to the finite and the infinite to the infinite; indeed, I could not do otherwise. Thus I concluded and had to conclude that force is force, matter is matter, will is will, infinity is infinity, nothing is nothing; and I could not get beyond that" (59). How does the man break free of this principle of identity? By taking on a position of despite-me, for-another; by forgiving an infinite number of times and thus becoming a finite vessel of the infinite. Thus, according to the theological position that lies at the heart of the novel, redemption is an open-ended process, one distinguished by the endless repetition of forgiveness. And so Tolstoy concludes his novel of redemption and resurrection without imposing on it any closure, ending it with a beginning: "A completely new life began for Nekhlyudov, not so much because he had entered into new conditions of life but because all that happened to him from that time on assumed a meaning entirely different from what had been before. How this new period in his life will end, the future will show" (458). This orientation toward the future is what makes Tolstoy's theology a theology of process and therefore of presence, and not one that is rooted in some redemptive event that has occurred in the past. The novel's open-ended aspect, moreover, opens up a position from which it calls us into question. We have neither the comfort nor the luxury to dismiss it as a social commentary or to approach it on strictly aesthetic grounds. In its interaction with the life of the soul it interacts with our lives.

Whether we take Tolstoy's theological position to be heretical or inspired, that higher principle that rules his vision of life also rules his art. Like the image of Christ overlooking the prison and courtroom scenes in the novel, a higher truth peers over this novelist's shoulder as he sets his pen to the page. While it is true that his is a human response to a human reader, the theological dimensions of that response introduce a third presence, another Reader, in whose name Tolstoy and his audience are gathered. Thus his sense of human responsibility entails that special responsibility that Bakhtin invokes when he says, "Wherever the alibi becomes a prerequisite for creation and expression there can be no responsibility, no seriousness, no meaning. A special responsibility is required. . . . But this special responsibility can be founded only on a profound belief in a higher truth, . . . the belief that another, higher being responds to my special responsibility, that I do not act in an utter void. Apart from this belief there can be only empty pretense" (*Estetika* 179). It is not through his solutions, therefore, that Tolstoy implicates us; addressing the theological aspects of his art, we are questioned by the very questions he raises. What we decide, then, about his lived theology or his view of redemption also entails a decision about our own lives, about our own exile and redemption.

But such questions are not easily lived with, for they question us at the very heart of our identity, creating a rupture in that discourse that constitutes our apparent attachment to ourselves and to life. Indeed, the question is itself the rupture. If, as Henri Bergson has said, religion is "that element which is called upon to make good any deficiency of attachment to life" (210), then the rupture is a rupture of religious discourse. Tolstoy's questioning of Russian Orthodox theology had such an impact on one of twentieth-century Russia's most influential religious thinkers: Pavel Florensky. "When I graduated the gymnasium in the summer of 1899," says Florensky, "I went through a spiritual crisis when I realized the organic nature of the knowledge of physics. In such a state I came under the influence of L. Tolstoy" ("O literature" 146). From the depth of that rupture Florensky took up the task of restoring life to a theological discourse that had become exiled from life.

PART THREE
The Rupture of Religious Discourse

5. Pavel Florensky's Antitheology

"The imaging of God," writes Karl Jaspers in *Truth and Symbol*, "is called theology. Theology never gets further than an intellectual conception of the language of cyphers" (75). Viewing theology in these terms, as "an intellectual conception of the language of cyphers," Jaspers places it in a speculative tradition. The truth of the cipher or the symbol, on the other hand—the truth of that which is a revelation of God—transpires in a living encounter with a living God. We have seen this at work in the lived theology of Tolstoy's *Resurrection*; God must be lived, not just studied within the confines—indeed, within the exile—of intellectual walls. In contrast to the speculative tradition, a theology of truth that is lived and living here presents itself as an antitheology, one that attempts to move beyond the intellectual conception. "As for me," Levinas echoes such a position, "I do not seek the meaning of the term 'God'—at once the most understandable and the most mysterious—in some theological system. I will try to understand it on the basis of a situation . . . " (*Nine* 130). What may thus be understood as an antitheology becomes for Pavel Florensky a theology of truth that places the human being *in situation*. Throughout the discussion in this chapter, this accent on being in a situation will have implications for anyone who is concerned with the nature of truth in life. As always, we are not studying a specific work by a specific figure; rather, we are drawing on Pavel Florensky in order to arrive at another level of understanding a spiritual aspect of the problem of exile.

. In their analytical biography of Mikhail Bakhtin, Katerina Clark and Michael Holquist point out that Bakhtin and Florensky "are perceived by many intellectuals in the Soviet Union as the major Russian thinkers of the twentieth century" (135). While the critical studies of Bakhtin have been fairly extensive in the West, examinations of Florensky's work have been rather scant by comparison. Yet within the context of the concern at hand, Florensky's thought is perhaps more critical to an exegesis of exile. Born in what is now Azerbaijan in 1882, Florensky entered Moscow University in 1900, where he spent four years studying physics and mathematics. From there he went to the Moscow Theological Academy, from which he graduated in 1908. In 1911 he was ordained a priest in the Russian Orthodox Church, and he served as a pro-

fessor at the Theological Academy from 1908 to 1919. In 1933 he was ar-
rested during one of the Stalinist purges and was exiled to Siberia,
where he is reported to have died in 1943 under circumstances that remain mysterious.

Although Florensky is known for his considerable talent in physics,
mathematics, and linguistics, his most influential work is *Stolp i utverzhdenie istiny* (*The Pillar and Foundation of Truth*), which was first published
in 1914. Subtitled "An Attempt at an Orthodox Theodicy in Twelve Letters," this theological investigation takes its title from the passage in
Paul's first letter to Timothy that reads, "I am writing these instructions
to you so that . . . you may know how one ought to behave in the household of God, which is the church of the living God, the pillar and bul-
wark of the truth" (1 Timothy 3:14–15). In sharp contrast to Tolstoy,
there is no doubt in Florensky's soul that the Orthodox Church is just
such a pillar and foundation, but in the work at hand his explicit concern lies more with the nature of truth than with the institution of the
Church or with what Tolstoy referred to as its dogmatic theology. Since
truth in this instance is definitively linked not only to the Church but to
"the living God," Florensky's interest is theological—or rather, it is antitheological, since he pursues the lived and not the speculative. As conceived by Florensky, truth is not to be viewed simply as a datum or fact
about the world or even about God. Rather, he notes, "our Russian
word for 'truth' [*istina*] is linguistically tied to the verb 'is' [*est'*] (*istina—
estina*), so that, in keeping with the Russian understanding of it, 'truth'
entails in itself a concept of absolute reality. Truth is 'the real,' the actually existing" (15). On the basis of this observation he goes on to adopt
the premise that "truth, in the Russian comprehension of it, is an 'abiding existence,' something 'alive,' a 'living being,' 'breathing,' that is,
possessing the essential characteristic of life and existence" (17). Florensky's theology of truth, therefore, is a theology that is not confined
to speculation on the Russian Orthodox view of God but rather goes beyond the peculiarities belonging only to Russian Orthodoxy and into
the heart of life itself. It is in this sense that the theology of Florensky is
an antitheology.

The emphasis on life lends Florensky's theology of truth an existential aspect that reflects Kierkegaard's assertion that "the truth consists not in knowing the truth but in being the truth" (*Training* 201). Florensky himself iterates such an existential stance with respect to truth
when he declares, "I do not know whether or not the Truth exists. But
with my every fiber I sense that I *cannot* be without it" (67). Human
essence, in other words, and the essence of truth are of a piece; created

in the image of the Holy One, the human being is created in the image of truth. It is not surprising, then, to find that this existential attitude leads him to adopt a phenomenological method in the pursuit of his investigation, a method underscoring the contrast between Florensky's antitheology and the theological tradition of speculation. In his address to his reader, for example, he describes the methodological nature of his work by saying, " 'Living religious experience is the sole legitimate means of knowing the doctrine'—thus would I express the general endeavor of my book. . . . Only by turning to direct *experience* can one review and evaluate the spiritual treasure of the Church" (3). Not dogma but experience: setting out more from living revelation than from theological speculation, Florensky's thought is more dialogical than dogmatic; it is characterized more by quest and question than by fixed formulas and ready answers. To be sure, the epistolary form of his work suggests such an approach. "I am writing you 'letters,' " he notes, "instead of composing an 'essay' because I am *afraid to affirm* and prefer to ask" (129). Like those thinkers examined in previous chapters, Florensky is wary of the fixed formulas and ready answers that not only fail to redeem the soul but drive it deeper into exile. As for the one to whom his letters are addressed, that figure remains ambiguous. The fact that he refers to the recipient of the epistles as his "winged Friend," however, may lead us to identify that person as the person of the truth itself. After all, he states that the letters are written not for his own sake but for the sake of his "winged Friend" (70), suggesting that the letters are not just a form of address but a means of answering a voice that he has heard. And, given his assertion that "the truth is revealed to me as truth by means of my affirmation of it" (24), it is reasonable to surmise that it is the truth itself that engages Florensky in his quest for truth.

Because Florensky's notion of truth pertains to what is lived rather than to what is known, an examination of his theology of truth will reveal something not only about the meaning of a concept but also about a manner of pursuing or generating meaning in life. Meaning, Bakhtin has said, is a response to a question (*Estetika* 350), and, as one who prefers to ask, Florensky takes us into the midst of meaning as it might be lived through quest and question. Proceeding from the dialogical format of his text, we are led first of all to a living truth as it emerges at the center of those human and divine relationships that are the vessels of life. Like life itself, truth arises in a realm between two, within a human relation that derives its substance from its relation to the divine. Since the life of relation is not fixed into a static mold but inheres in a

continual process of becoming, we shall find, moreover, that Florensky's antitheology entails a tension between what *is* and what is *not yet;*
here antinomy (a term that Florensky uses to denote the difference between two beings) overtakes identity as a distinguishing feature of that
truth that is lived rather than known. And what is the substance of the
relation that derives its life from a living truth? It is love, the very thing
that Tolstoy ultimately opposes to dogmatic theology, here conceived
not as a feeling or an emotion within the individual but as a presence
between two whose relation harbors a revelation of the holy. And, it will
be shown, love is a manifestation of wisdom, inasmuch as it is a revelation of truth. Let us consider, then, these concerns that are central to Florensky's theology of truth.

Human and Divine Relation

Drawing on his background in linguistics, Florensky establishes those
dimensions of truth that belong to human and divine relation by explaining the nature of truth as it is conceptualized in the Russian, Hebrew, Greek, and Latin languages. Thus turning to these languages, he
explains:

Truth for the Hebrew is actually "the faithful word," "fidelity," the "promise of
hope." . . . Truth is the indispensable promise of God. . . . Truth, therefore, is not
conceived of ontologically, as it is among the Slavs, and not gnosiologically, as
among the Greeks, and not judicially, as among the Romans, but historically, or
better, as belonging to sacred history. Thus it may be noted that the four con-
cepts of truth that we have formed in their shades of meaning can be set up in
pairs in the following manner: the Russian *Istina* and the Hebrew *Emet* are primarily related to the *divine substance* of Truth, while the Greek *Aletheia* and the
Latin *Veritas* are primarily concerned with its *human form.* On the other hand,
the Russian and Greek terms are of a philosophical character, while the Latin
and Hebrew are sociological. By this I mean that in its Russian and Greek concept Truth has an *immediate* relation to each *individual*, while for the Roman and
the Hebrew it is *mediated by society.* [22]

In order to clarify these interrelations that characterize truth, Florensky
sets up the following matrix (22):

	Divine Substance	Human Form
Immediate Personal Relation:	Russian *Istina*	Greek *Aletheia*
Relation Mediated by Society:	Hebrew *Emet*	Latin *Veritas*

From these remarks and the matrix that evolves from them one can see
that Florensky's theology of truth is not confined to a reflection on di-

vine attributes but necessarily includes a human realm—*our* realm—of relation, both communal and individual, which is linked, through truth, to a divine relation. If exile is exile from human and divine relation, then it is also an exile from truth. A condition of exile is thus opposed to a communal condition, where the relation of person to person intersects with the relation of person to community. And at the point of intersection stands the divine center of truth.

Much like Buber in his insistence that "I require a You to become" (*I and Thou* 62), Florensky regards human relation not just as something in which a single human I participates but as the event through which the human being is established as one who can say, "I." He argues, for example, that "the purely subjective, isolated, and blind *I* of the monad exhausts itself for the sake of the *Thou* of the other monad, and through this Thou the I becomes purely objective, that is, proven" (325). Thus the human being arrives at himself by way of another human being, and one can traverse this path in truth only by being for the other, that is, by living for the sake and the sanctity of the other person. The individual establishes a presence in life only through the absolute vulnerability that lies in a readiness to offer up all to the other, all and for nothing. Recall in this connection Levinas's assertion that "the one-for-the-other characteristic of the psyche, signification, is . . . a vulnerability and a pain exhausting themselves like a hemorrhage, denuding even the aspect that its nudity takes on, exposing its very exposedness, expressing itself, speaking, uncovering even the projection that the very form of identity confers upon it. It is the passivity of being-for-another, which is possible only in the form of giving the very bread I eat" (*Otherwise* 72). Without this vulnerability there can be no meaning; without this signification, where the I of the individual *stands for* the dearness of the other person, the I can have no significance. And if the I is unable to thus take on meaning, unable to stand for something before the Thou, then there is no truth to be known. Florensky asserts, therefore, that "the mystical union of *two* is the condition for knowledge, that is, the manifestation of the knowledge of the Spirit of Truth" (430). Because this knowledge rests on a relation between two, what is known is neither "in here" nor "out there" but between. The Spirit of Truth, then, is not like the blood that circulates in our veins but is rather like the air by which we draw the breath of life in a breathing of life into the other, for the sake of the other. It is the *pneuma*, the *ruah*, the *dukh*—words that mean both "spirit" and "breath" in Greek, Hebrew, and Russian—of human relation. Here too one can see what is antitheological about Florensky's theology of truth; the theological concern for God is tied to the human concern for the other person.

One important implication of this position is that the relation of two comprises a *single* presence. One does not imply two; rather, two are required to constitute one. It is this one, this oneness, created by two, moreover, that introduces a third element to the relation. Says Florensky, " '*Two*' is not '*one added to one*' but something of a greater essence, something of a much more significant and more powerful essence. '*Two*' is a *new* unification in the chemistry of the spirit, when '*one added to one*' (the parable of the 'leaven') is qualitatively transformed to form a *third*" (420). When truth is an issue at work in the encounter, the encounter that characterizes human relation entails the revelation of a third party. To be sure, it is only through this adding of one to one that a third presence, or the Third Himself, may be manifested, and He is manifested as the source of the individual's very being. Florensky makes this point by explaining, "The self-evidence and the self-grounding of the Subject *I* as Truth is its *relation to a He through a Thou*. Through the *Thou* the subjective *I* becomes the objective *He*, and in the latter lies its affirmation, its subjectivity as *I*. *He*, is the *I* made manifest. Truth contemplates Itself through Itself within Itself.... Truth is the contemplation of Itself through the Other within the Third" (48). Wherever Florensky invokes "the Third" he has in mind the divine; if the human being arrives at himself or herself by way of another human being, so does the I approach the divine by way of the human. The movement of that approach is the movement of truth. Indeed, truth is precisely the movement of the approach, the drawing nigh unto truth; it is the passage through the human on the way to the divine. Seek the human, and you will find the divine, for this seeking is itself a finding. Become an I through the utterance of Thou, and you will encounter the He who abides in and makes possible the utterance of every I—the He whose one utterance of the truth uttered at Sinai was *anokhi*: I. "God, at Sinai," says Elie Wiesel, "uttered just one word, *Anokhi*, I, but that word contained all the words which man, from the beginning, and till the end of time, will have spoken" (*Kingdom* 30). And, containing all words, that I contains every I to whom the He is revealed in a saying of Thou.

Just as there is no human subjectivity apart from a relation to another human subject, so is there no human subjectivity without the relation to the divine Third. Indeed, there is, according to Florensky, but a single subjectivity, which is the "Subject of Truth" (49) that is grounded in this relation of three. This is how we are to understand the Kierkegaardian principle that truth is subjectivity. It "is a *single essence about three hypostases*," Florensky declares. "Not three essences but one; not one hypostasis but three" (49). The three components of the Trinity unfold as the components necessary to the union of human and divine relation. To say, as Florensky does, that there is a single essence is to assert that there is a single presence, that is, a single spirit between self and other, there as the polarity that brings unity to the poles. Thus, in its relation to the human other, the self is inspired, inspirited, with the divine. To affirm, moreover, that there are three hypostases is to maintain that the oneness of God does not obliterate difference but transforms it into nonindifference. And the primary manifestation of truth as nonindifference in the human realm is in the relation of friendship. "Friendship," says Florensky, "is not only psychological and ethical but is above all ontological and metaphysical. Thus those with the most profound insight into life have viewed it throughout the ages. What is friendship? It is a knowledge of the Self through the Friend in God. Friendship is an awareness of the self through the eyes of the other, but before the face of a third, namely the Third" (438–39). The divine relation assumes its personal cast in the light of the personal nature of the human relation; that is, through the human relation God is revealed as Person, and not as a principle, and this notion of God as Person is antitheological. Instead of the First Principle—that deaf and mute idol known as "the god of the philosophers"—we have the First Person, the I, of all subjectivity and of the subjectivity that is All.

The term "first person" in its grammatical usage has a highly suggestive connotation in Russian; there it is *pervoe litso*, where *litso* not only may mean "person" but is also the word for "face." Truth is not simply some*thing* we must face but some*one* with whom we stand *face to face*. Because truth is subjectivity, the question that confronts him who would step before the countenance of the truth is not "*What* is the truth?" but "*Who* is the truth?" To this question Florensky replies, "The Abiding One alone is *aletheia*. Truth-*aletheia* is the Never-to-Be-Forgotten, that which is not erased by the torrent of Time; it is the Stronghold that cannot be devoured by the maw of Death, the Essence of the preeminently existing, in which there is no trace of nothingness" (193). What reduces the trace of nothingness to nothing? It is memory. To recall the words of the Baal Shem Tov, founder of Hasidism, "oblivion is at the root of exile the way memory is at the root of redemption" (see Wiesel, *Souls* 227). The holy manifests itself in the mode of memory, for memory in this case is memory of what there is to hold dear; it is the memory of the way home that leads us out of exile. In its association with redemption the memory of the Never-to-Be-Forgotten is tied to a response that affirms what there is to hold dear, to be sure, the Hebrew word for "redemption," *teshuvah*, also means "response." Florensky's accent on the memory of the Abiding One takes this redemption and response to the interior of the human being and of human life. "All forms of *teshuvah*," Adin Steinsaltz explains, "have a common core: the belief that human beings have it in their power to effect inward change" (*Teshuvah* 3–4). This interior, which is essential to dwelling in the world, is externalized through a response to the human other in an embrace of the divine Third; it is a love for that which is all love. The Abiding One abides precisely in that response, in that love, in the *between* space of that embrace. "Without the remembrance of God," Florensky maintains, "we die. Yet our very remembrance of God is made possible through God's remembrance of us. . . . If it should now be asked whether the phrase 'eternal memory' requires a *genetivus objectivus* or a *genetivus subjectivus*, then, on the basis of what has been said, it must be acknowledged that *both* meanings are included here; for 'my eternal memory' signifies God's 'eternal memory'" (195). This confluence of the object and the subject of memory is the basis of the confluence of the human and divine relation. Here relation is remembrance, and remembrance is redemption.

The determination of the self or the soul of the human being through the human and divine relation establishes the I's need for the Thou in order to become I. That is, the I requires the not-I in its effort to become what it is and thus to initiate that return to the interior that would bring the human being out of exile. The depth and substance of my soul lies in my capacity to get rid of my ego for the sake of the other. Florensky's theology of truth, therefore, rests not on the identity of I = I, which is a threat to truth, but on the antinomy of I = not-I, which is an expression of truth in its theological—or rather antitheological—aspects. The human and divine relation that brings about the shift from self to other thus brings about a shift from identity to antinomy. Let us now pursue that shift.

From Identity to Antinomy

It is the association between truth and life that leads Florensky to declare, "The law of identity is the spirit of death, emptiness, and nothingness" (27). Why? If we recall Bakhtin's statement in his *Estetika slovesnogo tvorchestva* (*Aesthetics of Verbal Art*), it may provide us with a clue. "The definition given to me," he writes, "lies not in the categories of temporal being but in the categories of the *not-yet-existing*, in the categories of purpose and meaning, in the meaningful future, which is at odds with anything I have at hand in the past or present. To be myself for myself means yet becoming myself (*to cease becoming myself . . . means spiritual death*)" (109). Only a corpse is equal to itself, for only a corpse is what it is, removed from the realm of the yet-to-be; the living soul, however—the soul who does not know the truth but is in the process of becoming the truth—is what it is *not yet*. On this view the opposite of truth is not simply a lie—it is death. In the context of religious discourse the opposite of truth is sin, where sin is not so much a transgression as that state of death, emptiness, and nothingness that distinguishes the self-centeredness of self-identity. Says Florensky, "Sin is the unwillingness to depart from the state of self-identity, from the identity of 'I = I' or, more precisely, 'I!' The affirmation of the self as a self, *apart from* its relation to the *other*—that is, to God and all His creatures—this accent on the self *outside of* a departure from the self is the root of all sin" (177). What Florensky describes is what we have seen in the narcissistic self-consciousness that defined the nothingness of the superfluous man; his sin, that is, the thing that constituted his exile from the human community, lay in a clinging to the self by which he lost himself. "Sin," Kierkegaard states it, "is this: *before God*, or with the conception of God, to be in despair at not willing to be oneself, or in *despair at willing to be oneself*" (*Sickness* 208). To be in a state of sin, in short, is to be outside of the human and divine relation in which I become who I am by becoming more than I have been, for the sake of the other.

The fall into sin, as Florensky views it, is therefore a fall into the self-identity of an autonomous selfhood. This is the distance, the exile, from God that Florensky describes in his description of hell: "Selfhood has received what it wanted and continues to want: to be its own form of the absolute, to be independent of God, affirming itself over against God. This independence, this absolute, negative freedom of egoism, is given to it. It wanted to be solitary, and it became solitary; it wanted to feed on itself, and it became self-consuming. Henceforth there is neither God nor anything else other than itself, nothing influences it. It is 'as God' " (242). This longing for the "I am I!" of selfhood is born in fear. It will be recalled, for instance, that when God puts to Adam the question He puts to every soul—Where are you?—Adam's reply is "I was afraid . . . I hid myself" (Genesis 3:10). What exactly is the fear that compels the man to hide himself, to cling to himself in isolation from the other, and thus to lose himself? It is a fear of the absolute vulnerability that defines a person who can be a person only by offering himself up for the sake of another. We must note at this juncture an important distinction between the subject or the self and subjectivity. Subjectivity is not the self but rather arises in that relation of the self to the other in which the self is subjected to the other. Subjectivity, in other words, emerges in a space between I and not-I, between one person and another (person or God): subjectivity is antinomy. In the relation to the other, the person who would become the truth must become something more and therefore something other than what he is; this entails assuming a position of vulnerability with respect to the other person. Here, to recall the words of Levinas, the subject "is exposed to the other as a skin is exposed to what wounds it, as a cheek offered to the smiter. . . . The subjectivity of a subject is vulnerability, . . . an exposedness always to be exposed the more, an exposure to expressing, and thus to saying, thus to giving" (*Otherwise* 49–50). This ex-pressing of the self who endeavors to live in the truth is a tearing away of the self from itself, as one would snatch a piece of bread from the mouth and offer it to the other, in an act of self-negation or self-effacement before the face of another, whether human or divine. Thus, in the life of the soul who lives in a process of becoming, thesis and antithesis are tied together.

In its linkage to the life of the soul, then, truth is itself tied to antinomy. "*Truth*," Florensky states it, "is a judgment that also contains in itself the limit of all its abrogations, or, put differently, *truth is a self-contradictory judgment*. . . . Thesis and antithesis *together* form the expression of truth. In other words, truth is *antinomy* and cannot be otherwise" (147). Thesis and antithesis *together*: this is not a dialectic by which we have first one thing and then another to come up with a third. The saying of "*Hinehni!*—Here I am!" is a going forth; from the standpoint of truth, presence is movement. Because truth belongs to a process of becoming and not to the acquisition of certain information, the antinomy of truth is the antinomy of I and not-I gathered into a single being, the contradiction of what I am and what I am yet to become. To be here and only here, outside of a context of where I am yet to be, is to be nowhere; this identity of I = I is the place of exile from which Florensky charts a path of return not to what was but to what is yet to be. Exile is the stasis of identity; dwelling happens within a dynamic of return, which means becoming more than what I am by moving into a place where I ought to be. Since this process of becoming is a process, the truth that one would become is tied to a fundamental movement of transformation. As suggested above, truth is this approach toward the truth, both the approach and the thing approached, both moving and immovable or immutable. Hence truth, in Florensky's words, "is the movement of the immovable and the immobility of what moves. It is the unity of opposites. It is the *coincidentia oppositorum*" (43). In its immobility truth draws us toward it; in its movement it moves us along. Just as prayer is not simply addressed to God but is itself divine, so truth is not simply what we seek at the end of the road but is itself the road traveled—or rather, it is the traveling of the road. Levinas expresses this idea, "What enables the soul to rise to truth is nourished with truth" (*Totality* 114). Because this collapse of identity into antinomy comes with movement, it bears certain implications for how we view the one who moves: the human being is neither here nor there but in the *between* space of relation. The movement, therefore, entails not just a shift from one place or time to another but a transition from within to without— or a transformation of within into without. And this makes it a movement of the body as well as the soul.

Here too the antinomy reveals itself, as Florensky points out: "What is usually called 'the body' is nothing more than an ontological *surface; beyond* it, on the other side of this *covering*, lies the mystical *depth* of our being. To be sure, everything that we call 'external nature,' all 'empirical reality,' including our 'body,' is merely the surface of a division of two depths of being: the depth of the 'I' and the depth of the 'not-I.' Thus it cannot be said whether our 'body' belongs to the I or to the not-I" (265). This division of two depths of being comes to bear in the process of stepping before the face of the other; it cannot be said whether the body belongs to the I or to the not-I because it is the other who defines the position and the substance of the body. The spatiality of height and depth that truth introduces to being lies in that between space that distinguishes the relation of the self to the other; and the spatial dimension of *between* is established by the spatial presence of the body. In the words of Levinas, the responsibility for another that defines the human individual "has meaning only as a being torn from the complacency in oneself characteristic of enjoyment, snatching the bread from one's mouth. Only a subject that eats can be for-the-other" (*Otherwise* 74). In my body of flesh and blood, I initially appear to another subject as an object; my body is your bread. To an extent, Sartre's statement holds true: "the Other is revealed to me as the subject for whom I am an object" (460). One can see, then, how antinomy is tied to relation. "A friend," Florensky notes, for instance, "is not only an I but is also *another* I, the *other* for the sake of the I. The I is a unity, and everything that is *other* in relation to the I is not-I. A friend is the I who is not-I: a friend is a contradiction whose very concept rests on an antinomy" (439). Another term for not-I in this case is Thou; a friend is the one who says and to whom is said, "Thou." Initially appearing before the other as an object (and this is what Sartre overlooks), I become a subject in the utterance of Thou, which is an offering of my whole being, body and soul, to the other. It is my self-effacement that imparts to me a face.

In this renunciation of the self Florensky sees a paradigm for the relation of God to humanity: God is He who becomes not-God out of love for that humanity to which He joins Himself through the figure of Christ, and the flesh of Christ, in turn, becomes the Bread of Life. Thus the truth I seek in my relation to the other lies in an imitation of God's own self-renunciation; this is what lies at the heart of the *imitatio Dei*, and in this way one may become perfect as God is perfect. "Self-negation," says Florensky, "is the only thing that draws us close to the likeness of God. . . . *A* cannot be not-*A*. It is *'impossible,'* and yet it is *'beyond doubt!'* Love transforms the *I* into *not-I*, for true love lies in the renunciation of the intellect" (163). What Florensky calls "the renunciation of the intellect" is a renunciation of the egocentrism that distances one person from another in the way that logic is often at a distance from life; here the intellect is the mark of the lie of identity. The life of the intellect is a life in the dative case, as it were; the eyes open and look around, ruled by the "to me" and "for me" of self-interest. Since, on Florensky's view, identity is the lie and antinomy the truth, love transforms the I into truth. Or perhaps better: truth is the movement of love's transformation of the soul into the likeness of God, where I equals not-I. And so we hear Florensky declare, "Contradiction! It is forever the secret of the soul, the secret of prayer and love. The closer we come to God, the more distinct the contradiction" (158). Closeness to God, as signified by prayer and love, entails a proximity to truth as it is revealed in the relation to the other, where proximity is conceived more in spiritual than in spatial terms. One is reminded that the Hebrew word for "sacrifice," *korban*, is a cognate of *karov*, which means "near": sacrifice, the act of making sacred, is a drawing nigh unto the Holy One. Again, this drawing nigh is not a spatial step forward but love's transformation of the I into not-I, of the I into the antinomy of truth. It is love that makes the sacrifice a sacrifice. Hence Kierkegaard insists that "when God requires Isaac" of him, Abraham "must love him if possible even more dearly, and only on this condition can he *sacrifice* him; for in fact it is this love for Isaac that, by its paradoxical opposition to his love for God, makes his act a sacrifice" (*Fear* 84). Here, perhaps more graphically than anywhere else, we have an illustration of that theology which is an antitheology. Abraham does not reflect on God—he offers in sacrifice to God that which he holds most dear.

Thus we see how the shift from identity to antinomy is brought about: it is through love as a primary ingredient of faith and hope. "The stagnation of the law of identity," Florensky expresses it, "is overcome by the threefold achievement of faith, hope, and love. The *I* ceases to be *I*, *my* thought ceases to be *my* thought; I refuse the self-affirmation of 'I = I' by means of an *inscrutable act. Something* or *Someone* helps me out of my self-isolation. . . . The Truth itself impels me to seek the Truth" (68). The antinomy of truth is the constitutive feature of human and divine relation as a relation of love. Like truth, love is not one feeling among an inventory of feelings but is a presence between two. If truth is something we seek to know, then to know the truth is to love the other; this is what makes the love for the other an act of knowing or *daat* in Hebrew, which implies a joining with somehting or someone. "That which is truth for the subject of knowledge," Florensky argues, "is the love of truth for the object of knowledge. . . . The manifestation of truth is love. . . . My love is the action of God within me and of me in God" (75). And what, we ask, is born of this coupling of love and truth as forms of knowing the other? It is wisdom. Love, far more active than speculative, is a manifestation of that wisdom that is a knowledge of truth. This brings us to the third point in our investigation of Florensky's theology of truth.

Love as a Manifestation of Wisdom

At this juncture we take up a consideration of the concept for which Florensky is perhaps most famous: the notion of wisdom in the form of Sophia. Wisdom or "Sophia," Florensky writes, "participates in the life of the Trihypostatic Divinity; it enters into the Trinitarian womb to join with Divine Love. But, as a *fourth*—as something created and therefore a Personality of a singular essence—it does not *'form'* the Divine Unity. It *'is'* not Love, but it simply *enters* into the intercourse of Love; it is *able to enter* into this intercourse in accordance with the ineffable, inscrutable, incomprehensible humility of the Divinity" (349). Sophia is the wedding of love to the Divine Unity and of the Divine Unity to humanity; this is why, Florensky notes, the concept of Sophia among the Church Fathers is nearly always associated with the Word (370). And the Word is heard in an act of response, received in an act of giving; what is thus received is born, "a Personality of a singular essence." Without this joining of humanity with the Divine Unity—without the Divine Word becoming flesh—neither creation nor the human life that unfolds in the midst of creation can have any meaning or truth. Viewing Sophia as a fourth element tied to the Trinity, Florensky goes on to say that "from the standpoint of the Hypostasis of the *Father*, Sophia is ideal *substance*, the basis of creation, the power and the strength of being; if we turn to the Hypostasis of the *Word*, then Sophia is creation's *reason*, its meaning and truth; and finally, from the viewpoint of the Hypostasis of *Spirit*, we have in Sophia the *spirituality* of creation, its holiness, purity, and chastity, that is, its beauty" (349). Like truth, wisdom takes on its significance—that is, its power to signify—through a divine relation that is manifested in human relation. In its capacity for signification it is not so much a sign of one thing or another but is rather a sign of that giving of signs that generates meaning; it signifies, in other words, the self's offering of itself to the other and for the other in an affirmation of the dearness of the other, through Sophia matter is transformed into spirit each time one person meets the needs of another, as when snatching the bread from the mouth and offering it to the other. The knowledge that distinguishes wisdom, then, is not only a knowledge of what there is to love, to live for, and to die for, beyond that, it is itself a mode of loving, a love for that which is all love.

This implication of Florensky's view of wisdom underlies his assertion that "God or the Truth not only *has* love, but, above all, God *is* love" (71). Entering into the intercourse of love, Sophia engages God; through that intercourse truth is known. The relation is marital, and the ideal marriage is an expression of that relation. Just as truth is essential to wisdom, so is love essential to truth; and all three are essential to the path that takes us out of exile. To suggest that God or the Truth is love, moreover, situates God not in the beyond of speculative theology but in the *between* of antitheology, in that human realm created through the relation of the soul to God, to the other, and to itself. And since, as we have seen, there is but a single relation that includes all three participants, there is only one *between* space. This oneness belongs to the Oneness of God and brings to the relation a certain reciprocity; the soul suffers what it inflicts, and the movement below has its corresponding movement above. One is reminded of the Hasidic saying that God is the shadow of man. "Just as a shadow," Wiesel explains, "follows the gestures and motions of the body, God follows those of the soul. If man is charitable, God will be charitable too. The name of man's secret is God, and the name of God's secret is none other than the one invented by man: man. Who loves, loves God" (*Souls* 31). When Florensky states, therefore, that "Sophia is the *Memory of God*" (390), we are to understand this to mean both God's memory of us and our memory of Him; to remember God is to be remembered by God. And God remembers us through our memory—our concern, compassion, and consideration—of the other. *"Love for one's brother,"* says Florensky, *"is absolutely impossible* for human strength alone. It is a matter of Divine strength. Loving, we love through God and within God" (84). Because Sophia or wisdom is the memory of God in this double sense, there is no loving God without loving the other and no loving the other without loving God. Wisdom, then, is a form of dwelling that begins where exile ends: it is a dwelling in that love for our fellow human being that is a love for the One who is all love. If exile ends with a movement elsewhere, that elsewhere is the site where this encounter takes place. To say Thou with one's whole being (and love happens only through one's *whole* being) is to behold the truth of being.

Thus Florensky offers yet another expression of that wisdom that he calls Sophia: "Sophia is the true Creation or the creation in Truth, *preliminarily as a hint* of the transformed, spiritualized world, as a manifestation invisible to others. . . . This revelation is consummated in the personal, sincere love of two—in friendship, when he who loves is given *preliminarily,* without the *act,* in a breaching of self-identity, taking away the border of the I, departing from the self and finding the I in the I of another, of the Other. Friendship, as the mysterious birth of the Thou, is the means by which the Truth is revealed" (391). Here more clearly than ever truth reveals itself not as an object of theological knowledge but as a moment of spiritual becoming, of finding oneself in the One who alone can say I and who therefore determines the truth of all I-saying. When the soul finds itself in this Other, the Other breathes life into the soul; thus Sophia happens as a moment of creation. The soul is precisely what is created through wisdom's participation in the Creation. That participation, moreover, is also an assignation—a commandment that brings with it a mission—so that the difference between self and other, between self and God, is transformed into nonindifference. As soon as I encounter the God who is Truth and Love, He lays claim to me and thus draws me into Him as He enters me in that act of knowing that is wisdom. As a manifestation of love, therefore, wisdom is "the essential knowledge of the Truth" that Florensky describes when he declares,

The essential knowledge of the Truth, that is, a joining with the Truth itself, then, is a genuine entry into the womb of the Divine Trinity, and not just an imaginary contact with Its external form. Thus true knowledge—knowledge of the Truth—is possible only through . . . an apotheosis of the human being, through the acquisition of love as the essence of the Divine: he who is not with God does not know God. In love and only in love is a genuine knowledge of the Truth conceivable. The reverse is also the case. A knowledge of the Truth is realized through love: he who is with love cannot help but love. [74]

Thus having no choice, we are set free from our exile in finitude, which, as Feuerbach has said, "is only a euphemism for nothingness" (6). While difference announces my finitude, that nonindifference that is love transforms me into a vessel of the infinite. When wisdom manifests itself as love, the human being is stamped with the image of the divine.

And yet it is the divine that brings about this manifestation and transformation; it is God who creates us in His likeness. Says Florensky, " 'Believe in the Truth, find yourself in the Truth, love the Truth'—that is the voice of the Truth itself invariably resounding in the soul of the philosopher" (72). The notion of the philosopher is here taken literally: the philosopher is he who lives in the love of wisdom and in the wisdom of love. Impelled by the One whom he seeks, the philosopher is the nonindifferent one; he is inspired or in-spirited by the Other and with the Other, by means of his loving relation to another. Thus "only what proceeds from God," as Jaspers puts it, "can seek Him" (*Glaube* 31). In the between space of relation, where love is a manifestation of wisdom, the self discovers the bridge of subjectivity that leads to itself as an instance of the truth. Indeed, the truth is both the self and the bridge. "Love for one's brother," Florensky asserts, "is the appearance to the other, the *crossing over* to the other, as if *flowing into,* entering into, that Divine life which binds God to the subject and by which we recognize the authority of the Truth" (91). One is reminded that in Hebrew the word for "Hebrew," *ivri,* is a cognate of *avar,* which means "cross over." To become a Hebrew is to undertake this crossing over into the life of the divine, making one's humanity into an expression of one's bond to God as it is revealed in human relation. To become a Hebrew, in short, is to become a bridge, so that I am situated neither here nor there but, again, *between.* In this crossing over—in this transformation of the self into a bridge—as Florensky suggests, the authority of the ego is eclipsed by the authority of truth. Here the human being dies away from the strictly empirical reality of the ego to be reborn in the spiritual reality of truth. "True love," Florensky expresses it, "is a departure from the empirical and a *crossing over* into a new reality" (90). That new reality is the new life announced in wisdom's manifestation of itself as love; there the soul becomes a moment in the life of the spirit, a revelation of what Florensky calls the Spirit of Truth. When the self dies to be reborn into that new reality, then, the duality of difference collapses into the unity of nonindifference, if only for a moment, and death is no more.

This dying away from duality is the tearing away of the self from itself that Florensky describes when he writes, "The membrane of selfhood that is between those who love is torn apart, and each looks into the other as though looking into himself, into his own most intimate essence, into his own *other I*, which nonetheless is not distinct from his own I" (433). As Shakespeare once expressed it, "Two distinct, division none; / Number there in love was slain" (1229). The membrane of self-hood, which is the wall imposed by the numerical duality, is the tomb of exile from which the spiritualized self emerges in a movement of re-turn. In the tearing of that membrane, in the rolling away of that stone, the human being grows wise; growing wise, he or she becomes an event in the life of the truth that is the origin of all life and that is manifest in the love for God. Thus taking love to be a manifestation of wisdom, Flo-rensky generates an antitheology, or a theology of a lived truth, that em-braces humanity. "In Florensky's instance," Robert Slesinski notes, "what began as an epistemological inquiry into the ultimate criterion of truth ended up as a metaphysical reflection on the nature of love" (233). Forging his epistemology and metaphysics into a theology of truth, Flo-rensky arrives at a position from which there can be no theology that does not include humanity, no "science of God" that is not also a sen-tience of man. This is how we are to understand the antitheological na-ture of his thought. Rather than soar into the heavens, Florensky draws heaven down to earth and raises the earth up to heaven. And so what was intimated in an examination of human and divine relation and then elaborated in the discussion of identity and antinomy is finally con-summated in a consideration of love as a manifestation of wisdom. Ap-proaching the end of this chapter, we discover that these elements of Florensky's antitheology are equally elements of human life as a reve-lation of the origin of life.

Near the conclusion of *The Town beyond the Wall* Elie Wiesel relates a leg-end that tells us that one day God and man agreed to change places for only a second, so that each might better understand the other. God be-came a man, and the man took the place of God, only to avail himself of the Divine powers and refuse to go back to his previous state. And so neither God nor man was ever again what he had appeared to be. Now the liberation of the one was tied to the liberation of the other, and the two of them continue their ancient dialogue charged "with infinite yearning" (179).

If Florensky's antitheology expresses anything, it is this infinite yearning of God for man and of man for God. That yearning is the yearning of truth for itself; that yearning is itself truth. It finds its voice not so much in the speculative discourse of traditional theological tracts but in the outcry that emerges, for example, when Florensky writes, "To set out and not to set out, to seek and not to seek, to hope and to despair, to be fearful of squandering the last ounce of strength and, because of this fear, to squander it tenfold, running back and forth. Where is the way out? Where is the refuge? To whom, to what, is there to turn for help? 'Lord, Lord, *if* You exist, help this insane soul, come, lead me to You! Whether I want it or not, save me . . . let me see You. Draw me nigh through strength and suffering!' In this outcry of utmost despair lies the beginning of a new level of philosophy, the beginning of living *faith"* (67). And the beginning of living faith is the end of speculative theology. "The discourse of faith," says Florensky, "is not at all the discourse of theology" (336). Thus Florensky's theology of truth is finally antitheological, and in this lies its strength. For it places truth beyond its pillars and foundations, which ultimately succumb to the law of identity, and returns it to the antinomy of that relation in which love joins the human and the divine. And only when these two are joined can there be a healing of the rupture of exile.

Thus the discourse that might put an end to exile is one that would overturn the speculative discourse of rationalism that we have inherited from the Greeks. As Dostoevsky's underground man discovered, the principle of "twice two equals four" that distinguishes reason is the beginning of death (118–19), and death lies curled up at the core of life's rupture from life. It is death disguised as reason that creates the rupture of religious discourse. Suddenly the human being collides with the realization that the Tree of Knowledge is not the Tree of Life, that God spoke the truth when He declared, "On the day you eat of this fruit you will surely die" (Genesis 2:17), and that, in the words of Shestov, "the serpent was the deceiver" (*Job* 87). Like Florensky, Shestov takes the love of wisdom that defines philosophy to be a love for life—or rather a movement toward life in a transition from the speculative to the existential, from Athens to Jerusalem. The watchword that guides him is the same as the outcry that issues from Pascal: "The God of Abraham, the God of Isaac, the God of Jacob—not the god of the philosophers!" (19). Let us now follow this thinker who leaves behind the god of speculative philosophy to pursue the biblical God in a return from the exile of Athens to the kingdom of Jerusalem.

6. Shestov's Return from Athens to Jerusalem

In the last chapter we found that, although Florensky places his accent on love as the essence of a living truth, he does not reject reason as a source of insight into life; despite his difference with Tolstoy in his view of the Church, the two of them have at least that much in common. It will be recalled further that Florensky is not averse to using the word *knowledge* in his discourse on life's truth, even though he does employ that term in a special sense, more along the lines of knowing a loved one than knowing a fact. In contrast to Florensky, Lev Shestov associates words such as *reason* and *knowledge* with the Tree that brings death and whose roots are planted in the soil of the Greek speculative tradition. Yet, like Florensky, Shestov opposes thought arising from revelation to thought ruled by rationalistic speculation. And, like Florensky, he is more concerned with the existential actuality of life and death than with the abstractions that operate within the safe confines of reflection. Indeed, while we noted certain affinities between the thinking of Florensky and that of Kierkegaard in the previous chapter, here it will be evident that Shestov's reading of the Dane had an important impact on his thought after 1930, during those years when he was writing *Afiny i Ierusalim:* these two cities, Athens and Jerusalem, signify for Shestov the contrast we have made between exile and dwelling. And yet, as we examine Shestov's undoing of the categories of speculative philosophy, we must note his rejection of a terminology that to some extent was acceptable to Florensky. Shestov takes a more narrow view of reason and knowledge than Florensky does and associates those notions with a syllogistic, materialistic mode of thought determined by the knowing of information and ruled by the law of contradiction. Whereas Florensky was guided by the Church's doctrine of the Trinity, Shestov takes the biblical tale of the Fall as the primary basis for his return from death to life, from exile to the Promised Land, from Athens to Jerusalem.

In the introduction to Shestov's *Umozrenie i otkrovenie (Speculation and Revelation)* his friend Nicolas Berdyaev describes him as "a philosopher who philosophized with his whole being, for whom philosophy was not an academic specialty but a matter of life and death" (1); and he goes on to explain that "the fundamental theme of Shestov's thinking" is "the conflict between biblical revelation and Greek philosophy" (2). The one volume in which that conflict is most thoroughly explored, with all its implications for life and death, is *Athens and Jerusalem*. Having completed this work, which is generally considered his masterpiece, about a year before his death on 20 November 1938, Shestov ended the seventy-two years of his life with his most profound articulation of what threatens life and what may restore it. Judging from an entry in his "Dnevnik myslei" (Diary of Thoughts) dated 11 May 1920, he may have first experienced a real threat to life in 1894: "This year [1920] it is twenty-five years since the 'disintegration of the bond of ages,' or more precisely, it was twenty-five years last fall at the beginning of September. I'm writing it down so I will not forget. The most important events in one's life—and no one else knows anything about them—are easily forgotten" (252). Perhaps it was at that point, in September of 1894, that Shestov began his lifelong struggle to move from Athens back to Jerusalem. And yet, by "most important events in life" he refers to certain turning points not just in his own personal life or in Russian life but in the life of any human being; once again, then, our examination of a Russian thinker is laden with implications for the human community as such.

But what, we ask, does this movement entail? For one thing, it is a matter of transforming the mode of thought from one shaped by the Aristotelian categories of reason to one ruled by the passion of faith. Looking at *Athens and Jerusalem*, we find that Shestov's purpose in writing the book, as he states it, "is to put to the test the claim to truth made by human reason or speculative philosophy. Knowledge here is not taken to be the ultimate goal of human kind. Knowledge does not justify being but must itself receive its justification from being. . . . [The aim of this book is] to throw off the power of the soulless and utterly indifferent truths into which the fruits of the Forbidden Tree have been transformed" (19). The conjunction of Athens and Jerusalem, therefore, implies much more in the way of conflict than in the way of comparison; it is not Athens *and* Jerusalem but Athens *over against* Jerusalem, just as reason stands over against faith, necessity over against freedom, the Tree of Knowledge over against the Tree of Life. "Is it really facts that we seek, that we are in need of?" Shestov asks. "Aren't facts just a pretext, even a shield, behind which are hidden altogether different longings of the spirit?" (*Afiny* 8). Facts represent the finite, or that equation of the finite to itself that, as Tolstoy discovered, turns the human being over to nothingness (*Confession* 59). In its longing for life, however, the spirit would undo the logic of identity, of $A = A$, to equate the finite with the infinite, as when the human relation manifests a relation to the divine. Facts represent the parameters of impossibility as delineated by the laws of reason, ethics, and natural necessity, by those limitations on life that may initially arise as fortress walls but turn out to be the walls of a tomb. The spirit, however, moves beyond those confines toward the ever-expanding horizon of possibility. In a word, Athens here signifies the death that Shestov associates with nothingness and necessity, while Jerusalem signifies the life that he ascribes to the open-ended truth of faith forever yet to be revealed. Like Kierkegaard before him, Shestov insists that faith is a "mad struggle for possibility" (*Kierkegaard* 95)—"mad" because it is indeed a matter of life and death that transforms A into not-A.

Thus we have the basic terms that define the encounters and collisions in Shestov's *Athens and Jerusalem*, as he undertakes his own mad struggle to dispel the specter of speculation with the voice of revelation. "When reason weakens," he declares in *Speculation and Revelation*, "when truth dies, when the light is extinguished—only then do the words of revelation become intelligible to man. And, vice versa. As long as we have light, reason and truth, we drive revelation away from us" (59). "Light" in this instance is the "natural light," which Shestov views as a darkness that reason would pass off as light; and "truth" is that counterfeit that is confused with necessity and fact, regarded as the object of knowledge rather than the essence of life. The movement from Athens to Jerusalem, then, entails a battle that Shestov wages against the evidence of the eyes, as they are opened upon eating the fruit of the Tree of Knowledge—the fruit that leads to death. But, says Shestov, the Angel of Death, the Angel with a Thousand Eyes, sometimes visits a man not to take him but to leave him with a new set of eyes (*Job* 29). It seems that upon the "disintegration of the bond of ages" Shestov was left with a new set of eyes that led him to his clambering for possibility; it was his eating the fruits of the Tree of Knowledge that made visible the Tree of Life and thus brought on the realization of what was lost. With Shestov, the rupture of religious discourse becomes a discourse of rupture that would overcome a condition of exile not by turning back but by pursuing it to its end, in a movement of return that is a going forth. Let us, then, take up that path that Shestov charts from Athens to Jerusalem and see whether the exile might indeed find some return to a life couched in revelation.

Reason over against Faith

In his *Meditations on First Philosophy* René Descartes, the father of modern speculative philosophy, writes, "Whenever I restrain my will in making judgments, so that it extends only to those matters that are clearly and distinctly shown to it by the intellect, it can never happen that I err, because every clear and distinct perception is surely something" (40). To which Shestov replies, "The clear and distinct lead us not to the real but to the illusory, not to existence, but to the shadow of existence" (*Afiny* 47). Such is the specter of speculation, a mode of thought grounded in seeing, as the word itself suggests; in Russian the term for "speculation" is *umozrenie*, which literally means "seeing with the mind." It implies the distance of the spectator from what he views. Here there are no witnesses but only observers; there is no I interacting with a Thou but merely one It gazing upon the other and turned to stone by its gazing. One recalls the story of how Thales of Miletus set Western philosophy into motion some 2600 years ago. As he walked along gazing at the stars one night, he fell into a pit. Upon climbing out he resolved never to take another step without first being sure of the firm ground under his feet. Thus, keeping his eyes on the ground, Thales lost sight of the heavens; ever looking before he would leap, he never made the decisive leap. But how far can the man go without encountering the pit? And what then can he do but stand paralyzed at its edge, mutely staring into its depths? And yet he struggles to construct an artificial ground, a ground of artifice. Speculative philosophy trades in guarantees, peddling insurance policies that promise security to the eyes when the heart knows there can be no security. One day the illusory ground crumbles, the ineluctable pit yawns, and no life insurance can make it otherwise. The will that Descartes would restrain is precisely the passion that stirs upon gazing into this abyss, and this is the passion, the passion of a Job, that Shestov attempts to introduce to thought.

In *Na vesakh Iova* (*In Job's Balances*) Shestov writes, "Reason presents its demands without regard to the heart, and so does the heart without regard to reason. What is this mysterious 'heart'? With Job it says: if my grief were laid in the balances, it would be heavier than the sand of the sea. Reason replies: the grief of the whole world cannot outweigh even a single grain of sand" (297). One must be careful here not to reduce this distinction to intellect versus emotion or caprice. In a statement that says what Shestov intends, Florensky points out that the Russian word for "heart," *serdtse*, "signifies something central, something internal, something in the middle—the organ which is the core of living being, as in accordance with its place and its activity" (*Stolp* 269). The heart is the organ of the blood, and the blood is the medium of life, as it is written (Genesis 9:6). The opposition, therefore, is one of life over against death, of movement over against paralysis, without which there can be no return from exile. "In the Bible," says Shestov, "God created the living person out of the dust, but our reason strives with all its powers to transform the living person into soulless dust" (*Speculation* 84). Opposite Him who breathes the spirit of life into the human being we have an allusion to Hellenism that brings to mind the image of Helen in Marlowe's *Doctor Faustus*, where the title character cries out, "Her lips suck forth my soul—see where it flies!" (71). Embracing biblical revelation, Shestov portrays reason not just as a mode of knowing but as the enemy of the soul. Despite Descartes's insistence that the notion of the mind is "much more distinct" than the notion of the body (34), rationalism is materialism set up in opposition to a God who is Spirit and to a man who is soul—the grief of the whole world cannot outweigh even a single grain of sand. And so in *Athens and Jerusalem* Shestov maintains, "Reason wants to be the creator, the sole creator, of everything" (245). Yet, like Cain, reason usurps Creation and the Creator not through the creation of life but through the reduction of life to soulless dust.

In his book on Kierkegaard Shestov elaborates on this point, saying, "In contrast to Spinoza and those who before and after Spinoza sought 'understanding' *(intelligere)* in philosophy and put human reason in a position to judge the Creator Himself, Job teaches us by his own example that in order to grasp the truth, one should not refuse or forbid oneself *'lugere et detestari'*[to weep and to curse], but should proceed from them. . . . Job's wails seem more than mere wails (i.e., meaningless, useless, tiresome cries). For him these cries reveal a new dimension of truth" (17–18). Those cries issue from the heart as Florensky describes it above, from that core in which the exile from life is most painfully felt. For the one who has been tempted by the *intelligere* of reason, this exile becomes a point of departure for seeking the truth, the place where the soul opens up like a wound in an effort to find healing. Thus we may better understand the saying in the *Mekilta* that "the Holy One, blessed be He, . . . heals with the very same thing with which He smites" (239). By "new dimension of truth," of course, Shestov means *the* dimension of truth, which is opposed to the lie of reason. "Reason does not and cannot have a single universal and necessary truth," he asserts in *Athens and Jerusalem*, "nor is it given to reason or to anyone else except the Creator to inscribe laws into the structure of being" (213). The lie of reason is that it would assume a false, monological authority that promises an equally false and insidious authority to its thralls. Seneca's famous remark, "If you wish to subject everything to yourself, then subject yourself to reason," Shestov argues, amounts to the satanic temptation, "All these things will I give you if you bow down to me" (*Afiny* 196). Once the eyes are opened, they long to have what they see, and reason is ready to strike a bargain, offering the human being everything in exchange for his or her heart and soul. Thus speculative philosophy, like the serpent of old, plays on what is "pleasing to the eye" (Genesis 3:6)—from Philo, who attempted to "correct" the Scriptures by changing the voice of God into a vision of God (see Sandmel 139ff.), to Husserl, who declared that "if phenomena have no nature, they still have an essence, which can be grasped and determined in an immediate seeing" (110). Indeed, the point of reason's *comprehendere* is precisely to grasp, to lay hold of, to have rather than to be. The one who is tempted to trade his soul for the world gazes upon what he would possess in an act of comprehension.

Shestov points out the consequences of this grasping and grabbing when he says, "Philosophy has always been, has always wanted to be, reflection, *Besinnung*, a looking around and looking back. . . . And looking back paralyzes" (*Afiny* 35). But just as Lot's wife was turned to salt in an act of looking back, so does reason, again, turn the human being to dust. We find once more that, like Thales, he who looks does not leap. Over against this looking back that characterizes reason is the going forth that distinguishes faith. "One must escape from reason," says Shestov, "without trying to find out beforehand what the end of the journey will be. . . . When it was necessary for Abraham to go to the Promised Land, writes the apostle Paul, he went, not knowing himself where he was going" (*Kierkegaard* 100). Abraham's going forth without knowing where he was going is the basis for Paul's reference to him as the father of faith (see Hebrews 11:8). To be sure, this movement from a place of exile toward the Land of the Promise is what makes Abram into Abraham, with the letter *hey* that signifies the name of God inserted into his own name and therefore into his own being. Thus the truth essential to faith is revealed not as what he knows but as what he is or is in the process of becoming, in the very midst of his name. That which distinguishes Abraham as the father of faith also marks the mode of philosophy that Shestov seeks to establish. What is this faith that is of decisive importance to Shestovian philosophy? He offers one definition in his book on Kierkegaard: "Faith is not reliance on what has been told us, what we have heard, what we have been taught. Faith is a new dimension of thought, unknown to and foreign to speculative philosophy, which opens the way to the Creator of all things, to the source of all possibilities, to the One for Whom there are no boundaries between the possible and the impossible" (27). Thus the demarcations and delineations outlined by the eye of speculation are erased by a mode of thought that, as in the case of Oedipus, blinds itself to the self-evident, to everything

that the natural light would posit as clear and distinct. The eye beholds
the necessary and the impossible and can only stare in mute horror. But
faith enables the human being to pluck out the eye that offends the soul
and to declare, with Abraham, "*Hinehni*—Here I am," reestablishing a
dialogical human presence that had been eclipsed by the fixed formulas of monological reason. Shestov's philosophy, in a word, is a philosophy of presence, and that makes it a religious philosophy, one that
arises from the religious problem of dwelling in the world.

The aim of such a philosophy is neither to know nor to grasp but to
return to a relation to the Creator whom reason would overthrow.
Shestov makes this point in *Athens and Jerusalem* when he says, "Religious philosophy is a being born into a boundless tension by turning
away from knowledge, through faith; it is a surmounting of the false
fear of the unlimited will of the Creator, a fear suggested to our fore-
father [Adam] by the tempter and inherited by us all" (21). While speculative philosophy keeps its eyes focused on the firm ground, religious
philosophy looks upward in its movement onward—and inward: for
the religious philosopher, Within and Above are synonyms. The language of birth and creation here suggests that when thought is ruled by
faith the philosophical accent lies not on knowing but on living in such
a way that one's life is defined by a relation to the Creator of life. Such
a view of religious concern as a concern for life makes religious philosophy, as Shestov conceives it, an existential philosophy, the basis of
which, he says, is "*justus ex fide vivit*"—the righteous shall live by faith
(*Afiny* 217; cf. Habakkuk 2:4). Living by faith, the righteous live within
the contexts of human relation expressive of a relation to the divine,
where the self returns to itself—and therefore returns from exile—by
way of the other. "For that quality by virtue of which a man has faith,"
says Kierkegaard, "is not the one in which he is different from another
man, but that wherein he is identical with him" (*Edifying* 5). In
Kierkegaard and the Existential Philosophy, moreover, Shestov posits a definitive link between faith and existential philosophy, declaring that
"existential philosophy, which is so closely united with faith that only
in the presence of and through faith can it do its work, finds in faith that
new dimension of thought which sets it apart from theoretical philosophy" (223). And it is thus set apart by a movement into a life grounded
in human and divine relation. Who, then, are the righteous? They are
those who, in keeping with the injunction to choose life (see Deuteronomy 30:19), choose a truth whose essence lies in a relation to God that
is revealed in the midst of human relation.

Kierkegaard renders the distinction between the speculative and the existential as a distinction between the objective and the subjective, explaining that "objectively, reflection is directed to the problem of whether this object is the true God; subjectively, reflection is directed to the question of whether this individual is related to a something *in such a manner* that his relation is in truth a God-relationship" (*Postscript* 178). In *Athens and Jerusalem* Shestov adopts this line of thought by saying, "Within the 'limits of reason' one may create a science, a lofty morality, even a religion, but in order to find God one must tear oneself away from the seductions of reason, with its physical and moral constraints, and go to another source. In Scripture it is called by the mysterious word 'faith,' that dimension of thought through which truth joyfully and painlessly gives itself over to the everlasting and uncontrollable disposition of the Creator" (20). One striking implication of such an approach to philosophy is that it makes the philosophical endeavor into something akin to prayer; like prayer, philosophy is here seen as an effort to draw nigh unto the Holy One, as a struggle to emerge from that exile that is a distance from the Origin or the Creator. This implication may also shed light on the mystery of "the mysterious word 'faith,' " since both faith and prayer are not only in God and for God but are also *from* God. "By himself," says Shestov, "man can no more obtain faith than he can his own being" (*Afiny* 61). As for prayer, one will recall, for example, Paul Tillich's assertion that "it is God Himself who prays through us, when we pray to Him" (*New* 137), an idea that may also be found in Augustine's *Confessions:* "When men see your works by your Spirit," prays the Saint, "it is you who see through their eyes" (342). God is never an object but is all subject, revealed through His disturbance of the witness, whether that witness is engaged in prayer or in the philosophy of which Shestov speaks.

It is this disturbance, this troubling of the waters, that Shestov views as the movement of faith. So regarded, one can see why biblical faith, in the words of Shestov, "has absolutely nothing to do with obedience, and that every 'thou shalt' lies in those regions where the rays of faith do not penetrate" (*Afiny* 146). The "thou shalt" of which Shestov speaks is an expression of a necessity that pertains not so much to the Decalogue as to the delineations of impossibility, of necessary and universal truths. Counterposed to reason, therefore, faith is the contrary of necessity. "Faith, only faith," Shestov insists, "can tear man out of the power of the necessary truths that took possession of consciousness after he had tasted the fruits of the forbidden tree. And only faith gives man the courage and the power to look madness and death directly in the eyes and not bow down will-lessly before them" (*Speculation* 221). Faith, in other words, is here opposed to those forms of idolatry disguised as rational and natural necessity. In *Athens and Jerusalem* Shestov sets up an opposition between necessary truths and the truths of faith that implies an additional opposition, one of necessity over against freedom. "The truths of faith," he argues, "are recognized by this sign: that they know neither universality nor necessity, nor do they impose universals or necessities. They are freely given and freely received; they justify themselves before no one, nor are they certified by anyone" (262). Freely given and freely received means given and received outside of the constraints of reason and necessity; faith opens up a horizon of possibility and therefore of freedom that reason and necessity had occluded. Let us consider, then, this dimension of the tension that Shestov poses in the opposition of Athens to Jerusalem.

Necessity over against Freedom

"Speculative philosophy," writes Shestov, "cannot exist without the idea of necessity; necessity is essential to it, just as air is to a human being or water to a fish" (*Kierkegaard* 20). Why? Because without the if-then mode of thought that characterizes the notion of necessity, speculation can make no deductions and is therefore unable to see the ground before it. The notion of necessity provides the illusion of certainty and solidity that comes with impossibility; the necessary is not just the actual but also includes the impossible, as it is described, for instance, by Dostoevsky's underground man. "Under certain circumstances," he cries, "these gentlemen may bellow like bulls, and let us suppose that this brings them the greatest honor. But as I have already said, in the face of the impossible they immediately fall silent. The impossible means the stone wall! Which stone wall? Why it goes without saying, the laws of nature, the conclusions of natural science, mathematics" (*Zapiski* 142). The stone wall is not discovered—it is posited, even worshiped, by reason because reason is in need of it; the necessary is necessary to reason, which is as cold, distant, and indifferent as the stones in the wall it constructs. Couched in the categories of necessity, the discourse of reason is the opposite of the discourse of life; it summons no dialogical response but rather issues only its monological decrees. Hence, from the standpoint of reason, only the necessary may be known, only the wall of stone. But, says Shestov, if we "drive Necessity from the world," such "knowledge will become a dream that is as infeasible as it is unneeded"

(*Afiny* 55). By "knowledge," of course, he means those conclusions of reason that define necessity, that is, that demarcate the limitations of possibility in the world. In short, that which may be known, in this context, is that which is determined to be finite. This, indeed, is exactly where consuming the fruits of the Tree of Knowledge places the human being: in the midst of the finite and outside the presence of the Infinite One. Once this knowledge becomes a "dream," the voice of the soul speaks from another dream, from beyond the stone wall that isolates us from Eden; necessity proves to be the finite made unreal, so that, with Tertullian, Shestov may declare, "*Certum est quia impossible*"—it is certain because it is impossible (*Afiny* 169). The calm to which reason pretends is far less substantial, far more alien to human being and to human life, than the passion that breeds such an outcry.

To identify necessity as the finite made unreal, however, is not to say that it is nonexistent. In a statement reminiscent of Feuerbach's remark that finitude is a euphemism for nothingness (6), Shestov notes, "However much reason may sing the praises of freedom, it still wants to, and has to, fit into the mold of Necessity. This Necessity is indeed that Nothingness which we must say exists, for although it is nowhere and there is nowhere to search for it, it still in some mysterious fashion bursts forth into human life" (*Kierkegaard* 110–11). In order to acquire a better sense of this nothingness that is at once everywhere and nowhere, it may prove helpful to add to Shestov's comment Levinas's description of what he calls the "there is." The "there is," he explains,

is the phenomenon of impersonal being: "it." My reflection on this subject starts with childhood memories. One sleeps alone, the adults continue life; the child feels the silence of his bedroom as "rumbling," . . . as if the emptiness were full, as if the silence were a noise. . . . It is a noise returning after every negation of this noise. Neither nothingness nor being. I sometimes use the expression: the excluded middle. One cannot say of this "there is" which persists that it is an event of being. One can neither say that it is nothingness, even though there is nothing. *Existence and Existents* tries to describe this horrible thing, and moreover describes it as horror and panic. [*Ethics* 48–49]

Although Levinas resists the term *nothingness*, his notion of the "there is" is very much like the necessity that Shestov associates with nothingness. Indeed, Levinas resists calling it "nothingness" because, as Shestov pointed out above, in some mysterious fashion it bursts forth into human life. Much like Levinas in his reference to horror and panic, moreover, Shestov cites dread as the sign of the bursting forth of nothingness (*Afiny* 148), a dread that comes both from beyond and from within. If speculative philosophy has its origin in "the consciousness of impotence before necessity," as Shestov claims (*Speculation* 224), impotence manifests itself as the dread of nothingness and the nothingness of dread.

Here, with the help of Kierkegaard, the opposition between necessity and freedom, as well as the association between necessity and finitude, may become more clear. "Dread," he explains, "is the dizziness of freedom which occurs when . . . freedom gazes down into its own possibility, grasping at finiteness to sustain itself. . . . The nothing of dread is a complex of presentiments which reflect themselves in themselves, coming nearer and nearer to the individual, notwithstanding that in dread they signify again essentially nothing, not, however, be it noted, a nothing with which the individual has nothing to do, but a nothing in lively communication with the ignorance of innocence" (*Dread* 55). Thus in the effort to get rid of nothingness we get rid of innocence, that is, we fall, and produce a sense of necessity that merely walls out the nothingness we dread. That wall consists not only of natural or rational necessity but also of ethical necessity; the Tree, after all, is the Tree of Knowledge of Good and Evil. "In the world ruled by 'necessity,' " Shestov holds, "man's lot and the single goal of every rational being lies in the fulfillment of duty: autonomous ethics weds itself with autonomous conformity to the laws of being" (*Afiny* 15). Like the necessary, the ethical belongs to finite and external forms and has nothing to do with the internal upheavals of the soul that characterize the faith of Abraham or Job. Like the necessary, the ethical demands the submission of the will not to God but to the code. While it may demand decency, it cannot engender sacrifice; while it may call for a certain treatment of our neighbor, it cannot summon love or compassion for him.

Shestov brings out the distance that ethics and necessity set up between one human being and another—which, as we have seen, creates a rift between the self and itself—when he says, "Ethics is not alone; behind its gibes and its indignation stands Necessity. Necessity cannot be seen; it says nothing, it does not jeer or reproach. It is impossible even to say where it can be found; it is as though it were nowhere at all. It only strikes, silently, indifferently, at the man who is unprotected, who obviously does not even suspect the existence in the world of the indignation, the anger, the horror of Job, Abraham, and Kierkegaard, and does not in any way take them into account" (*Kierkegaard* 87). The anger and the horror that Shestov accentuates are rooted in the dizziness of freedom that Kierkegaard alludes to above. From the standpoint of rationalistic necessity, everything is reducible to the material; love, hate, anger, faith, cynicism, good, evil—all of it amounts to chemical reactions and the interactions of molecules. While necessity makes this "all the same" into a distant indifference, freedom, in its passion, insists on a difference that is a nonindifference. Freedom comes to bear because in this dizziness life's need for decisiveness and resolve comes to bear. Shestov maintains that "necessity and the ability to choose between good and evil are not a sign of freedom, as Spinoza and after him Schelling and all of us suppose, but a sign of the absence, of the loss, of freedom" (*Afiny* 103). Once again, Levinas makes a point that sheds important light on the issue at hand. "The attachment to the Good," he writes, "precedes the choosing of this Good. How, indeed, to choose the Good? The Good is good precisely because it chooses you and grips you before you have had the time to raise your eyes to it. *Formally*, it thus challenges freedom; but if no one is good through free choice, no one is a *slave* to the Good. Precisely because the other who commands us is thus the Good, he redeems, by his goodness, the violence done to the 'freedom' before freedom" (*Nine* 135). If freedom means being free to choose between good and evil, then there is the false implication that, having chosen evil, I nonetheless remain free. Making such a choice, however, I am enslaved; evil is the absence of freedom. Only through my response to the Good that chooses me prior to all choosing on my part do I become free. And no code, ethical or otherwise, can answer for me. I must become present before the Good by opening up a place where it may become present; and that opening is the portal through which I may enter into a movement of return from my exile.

To become present is to create just such an opening, within oneself, for another. Once again we see why the existential philosophy that Shestov promotes is a philosophy of presence, for the absence of freedom is an absence of self, an eclipse or displacement of the self by the code. Freedom, then, does not lie in doing what the formula tells us to do; it allows no room for categorical imperatives. Freedom, as Shestov understands it, pertains to a way of being that is grounded in a relation to the One who is beyond all ethics (understood strictly as a behavior code), all natural necessity (understood strictly as physical laws), and therefore all explanation. "Indeed," writes Shestov, "the point of all 'understanding' and 'explanation' consists precisely in demonstrating that what is could not and cannot be otherwise" (*Afiny* 205). The point of such explanation, in other words, is to demonstrate that faith and the freedom it brings are at best pointless, at worst harmful. In explanation, then, lies the crux of the opposition between freedom and necessity. In his book on Kierkegaard Shestov establishes this opposition by saying, "So long as man is free, so long as man's freedom is not paralyzed, so long as man is free to do everything he wants to, everything he needs to, he does not make explanations. The man who explains is the one who does not have the strength to act on his own, who has submitted to a power outside himself. One who is free not only does not seek explanations, but with unerring perceptiveness guesses that the greatest threat to his freedom lies in the very possibility of explanation" (133). When reading these lines, one must be careful to place the accent on everything needful rather than everything desired; Shestov's notion of freedom is not to be confused with license. The realization of the needful, in fact, entails a certain demand for a higher form of obedience, one that Tillich describes when he says, "The demand to be obedient is the demand to be what one already is, namely, committed to the ultimate concern" (*Dynamics* 37). Nor should this ultimate concern be confused with the power outside myself that Shestov mentions; rather, it is a manifestation of the Holy One, whose presence is not simply "outside" the self but also cuts through the self.

Abraham, then, is free not because he wants to sacrifice Isaac but because he seeks what is needful to the relation to God. And so he does not speak; that is, he makes no explanation. To be sure, as Kierkegaard points out, "Abraham cannot *speak,* for he cannot utter the word which explains all (that is, not so that it is intelligible), he cannot say that it is a test, and a test of such a sort, be it noted, that the ethical is the temptation" (*Fear* 124). Studying the case of Abraham, one acquires a sense of the fear and trembling that underlie freedom, and one can see why Shestov declares that "the fear of freedom is a fundamental characteristic of our perhaps distorted but nonetheless real nature" (*Afiny* 58). What exactly do we fear when we fear freedom? According to Shestov, it is a fear "of groundlessness, of chaos, of unlimited possibility" (*Job* 215). For God, *all* things are possible, from Eden to Auschwitz. In freedom infinite possibility reveals itself as infinite vulnerability; only one who has shed the illusory guarantees and the false security of the rational and the necessary is free—free, that is, to the extent that he remains unafraid. "Thus," says Shestov, "fear emerges not as the reality of freedom but as the manifestation of the loss of freedom' (*Afiny* 149). Fear threatens freedom in its longing to see the firm ground beneath our feet and the choices laid out before us. Once again, Shestov argues, one discovers that "freedom as the possibility to choose between good and evil, which the Greeks knew and which was handed down to medieval and to modern philosophy, is the freedom of fallen man, freedom perverted by sin, the freedom that brought evil into the world, and it is powerless to drive evil from life" (*Afiny* 206). Powerless to drive evil from life, the perverted freedom confronts a choice but makes no decision, for the perverted freedom is paralyzed by necessity. A genuine freedom, on the other hand, is rooted in a responsiveness to the call to a higher relation. Such freedom moves by the light of destiny, just as necessity is petrified by the shadow of doom. "Freedom and fate are promised to each other," as Buber has noted, "and embrace each other to constitute meaning" (*I and Thou* 108). And so, says Shestov, "like everything that bears the mark of mystery, freedom harbors an inner contradiction" (*Afiny* 100), and the contradiction consists in this: freedom does not mean doing anything one desires but rather lies in the realization of what one must do—not out of necessity but in the light of the call to stand before the Creator and declare, "Here I am! Send me!"

Hence, Shestov affirms, "Freedom is the relationship of man to God" (*Afiny* 210). For only in this relationship to the Creator of life can meaning be something lived and not something merely known. What is freedom? It is, as Buber suggests above, a capacity to generate meaning, and therefore it is a capacity to dwell, free of the exile that is the opposite of freedom. On Shestov's view, then, one thing needful to life is not happiness born of virtue but meaning born of freedom. "Because freedom is freedom," he argues in his book on Kierkegaard, "we cannot know in advance what it will bring; it may be something good, but it may be something bad, very bad" (140). Meaning is tied to freedom through their mutual bond with what is not known and is therefore yet to be. This linkage underscores a point made earlier, namely that knowledge in the mode of speculative philosophy is a *Besinnung*, a looking back; only what is past and thus behind us can be known. What is thus already established threatens life because it threatens the process of becoming; it is the known, and not the yet-to-be-known, that creates the rupture or the condition of exile from life. "In their pursuit for knowledge," Shestov asserts, "the great philosophers lost their most precious gift from the Creator—freedom" (*Afiny* 19). And with the loss of freedom comes the loss of meaning, the loss of the yet-to-be, in short, the loss of life.

Knowledge over against Life

The title of this section, like the title of *Athens and Jerusalem* itself, implies an invocation of biblical imagery and therefore of a religious discourse opposed to its own rupture. One is not surprised, therefore, to find Shestov saying, "For the prophets and apostles faith is the source of life; for the philosophers of the Middle Ages enlightened by the Greeks it is the source of knowledge and understanding. How can one fail to recall the two trees God planted in the Garden of Eden at the time of the creation?" (*Afiny* 191). In *Speculation and Revelation*, moreover, Shestov draws on this contrast between knowledge and life to posit the calm of a corpse over against the movements of the living soul. "First," we read,

reason reveals to man what is possible and what is impossible, then the same reason suggests to him that it is folly to strive after the impossible. From this, finally, the conclusion is drawn: the highest good is spiritual calm. . . . The prophets, in contrast with the philosophers, never know any rest. They are anxiety incarnate. They cannot bear satisfaction, as if they felt in it the beginning of decomposition and death. . . . For the prophets there is, first of all, the omnipotent God, the creator of the heavens and the earth, and only then—truth. For the philosophers truth is first and then God. The philosopher submits both to Sheol and to death and finds in this "willing" submission his highest good; the prophet challenges Sheol as well as death itself to a fearful and final struggle. [40]

Like reason, knowledge is a form of rebellion that places a principle above God, a First Cause above the Creator, by placing necessity above possibility. Knowledge, in short, comes in an effort to become as God and thus usurp God. Hence knowledge views faith not as a passionate relation to God but as an acquiescent nodding of the head to what the intellect has yet to understand, that is, as a "willing submission" or a resignation to what reason deems necessary; that is what makes it a source of "understanding"; faith is not, in other words, what enables Abraham to set out for a place to dwell, even though he does not know beforehand where he is going. So we see what sort of rebellion is at work here: it is a refusal of decisiveness and is therefore a flight from presence.

Taking the side of the prophet—for whom, of course, exile is a chief concern—Shestov moves philosophy away from speculation toward revelation and thus heals the rupture of the holy word. Placing God above the "truths" of knowledge, he declares that "God does not 'know' anything; God creates everything" (*Afiny* 147)—which is to say, there is nothing other to God; every notion born of reason, ethics, or natural necessity is subject to erasure with but a word from God. In *Kierkegaard and the Existential Philosophy* we find one ramification of this position when Shestov states, "God signifies that the knowledge for which our reason strives so eagerly and to which it draws us so irresistibly does not exist. God signifies that there is no evil, there are only the primeval *fiat* ('let there be') and the heavenly *valde bonum* ('very good') before which all our truths, based on the 'law' of contradiction, the 'law' of sufficient basis, and the other 'laws' fade away and become shadows" (293–94).

Only from such a standpoint can it be maintained, as the Rabbi, for example, in Elie Wiesel's *The Gates of the Forest* maintains, that "a man who is put to the trial must give triple thanks to the Almighty: first for giving him strength to endure the trial, second for bringing the trial to an end, third for the trial itself" (201). The resolve required to join one's will with the will of the Holy One is a resolve for gratitude, which cannot be offered to an abstract First Cause but only to the living Creator. Like Augustine (see *Confessions* 148), Shestov rejects the Manichaeanism posed by the knowledge of good and evil—a knowledge that subverts the Good—and regards evil as a form of absence, as a nothingness that knowledge introduces to human life. "The first step of knowledge," as he expresses it, "is this: Nothingness, which is supposed to be Nothingness, and which is only Nothingness, breaks its way into the soul of man and begins to take charge there, as if it were in fact the master" (*Kierkegaard* 265–66). The first man clothes himself—and thus hides or protects himself—not just because he is ashamed but also because with knowledge he has acquired fear. The state of exile is a state of fear, as we see when God puts to Adam the question put to every human being—"Where are you?"— and he answers, "I was afraid" (Genesis 3:10). "Suddenly," says Shestov, "it turns out that knowledge cannot rest on itself and that it demands trust; and not only does it fail to allay terror— it arouses terror within us" (*Afiny* 85). Even knowledge needs its axioms, and axioms are by definition groundless; all groundwork, every guarantee, everything "clear and distinct" is an illusion.

Operating within the confines of a field of vision determined by reason, the eyes opened by knowledge perceive only a material reality; "rationalism," as Miguel de Unamuno has said, "is necessarily materialist" (80). If speculation knows only the specular, that is, only what it sees, then it sees only the necessity of death. Hence the fear in a handful of dust. We have found that where fear is present, freedom is absent, and this suggests a linkage between knowledge and necessity. "Where necessity is," Shestov notes, "there can be no freedom; therefore where knowledge is, there can be no freedom" (*Afiny* 125). Which ultimately means: where death is, there can be no freedom. The first man and woman are told that on the day they eat the fruits of the forbidden tree they will die, and on that day they are sent into exile: exile is exile to the necessity of death. The Tree of Knowledge is not the Tree of Life, and the fallen condition of the fallen man, his condition of exile, is signified by his discovery of the skull amid the wine cups and the roses. Yet this collision, this rupture, that erupts in a gasping, horrified "Can it be?" is precisely what engenders the break with speculative philosophy, since this is the encounter through which the man realizes that freedom is eliminated by the limitations of knowledge. "The essence of knowledge," says Shestov, "is limitation: this is the meaning of the biblical legend. Knowledge is a capacity, a constant preparedness to look around, ahead and behind. It is the result of the fear that if you do not look to see what is around you, you will fall prey to a dangerous and insidious enemy" (*Job* 226). This is where the lie of knowledge shows itself; indeed, Shestov believes that the question that decides all of philosophy is the question whether it is the serpent or God who is the deceiver: does knowledge bring death or doesn't it? By now one can anticipate Shestov's reply: "Where the fallen man"—that is, the knowing man—"perceives the path to salvation, death awaits him" (*Afiny* 137). And: "Everything the fallen man does for his salvation only brings him to the abyss" (*Afiny* 149). The knowledge born of reason—and not the "absurd"—is itself the abyss. "I am not like the gods!" cries Goethe's Faust after emptying the fatal Tree of all its fruits. "I am the worm that crawls in the dust, lives there and must feed on dust, and dies" (17). From out of this rupture Shestov's biblical, existential philosophy rises up: when the man would become as the gods, the gods flee the world and take with them the soul they breathe into the man. Drained of his soul, he is sent into exile.

Hence, writes Shestov, "from the moment when the gods abandoned the world, the Tree of Knowledge has forever hidden from man the Tree of Life" (*Afiny* 94). As the example of Descartes demonstrates (see his Second Meditation), knowledge tears the soul from the body, from the flesh and blood of the man. And is exile not exile from the blood, from the blood line, which is a man's life line? The Tree of Knowledge occludes the Tree of Life because it renounces what runs in the blood, insisting that we "turn away from everything to which our joys and sorrows, our hopes, longings, despair, and so on are bound. One must renounce the world and everything in it" (*Afiny* 18)—including one's own life, not to mention the lives of others. While knowledge that issues from Athens confronts us with a choice between good and evil, the Scriptures that arise in Jerusalem, upon which Shestov bases his thought, enjoin us, again, to choose between life and death. Just as the former is a rebellion in the mode of obedience, so is the latter embrace in the mode of command. To be sure, Shestov sets up this opposition when he asserts that "Seneca is right: in the *parere* [obey] everything is understandable, clear, . . . natural; while in the *jubere* [command] all is mysterious, arbitrary" (*Afiny* 32). The command here does not lie in that form of enslavement known as caprice; rather, it is the command of life, the command to choose a life lived in a relation to the Creator of life. Shestov describes it as the command of the Demiurge, declaring, "The more the Demiurge commands, the less one must obey [the laws of necessity]. The Demiurge beckons the man bound to the chains of Necessity to the ultimate freedom" (*Afiny* 54). For the command of the Demiurge is the command of that spark of the Creator that abides in the soul created in His image, which is the image of life. It is a command that comes both from within and from beyond the human being, a call of deep unto deep and of life unto life, that may be heard above the temptations of the serpent we hold to our breast. But on the day we consume the fruits of the forbidden Tree we surely die.

The man who falls prey to death cannot go back to his unreflective Edenic state, but he may move into a new "dimension of thought," as Shestov calls it. It will be recalled that Shestov sets up this opposition in *In Job's Balances* (252–53) as an opposition between Spinoza's "*non ridere, non lugere, neque detestari, sed intelligere,*" or "laugh not, weep not, curse nothing, but understand," (4) and Pascal's "*chercher en gemissant,*" or "seek with lamentation" (240). Elaborating on this distinction in *Athens and Jerusalem*, he writes, "The *ridere, lugere et detestari . . .* , which Spinoza rejects, is utterly nonexistent or, more precisely, has completely atrophied in the person *qui sola ratione ducitur* [who is led by reason alone]" (14). And yet, he insists, "No matter how much knowledge instills us with the notion that Necessity is all-powerful, no matter how much wisdom assures us that the virtuous man will find happiness even in the Bull of Phalaris, they can never succeed in extinguishing in man his *lugere et detestari*. It is from these *lugere et detestari*, these horrors of life, that the terrible 'Hammer of God' of the prophets and Luther is forged" (*Afiny* 153). The Hammer of God, which manifests itself in the "new dimension of thought," is the passion of faith that breaks down the stone wall of knowledge and announces itself in the lamentations of Job and in the silence of Abraham. This passion is the stuff of which the relation to God and therefore the substance of life are made. While knowledge and the reason it breeds would universalize the human being into a featherless biped, the passion that characterizes faith individualizes the human being as an I who lives in a relation to a Thou. Thus the finite becomes a vessel of the infinite, the individual an expression of the universal. Such, indeed, is the "paradox of faith," as Kierkegaard describes it: "the individual determines his relation to the universal by his relation to the absolute, not the relation to the absolute by his relation to the universal" (*Fear* 80). These are the categories that shape the "second dimension of thought," the living human being's thinking with his blood, over against the categories of reason inherited from the Tree of Knowledge.

Knowledge or understanding, as Shestov points out, "means renunciation of every 'who' " (*Speculation* 78), for it means the elimination of every question that may sustain that process of becoming that is essential to life. As we have seen, with knowledge comes fear, and fear is fear of the yet-to-be, fear of setting out without knowing beforehand what lies ahead, fear of becoming other than what we are—in brief, fear of any return from exile, which is a fear of life and the questions that give it meaning. Yet, as Wiesel has written, "the essence of man is to be a question, and the essence of the question is to be without answer. . . . The depth, the meaning, the very salt of man is his constant desire to ask the question ever deeper within himself, to feel ever more intimately the existence of an unknowable answer" (*Town* 176). And this is the essence of the life that unfolds in Shestov's philosophy. It is a life that is constituted by quest and question, posited over against the fixed formulas and ready answers of knowledge and beyond the limitations of explanation. "There are questions," Shestov maintains, "whose whole significance lies in their allowing no answers, for answers destroy them" (*Afiny* 235). When such questions are destroyed so is all that is most precious in life. "What is 'most important,' " we read in *Athens and Jerusalem*, "lies beyond the limits of the understandable and the explainable" (239)—that is, beyond the limits of answers that delineate the place, or the nonplace, of exile. What are some of those questions that forever remain questions and that therefore sustain what is most important and most dear? They are questions such as these: What do you stand for? What is the meaning of your life and your death? What do you hold dear?—all of which return us to the question to which we continue to return: Where are you? Since living entails the movement of becoming, this is a question that remains forever unsettled and eternally unsettling. For it is the question that decides where we stand in relation to God, to others, and to ourselves, the question that takes us to the heart of our exile and to the threshold of return. Yet no sooner is the movement homeward made than we have moved elsewhere, carried into the next moment, and once again we must respond, bearing witness to the essence of life with our very lives.

Just as knowledge is the opposite of life, reason, then, is the opposite of relation. And so finally we ask: What exactly is it that is "most important" and therefore most essential to those relations by which we draw the breath of life? Quite simply, it is love. "Without love," says Shestov, "all the gifts of knowledge amount to nothing" (*Afiny* 208). We are reminded of Florensky's insistence that "in love and only in love is a genuine knowledge of the Truth conceivable" (*Stolp* 74); of Tolstoy's claim that "we pass from death to life if we love our brother" (*O razume* 19); and of Dostoevsky's assertion that "love is higher than existence" (*Possessed* 679). Once more, the question underlying the problem of exile as it is adressed in Shestov's philosophy—Where are you?—suggests that his is a philosophy of presence, and presence is made of love. Although this word seldom appears in Shestov's discourse, it is the word that inhabits his every word. "If a philosopher is not a man," Unamuno has said, "he is anything but a philosopher" (15). And Lev Shestov is above all a man, one who is guided by a love for the human and for the Most High. In that love lies his most valuable lesson for those of us who would do philosophy in the shadow of the Tree of Knowledge and in a return to the Tree of Life. For only love can effect the the return from the exile of Athens to the kingdom of Jerusalem.

"Take ye therefore good heed unto yourselves," it is written in the fifth book of Moses, "for ye saw no manner of similitude on the day that the Lord spake unto you in Horeb out of the midst of the fire: Lest ye corrupt yourselves, and make you a graven image" (Deuteronomy 4:15–16). These words convey the opposition that Shestov poses between Athens and Jerusalem: it is the lifeless image of stone fashioned by the hand of reason, necessity, and knowledge opposite the voice and the fire of the living God, who is accessible only to faith, freedom, and life itself. In a word, the one difficulty confronting a philosophy that would have anything to do with life is idolatry. The problem of exile is a problem of idolatry; a life lived in exile is a life steeped in idolatry's death. Shestov, of course, is aware of this. "We are inclined to think," he observes, "that the prophets meant only idols of gold and silver. However, it is not a matter of gold and silver, but of the fact that man sets a work of his own hands in the place of God. Ideological, ideal idols were just as much hated by the prophets as idols of any crude material" (*Speculation* 47). Again, rationalism is materialism; materialism is universalism or what Shestov refers to as "omnitude"; and this omnitude is the idolatry of the ideal. "So long as we are in the power of the truths and the ideals of 'omnitude,' " Shestov declares, "we are doomed to all the terrors of being that lead us inevitably to eternal perdition. That is why 'omnitude' is our greatest and most terrible enemy, against which it is necessary to struggle to the death" (*Speculation* 163). Indeed, the strug-

gle with idolatry—the battle between Athens and Jerusalem—is *to* the
death because it is a struggle *against* death. Perhaps we can now better
understand Berdyaev's claim that Shestov is a man for whom philosophy is a matter of life and death—and why it is a matter that does not
concern Shestov alone.

The specter of speculation is the specter of idolatry, something unreal that passes itself off as the only reality. It is this idol that Shestov attempts to crush with the *malleus Dei*, or the Hammer of God, that he invokes when he says, "Under the blows of the *malleus Dei* the greatly
scorned *lugere et detestari* is transformed into a new power which awak-
ens us from the sleep of centuries and gives us the courage to engage in
the struggle with the terrible monster. The horrors through which necessity established itself are turned against it. And in this final, life-and-
death struggle perhaps man will finally succeed in returning to the true
freedom, the freedom from knowledge which was lost by the first man"
(*Afiny* 154). In this summons to return Shestov echoes the prophets' call
to *teshuvah*, to that redemption that comes in a movement of return and
in a leap of faith. Here we behold no similitude but only hear the voice
in the midst of the fire of this man's philosophy, a voice that calls out
from a place to which we are exiled by the philosophy we fashion. Thus
we are the ones who are called.

We have seen that in Florensky and Shestov the rupture that tears
the soul from its origins and rends the fabric of life is a rupture of religious discourse. For one person it engenders an antitheological discourse, for the other an antiphilosophical discourse; both oppose a dialogical discourse of life and of love to the monological discourse of
speculation. During the time of the Soviet labor camps (in one of which
Florensky met his end) this opposition takes on a new aspect, where the
religious concern is tied not only to a political concern but to a concern
for morality and responsibility as the keys to overcoming a political
problem. There the use of exile as a punishment of political crimes is as-
sessed in the light of a higher relation, which is the relation to God as it
is expressed in the ethical relation. Here, however, ethics is not the fixed
code that Shestov assails; rather, it becomes a mode of first philosophy
and therefore a passage to the Most High. We proceed next, then, to a
consideration of those texts written by people who endured an internal
exile and who addressed that political condition in the light of a metaphysical condition. And so we come to Part Four.

PART FOUR
The Exile Within

7. From Politics to Metaphysics: Solzhenitsyn's *From under the Rubble*

According to a Russian folk legend related by the prisoner Shukhov in Solzhenitsyn's *One Day in the Life of Ivan Denisovich*, God breaks up the old moon into stars each month when the moon fades away. "And why does God do that?" asks the Captain, who has just heard the tale. Shukhov replies, "Don't you see? The stars keep falling down, so you've got to have new ones in their place" (128–29).

One constellation of beacons made from a dying light appeared in Russia in 1909; it was the collection of essays titled *Vekhi*, which means "landmarks" or "reference points," bearings from which a direction in life may be determined. Consisting of articles by Nicolas Berdyaev, Sergei Bulgakov, Semyon Frank, and others, *Vekhi* issued a call for a return to spiritual, predominantly Christian values as the only path to salvation that Russia had left. Once the Soviets took over, however, those stars were forced out of the sky. Nevertheless in 1974 a new constellation appeared in Russian letters; it was the collection of essays titled *From under the Rubble*, edited by Alexander Solzhenitsyn and conscientiously modeled after *Vekhi*. In addition to Solzhenitsyn, its contributors included Igor Shafarevich, Evgeny Barabanov, Vadim Borisov, and two others, who wrote under the pseudonyms A.B. and F. Korsakov. Solzhenitsyn comments on the work after which his edition is modeled by saying, "The fateful peculiarities of the educated stratum of Russians before the revolution were thoroughly analyzed in *Vekhi* (*Landmarks*)— and indignantly repudiated by the entire intelligentsia. . . . But after sixty years its testimony has not lost its brightness: *Vekhi* today still seems to us to have been a vision of the future" ("Smatterers" 229). In its vision of the future, Solzhenitsyn adds, *Vekhi* "regards the moral doctrine of the individual as the key to the solution of social problems" ("Smatterers" 271). This brief statement harbors much more than it may seem at first glance, for here we see a transition from politics to metaphysics, from external policy to an internal condition expressive of a higher relation. In keeping with the authors of *Vekhi* and with thinkers such as Dostoevsky, Tolstoy, and Florensky, the contributors to *From under the Rubble* hold to a view of ethics as first philosophy; to the horizontal relations that distinguish politics they introduce the vertical relations that characterize metaphysics. What is needed, they maintain, is not a new political ideology but a new spirituality, not a new party but a new morality. Unless this internal shift can be made, then not only the Russians but all of humanity will continue to languish in an internal exile.

For most of the authors of *Vekhi* and *From under the Rubble*, spirituality means Christianity; this religion represents the metaphysics into which politics must be transformed if the human being is ever to achieve any true freedom. "This freedom," argues A.B., "is not man's 'natural' inheritance, but rather the aim of his life and a 'supernatural' gift. 'Servitude to sin' is how Christianity defines the normal condition of man's soul and it summons man to free himself from his servitude. The path of heroic spiritual striving is the only path that can lead man—and the whole of society—to freedom. The authors of *Vekhi* (*Landmarks*) wrote of these things" (147–48). The path to freedom, according to this view, begins with a moral direction, since only morality can instill human action with the sense and sensibility that distinguish genuine freedom from its counterfeit, which is merely caprice or license. In contrast to the spiritual striving that seeks meaning, politics seeks power. It is the edifice that Borisov describes when he writes, "The edifice that took two centuries to build on 'rational foundations' proved a useless and damnable dwelling. The 'temple of society,' to the horror of its architects, became a place of mass human sacrifice, equipped with torture chambers to the greater glory of the Future. It emerged that this laborious process of construction had *its own* aims, . . . the aim of *destroying man and the foundation of his human existence*" (223). But what is the foundation of human existence? It is morality steeped in spirituality, ethics grounded in metaphysics. The outcry raised in *From under the Rubble*, then, is not so much for a new political system as it is for a spiritual salvation. "To live in this country is impossible," writes Korsakov. "Here you can only seek salvation" (166). This statement points both to an internal condition of exile and to a path of return. And yet salvation manifests itself precisely as something sought, as something we strive for, rather than as something we have in hand. According to the authors of *From under the Rubble*, this seeking can happen only in a movement of religious repentance that arises from a deep sense of responsibility. And responsibility, in turn, is characterized by a certain ethical outlook on freedom.

Thus freedom, responsibility, and repentance are the key terms to be addressed in this essay. While these are issues that come to us in this instance from Russians, they are not confined to the Russians but, like the other questions examined in this book, have a universal significance for all who would seek a placing of dwelling in the truth. *Seeking* is the essential aspect of *dwelling*. As we have seen from Shestov and others, the confines of exile are made of fixed formulas and ready answers; the fixtures of exile are made of the material, which is defined only by what meets the eye. "What we see with our bare eyes today is not necessarily the real truth," Avieta expresses it in Solzhenitsyn's *The Cancer Ward*. "Truth is what *ought* to be, what will come about tomorrow" (337). This is why another one of his characters, Varsonofiev in *August 1914*, insists, "Important questions always have long, tortuous answers. And no one can ever answer the most important question of all" (476). What is the most important question of all? It is the first question put to the first man: Where are you? The struggle to respond to this question and thus to become present before God and man is the struggle for freedom, responsibility, and repentance. The stars made from an old moon invariably fall from the sky and summon us to generate the stars anew, so that we may find our way home. This is the struggle that most clearly defines these voices that speak from under the rubble in their effort to move from politics to metaphysics, from exile to presence.

The Moral Path to Freedom

"To do evil," writes Solzhenitsyn in *The Gulag Archipelago*, "a human being must first of all believe that what he's doing is good, or else that it's a well-considered act in conformity with natural law" (174). This confusion between good and evil arises as the result of a prior, deeper confusion between an ideology that *serves* the Good and an ideology that sets itself up *as* the Good. In the former instance the truth of the ideology is subject to the question of whether it indeed serves the Good; in the latter instance the ideology is beyond question, since it passes itself off as the unassailable Good. The human being who does evil while convinced that he is doing good is a person who has given himself over to the idolatry of ideology-worship, where the real question is not whether I am doing good or evil but whether I am serving the idol. This is why Barabanov insists that "ideology, however infallibly true it may seem, is incapable of liberating man" (192). Making our decisions for us, ideology, like Dostoevsky's Grand Inquisitor, demands that we lay our freedom at its feet, and with our freedom the morality that defines it. Opposite the ideology that eclipses the Good is precisely the Good, which, Levinas explains, "does not radiate over the anonymity of a collectivity presenting itself panoramically, to be absorbed into it. In concerns a being which is revealed in a face. . . . It has a principle, an origin, issues from an I, is subjective. It is not regulated by the principles inscribed in the nature of a particular being that manifests it . . . nor in the codes of the State. It consists in going where no clarifying—that is, no panoramic—thought precedes, in going without knowing where" (*Totality* 305). Going without knowing where, as Abraham did when he set out for the Promised Land—going on a quest and in the light of a question—is the initial movement of freedom.

The state (in its absolute state) is the very opposite of freedom whenever it is the incarnation of an ideology made absolute. "Thanks to *ideology*," Solzhenitsyn maintains, "the twentieth century was fated to experience evildoing on a scale calculated in the millions. This cannot be denied, nor passed over, nor suppressed. How, then, do we dare insist that evildoers do not exist? And who was it that destroyed these millions? Without evildoers there would have been no Archipelago" (*Gulag* 174). If "in no socialist doctrine," as Solzhenitsyn notes, "are moral demands seen as the essence of socialism" ("Breathing" 14), it is because the doctrine itself poses as the "moral" demand, so that anything done in the name of the ideological doctrine becomes justified. Thus, through their allegiance to the ideology, human beings are led to do evil in the conviction that they are going good. The danger inherent in any opposition to this authority is that the human being may set himself up as his own authority, exchanging the exile of imprisonment within the ideology for the exile of unlimited license. Says Levinas, "Modern man persists in his being as a sovereign who is merely concerned to maintain the *power of his sovereignty*. Everything that is possible is permissible" ("Ethics" 78). As we have seen, however, freedom does not lie in the external permissiveness of being able to do anything I want to do; rather, it lies in the self-restriction that comes with the realization of what I *must* do, of what the Good commands me to do. For only in this way can the meaning and direction essential to freedom be determined. Exile is a condition of enslavement, whether it be in the form of absolute restriction or absolute permission. And enslavement is a condition of being without meaning and direction, without a path to pursue.

Well aware of this, Solzhenitsyn argues that "unlimited external freedom is in itself quite inadequate to save us" ("Breathing" 18); once again we find the motif of salvation, which for these thinkers bears metaphysical implications. Over against the external freedom of permissiveness stands the internal relation to the Good; the moral path to freedom leads us inward. Therefore, says Solzhenitsyn, "we can firmly assert our inner freedom even in external conditions of unfreedom" ("Breathing" 22). The inner freedom—that is, the moral freedom—of which he speaks is the freedom of the soul that attends to its life by attending to the Good. "What d'you want freedom for?" Alyoshka asks Shukhov in *One Day in the Life of Ivan Denisovich*, where "freedom" means simply the release from prison. "What faith you have left will be choked in thorns. Rejoice that you are in prison. Here you can think of your soul" (198). Even in the prison camp it is possible to generate gratitude; and the one who can be thankful can emerge from exile. Thus in the prison camp that Solzhenitsyn knew so well his character Alyoshka discovers the truth of the statement concerning an inner freedom as a primary condition for any genuine freedom. For in the movement toward the inner freedom of the soul the person enters into the interiority of which Levinas speaks when he says, "Interiority is the very possibility of a birth and a death that do not derive their meaning from history. Interiority institutes an order different from historical time in which totality is constituted, an order where everything is *pending*, where what is no longer possible historically remains always possible" (*Totality* 55). Only beyond the realm of totality, which gives rise to totalitarianism, can the ever-pending truth become an issue in a person's life. For Alyoshka, as for his author Solzhenitsyn, the historical impossibility that became possible in a movement inward is the discovery of freedom in prison. Indeed, when the state is totalitarian, prison may be the only place where the inner freedom of the soul can be discovered, since it may happen that only in prison is the participation in a lie no longer required.

For Solzhenitsyn this idea is of the greatest importance: "If the absolutely essential task is not political liberation, but the liberation of our souls from participation in the lie forced upon us, then it requires no physical, revolutionary, social, organizational measures. . . . It requires from each individual a moral step within his power" ("Breathing" 25). The soul's path to freedom lies in a moral path to freedom, and the relation to the Good arises with the relation to the Truth. Both arise, moreover, before any point where freedom becomes an issue, for it is only in the light of the Good and the Truth that freedom *can* become an issue. Freedom, therefore, is not the freedom to choose between good and evil or truth and lie, since this would imply that even in our participation in evil or in the lie we are free. On the contrary, as Solzhenitsyn suggests, that participation is precisely the condition of exile and unfreedom from which every human being must free himself or herself. This liberation comes only by choosing the Good and the Truth that have already chosen us and that yet stand before us, calling upon us to take the moral step. Where does this step take us? It takes us into the relation to another person, which in turn is expressive of the higher relation to the Good. Here we discover, with Korsakov, an important distinction between the moral path and moralizing. "Nowadays," he laments, "there is no attempt to understand another's experience, not even that of a close friend; everything takes the form of a fashionable world-weariness and the moralizing sophistries of Ivan Karamazov returning his 'ticket.' Before I have even crossed the threshold of the Church, I hold her responsible for a child's tears, not taking the trouble to consider that, outside the Church, I will never find a meaning for those tortured tears" (160). One immediately wants to ask how any meaning for those tears can be found even within the Church. If there is an answer to such a question, it lies in assuming the responsibility that I would lay upon the Church; this is where the shift from moralizing to the moral path, from exile to freedom, occurs. For it is the Good and the Truth exemplified by the Church and by which I am implicated that makes those tears *matter*. In the Church— or rather in the *principle* upon which the Church is founded—spiritual impulse and moral imperative are of a piece.

Korsakov himself says as much when he asserts, "The kingdom and everyday life are not historical categories, but religio-cosmic ones, and in Orthodoxy they have to this day remained external to the idea of the creative impulse, its spiritual impulse and moral imperative" (184). Like Solzhenitsyn and other contributors to *From under the Rubble*, Korsakov here brings out the transition from politics to metaphysics, and the path that brings about such a transition is the path of ethics. The spiritual impulse introduces a dimension of height, the dimension of the *meta*, to the moral imperative that determines our relation to the other person. Levinas explains,

In its Otherness it [the Other] is situated in a dimension of height, in the ideal, the Divine, and through my relation to the Other, I am in touch with God. The moral relation therefore reunites both self-consciousness and consciousness of God. Ethics is not the corollary of the vision of God, it is that very vision. Ethics is an optics, such that everything I know of God and everything I can hear of His word and reasonably say to Him must find an ethical expression. In the Holy Ark from which the voice of God is heard by Moses, there are only the tablets of the Law. . . . The attributes of God are given not in the indicative but in the imperative. The knowledge of God comes to us like a commandment, like a *Mitzvah*. To know God is to know what to do. [*Difficult* 17]

The moral path to freedom is constituted by this manifestation of the metaphysical relation in the physical action. The commandment is given from on high, but it is not received until it is enacted below. Moral conduct thus becomes spiritual conduct. And so Solzhenitsyn argues, "We shall have to 'rediscover our cultural treasures and values' not by erudition, not by scientific accomplishment, but by our *form of spiritual conduct*" ("Smatterers" 273). The cultural heritage is rediscovered through action and not erudition because it consists of a living tradition. Tradition, moreover, is something living and not just an accumulation of customs because it is a means by which the origin of life's significance is revealed. While history is the history of the political, tradition is the history of the metaphysical, the history of God.

"Was this not at the heart of our old error," Solzhenitsyn raises the rhetorical question, "which proved the undoing of us all—that the intelligentsia repudiated religious morality and chose for itself an atheistic humanism that supplied an easy justification both for the hastily constituted revolutionary tribunals and the rough justice meted out in the cellars of the Cheka [secret police]?" ("Smatterers" 270–71). What is repudiated by those who embrace atheistic humanism is the tradition from which moral imperatives as spiritual conduct arise and through which the face of the other is made visible. The relation to the religious morality of tradition, then, is not simply a relation to the past, but it also entails a determination of the future. The moral path to freedom guides us into this future by way of a living past that is forever before us and not only behind us. Atheistic humanism not only repudiates the past but also demands the sacrifice of the future by insisting that we lay our children upon the altar of the political, ideological Moloch. In this connection Solzhenitsyn complains of certain Russians, "That the moral health of their children is more precious than their careers does not even enter the parents' heads, so [morally] impoverished have they themselves become" ("Smatterers" 249). Our children invariably suffer for our sins, down to the fourth generation, as it is written. At the heart of the community is the family, and at the heart of the family are the children. In our relation to our children we not only pass on a tradition and a teaching, but we incur a responsibility that extends beyond our children, beyond our children's children. The exile within lies within the family, as does the egress from exile. That which threatens us with exile, then, threatens the family. To be sure, Igor Shafarevich points out that the destruction of the family is a basic tenet of the socialism that is characteristic of atheistic humanism; and this project, he shows, is definitively linked to the eradication of religion ("Socialism" 31). What is the means of all this destruction? It is the abolition of the moral imperative and spiritual conduct, which, we can now see, is the abolition of freedom.

Over against this condition of enslavement and exile A.B. argues that "we must achieve the sort of spiritual condition that enables solutions to be dictated from within by the immutable laws of compassion and love. Mysterious inner freedom, once achieved, will give us a sense of community with everybody and responsibility for all" (150). The word *mysterious*, of course, suggests the metaphysical; one of the implicit and perhaps "practical" aims of politics is to do away with the mysterious. At the core of this "mysterious inner freedom," *within* and *above* become synonyms by virtue of a *between:* the relation between human beings expresses a relation to what is above human being, thereby imparting substance to the individual's inner being. "Only to the abstinent spirit," A.B. insists, "is truth revealed, and only truth liberates" (149). What comprises the abstinence and the truth of the abstinent spirit? According to Solzhenitsyn, it is self-restriction. "Freedom," he declares, "is *self-restriction!* Restriction of the self for the sake of others! Once understood and adopted, this principle diverts us—as individuals, in all forms of human association, societies and nations—from *outward* to *inward* development, thereby giving us greater spiritual depth. The turn toward *inward* development, the triumph of inwardness over outwardness, if it ever happens, will be a great turning point in the history of mankind" ("Repentance" 136–37). Again, this shift from outward to inward is a shift from politics to metaphysics; and it comes about in a shift away from the self, for the sake of others. The moral path to freedom, then, leads the self away from a stance of I-for-myself and into the position of I-for-the-other. Ethics emerges as first philosophy where this responsibility arises. Thus it turns out that, contrary to the cliché, freedom does not bring with it responsibility, but rather responsibility makes freedom possible. The truth that liberates is the truth of moral responsibility of each for all, in the light of a relation to One who is above all. Let us examine this idea more closely.

Responsibility

It was argued above that history in the mode of tradition bears a metaphysical aspect and that tradition is the history of God. The memory of tradition, therefore, is a memory of God, which is a mindfulness of the One who summons and thereby posits our responsibility; through this memory the holy manifests itself in the world. A primary means by which the holy is eradicated and exile is imposed on a people, then, is to undo memory. Both Elie Wiesel (*Evil* 155) and Primo Levi (31) have noted, for example, that the Shoah was largely a war against memory. But this war is not confined to the Shoah.

In *The Gulag Archipelago* Solzhenitsyn comments, "We forget everything. What we remember is not what actually happened, not history, but merely that hackneyed dotted line they have chosen to drive into our memories by incessant hammering" (299). This hammering is characteristic of an ideology that poses as the ultimate good. Denying any independent presence of the Good, the ideology insists that memory be dependent on itself, on the ideology; thus, eclipsing the Good, it eclipses memory. Because the life of the soul lies in its attachment to the Good, the soul dies when memory is obliterated. Hence, says Borisov, "a people can perish without being totally annihilated physically—it is necessary only to remove its memory, its thought and its word, and the *soul* of the people will die" (196). Further, he elaborates, inasmuch as history includes a history of a people's spiritual life, "the destruction of historical memory kills a people's spiritual yearning, . . . cripples its moral personality, undermines its faith in the possibility of the creative conquest of evil and its hope of rebirth" (211). Unlike political liberation, the rebirth of the soul requires a renewed moral direction, and morality requires the memory of the Good that precedes us. To the extent that history relates the tale of the Good and our relation to it, historical memory is a necessary component of moral responsibility and spiritual life. For historical memory conveys the memory of the immemorial, which is the memory of the absolute that precedes the first and that neither history nor memory can contain. Levinas explains, "Responsibility for my neighbor dates from before my freedom in an immemorial past, an unrepresentable past that was never present and is more ancient than consciousness of . . . " ("Ethics" 84). The metaphysical takes us to the metahistorical: no matter where I may locate an event in historical time, morality is an issue because a responsibility from on high precedes the event and thus makes it meaningful.

The difference between politics and metaphysics, then, can be seen in the different views of history that each tends to adopt. While politics often approaches history as something directed by the forces of a power struggle that is out of our hands, metaphysics, when tied to ethics, places the responsibility for history on the shoulders of each individual. "In the most vivid socialist doctrines," says Shafarevich, for example,"we usually find assertions that history is directed by factors independent of the human will, while man himself is the product of his social environment—doctrines which remove the yoke of responsibility which religion and morality place on man" ("Socialism" 58–59). Shafarevich utters "religion and morality" in one breath because, like the other authors of *From under the Rubble*, he maintains that one is necessary to the other and that both are essential to the life of the soul. Solzhenitsyn reiterates this position by declaring, "Man's hope, salvation and punishment lie in this, that we are capable of change, and that we ourselves, not our birth or our environment, are responsible for our souls!" ("Repentance" 110). Solzhenitsyn is bent on robbing his readers of their excuses. For historical memory, as the memory of the metaphysical, is the memory of those whose example proclaims that we are without excuse; therefore it is a memory of a responsibility that we have yet to meet. When studying the history of atrocity, many like to search for beacons of light in times of darkness, such as the Righteous Gentiles who saved a few Jews during the Shoah, in order to be consoled by the fact that evil is not absolute. But these righteous individuals, whose actions were not determined by birth or environment or even personal safety, can also be rather unsettling, since they take away our reasons not to act. "Every man," says Solzhenitsyn, "always has handy a dozen glib little reasons why he is right not to sacrifice himself" (*Gulag* 17). Yet the righteous who precede us and whose memory is the stuff of tradition undermine those reasons by imposing upon us the truth of our responsibility and our humanity. "If one is forever cautious," asks Volodin in Solzhenitsyn's *The First Circle*, "can one remain a human being?" (3). The righteous say no to this by saying yes to the truth of the Good.

In *From under the Rubble*, therefore, Korsakov asserts, "If the Truth does not exist, your existence has no meaning. So you go on repeating and whispering the words your countryman left for you and paid for with his life in one of the unknown camps of the north" (167). If the metaphysics of the Good consists of abstractions, its manifestation lies in the all-too-concrete suffering of its witnesses; it lies in the blood spilled into a frozen earth, from which a voice cries out not to God but to those of us who still have ears to hear. Exile is made of the excuses that lead us to turn our backs on those who summon us, often silently, in the mode of memory. The freedom that arises in and makes possible human dwelling in a human community lies in our answering to and for the righteous who precede us. Their past instills us with presence by calling us to account. The lesson that Korsakov would have us learn is itself an ancient one and has its origins in an immemorial past. Recall, for example, the two arks that the Israelites bore in the wilderness during their trek to freedom. One contained the tablets of the Torah and the other the bones of Joseph, who "accomplished all that is written on the Tablets lying in the ark of Him who lives eternally," Levinas explains. "The living God can be found among this free people in the desert only if the memory of him who has rigorously obeyed marches alongside" (*Difficult* 55). This memory of the one who precedes us, of the one whose bones lie buried in an unmarked grave somewhere in the north, announces our responsibility for the one who is now before us. For this memory is constituted not only by a recollection of the person but also by a remembrance of the sacred truth for which he lived and died. And the fact that so many have died for it attests to its unconditional, universal nature; the word *martyr*, indeed, means "witness." How is this sacred, unconditional truth, this testimony, to be approached? Through the unconditional, ethical approach toward the other human being. "I become a responsible or ethical 'I,' " Levinas states it, "to the extent that I agree to depose or dethrone myself—to abdicate my position of centrality—in favor of the vulnerable other" ("Dialogue" 27). The other is always the vulnerable one, the widow and the orphan and the stranger placed in my care. And I am always without excuse, deposed by my responsibility.

" 'Going towards God,' " Levinas argues therefore, "is meaningless unless seen in terms of my primary going towards the other person. I can only go towards God by being ethically concerned by and for the other person" ("Dialogue" 23). The unconditional nature of my responsibility to and for the other person lies in such a view of the relation to the other as the expression of a relation to God. This point is of extreme importance to Borisov, who writes, "The unconditional equality of persons before God was replaced by the *conditional* equality of human individuals before the law. . . . And it is here, in the admission of the *conditionality* of the human personality, that we find the root of its calamitous ordeals in our barbarous world. If the human personality is conditional, then so are its rights. Conditional too is the recognition of its dignity" (200). Here the political and the metaphysical come into conflict, and they engage one another in the face that is constitutive of the personality. "The *personality*," Borisov develops this point, "as opposed to the individual, is not a part of some whole, it comprehends the whole within itself. The personality is not a fragment of our nature, but embraces the whole fullness of nature; therefore the idea of personality *presupposes* the existence of a common measure in mankind" (210). It should be noted here that the Russian word for "personality," *lichnost'*, has as its root the word for "face," *litso*. The common measure of mankind announced in the face is the ethical measure; and through the ethical measure revealed in the face we meet with the metaphysical. For in the face we encounter the eyes of which Solzhenitsyn speaks in *The Cancer Ward* when he writes, "When eyes gaze steadily into eyes, an entirely new quality appears: You see what does not show at a fleeting glance. The eyes seem to lose their protective camouflage and the truth spills forth without words. They cannot hold it back" (385). Invoking a truth that flows from the eyes, Solzhenitsyn invokes a vertical, metaphysical relation that inserts itself into the horizontal, human relation. Levinas explains why: "Those eyes, which are absolutely without protection, the most naked part of the human body, none the less offer an absolute resistance to possession" (*Difficult* 8). Refusing possession by me, the eyes announce the absolute truth that lays claim to me, which is the truth of the absolute sanctity of the human being; this is what I am responsible for in my responsibility to and for the other person. Borisov recognizes this element of the absolute within the personal, saying, "We have forgotten the Christian origins of our idea of the 'personal' as of something that gives *every* individual his qualities of absoluteness, unrepeatability and irreducibility to other individuals—and this insensibility threatens ultimately to render meaningless the words we all so willingly use" (208). Here one is reminded of Buber's remark about the uniqueness of every living situation. "In spite of all similarities," he maintains, "every living situation has, like a new-born child, a new face, that has never been before and will never come again. It demands of you a reaction which cannot be prepared beforehand. It demands nothing of what is past. It demands presence, responsibility; it demands you" (*Between* 114). What makes every situation unrepeatable and what summons our responsibility is the face before which we stand; to be in a situation is to be situated before a face and summoned to answer to it by answering for a higher, absolute relation. "Responsibility," Buber states it, "presupposes one who addresses me primarily, that is, from a realm independent of myself, and to whom I am answerable. He addresses me about something that he has entrusted to me and that I am bound to take care of loyally" (*Between* 45). What is entrusted to us? What are we to take care of? The truth that flows from the eyes of the other; the truth that constitutes the essence and the sanctity of the human being. And because it is absolute, our responsibility is absolute.

This is Solzhenitsyn's point when he insists,

The realm of darkness, of falsehood, of brute force, of justice denied and distrust of the good, this slimy swamp was formed by *us*, and no one else. We grew used to the idea that we must submit and lie down in order to survive—and we brought up our children to do so. Each of us, if he honestly reviews the life he has led, without special pleading or concealment, will recall more than one occasion on which he pretended not to hear a cry for help, averted his indifferent eyes from an imploring gaze, burned letters and photographs which it was his duty to keep, forgot someone's name or dropped certain widows, turned his back on prisoners under escort, and—but of course—always voted, rose to his feet and applauded obscenities. ["Repentance" 118]

If the slimy swamp that Solzhenitsyn refers to is the Soviet Union, it extends far beyond the borders of Russia to cover the whole world. As always, our interest here concerns not just the Russian condition but the
human condition. All of us who dwell in the exile east of Eden know
what it is to rise to our feet and applaud obscenities. Solzhenitsyn, of
course, has a much larger point to make about the scope of our responsibility and the absence of all excuses: "Even in the most totalitarian
states, whose subjects have no rights at all, we all bear responsibility—
not only for the quality of our government, but also for the campaigns
of our military leaders, for the deeds of our soldiers in the line of duty,
for the shots fired by our frontier guards, for the songs of our youth"
("Repentance" 113). Each time our leaders lie, it is our lips that move.
Each time our soldiers raise their weapons it is our hands that move.
The shift from the political to the metaphysical is a movement into this
arena of infinite responsibility; only this infinity of responsibility can
oppose the totality of the totalitarian state.

While the authors of *From under the Rubble* cast their metaphysics in
terms of religion, they are well aware that here too danger lurks, if turning to religion is a turning away from the world. Barabanov, for example, notes, "The Christian's own religiousness has become his chief
preoccupation. And in this context the concept of the Christian's responsibility for the fate of the world has irrevocably lost all meaning. It
seems at times that we Christians deliberately do not want to understand our historical failure or to admit our historical sins" (185). Even
the Christians are summoned to recognize their responsibility, for they
too are in exile. Even the Christians are in need of repentance. For, according to the authors of *From under the Rubble*, repentance is the one
path that leads out of the exile within.

Religious Repentance and the Return from Exile

"Religion can hide from us as nothing else can the face of God," Buber
observes. "Dogma, even when its claim of origin remains uncontested,
has become the most exalted form of invulnerability against revelation"
(*Between* 18). Seeking a path of return from an exile within the homeland, the authors of *From under the Rubble* examine not only political op-
pression but also another problem: it is the problem of the Church that
falls prey to the condition of exile rather than open up a way out of exile. In the Russian Church under the Soviet regime, what Buber calls "invulnerability against revelation" assumes the form of indifference to a
higher relation. Instead of moving from politics toward metaphysics,

from the power struggle to the moral struggle, the Church succumbs to the temptation of making metaphysics into politics; thus doctrine is reduced to yet another ideology that worships nothing while demanding that it be worshiped. Realizing this, Barabanov writes, "We want to think that God speaks only through our Church organization, only through our rite, only through our doctrine and tradition. In this approach the Church easily becomes an idol" (190–91). Once the Church becomes an idol, it becomes a power broker, so that it sees its task not as a pursuit of truth but in terms of negotiating for at least some realm of dominion. Like the ideology that gives it a nod, the Church too becomes engaged in a war against memory; but without memory there can be no repentance, and without repentance there can be no return from exile. Therefore Solzhenitsyn points out, "The monstrous punishment of the Old Believers—the burnings at the stake, the red-hot pincers, the impalements on meat hooks, the dungeons—followed for two and a half centuries by the senseless repression of twelve million meek and defenseless fellow-countrymen, and their dispersal to the most uninhabitable regions of the country or even expulsion from the country—all of this is a sin for which the established Church has never proclaimed its repentance" ("Repentance" 116). When the truth is sacrificed in this way, people die. And the Church languishes in its indifference to that suffering and death, thus betraying all that it stands for.

It is with profound lamentation, then, that Korsakov cries, "Perhaps it is true, after all, that the Church fears those in power, that she bows to the earthly authorities and shows her gratitude to the atheist Moloch for not interfering with her and sparing her for the time being by pretending not to see that, in essence, she has nothing to offer twentieth-century man, that she is indifferent to the real suffering of our time" (154–55). If Heaven's authority on earth should assume such a stance of indifference, then the heavens themselves are clouded with the silence of indifference. The dimension of height is lost and with it all truth, all meaning, all sanctity of human being. What remains is the remnant of a modern philosophy that has come to shape modern politics and has exiled modern man to a wasteland. Korsakov is aware of this side of the issue as well, for he asserts, "Insisting that the Revelation, the Word, all that the Divine Liturgy and the writings of the Holy Fathers contain, are not enough to satisfy contemporary philosophers and contemporary man in general, we appeal to 'contemporary thought'—to Western philosophy, the Enlightenment and humanism, forgetting that all the wise words of the Enlightenment led only to the Paris Convention and the guillotine, even as the selfless purity of the Russian Nihilists and the

People's Will group led to the Lubyanka [secret police prison] and to Kolyma [labor camp region in Siberia]" (157). The voices to which the Church becomes deaf are the voices by which it is implicated. In both instances the reason is the same: under the rule of a totalitarian ideology, one finds both within the Church and outside of it the insistence that the only reality is a political reality, that anyone who turns to truth instead of power is a fool, that the realm of metaphysics—of the holy and the good—is not of this world. And yet, as Barabanov notes, Russian literature "has unfailingly borne witness to the profound malady of our secular culture, to the tragic absurdity of an existence without God, to man's indestructible urge to find the true light" (189). The voice of the "true light" is the voice that these voices from under the rubble would have us hear. And even—or especially—from beneath the rubble of the Church there is a voice to be heard, the voice that, according to these authors, brought the Church itself into being. It lays claim to every Russian who has ears to hear. It chooses the human being before he or she has had time to make a choice. The return from exile is not an option—it is a spiritual assignation.

Korsakov, like the other authors of this collection, embraces the notion of a Church within the Church, of a truth within the facade of what, in times of exile, appears to be a lie. This is a truth that announces itself through the history that the ideology would have people forget; it is a truth that turns history into tradition and politics into metaphysics. "The Russian Orthodox Church," says Korsakov, "was made manifest to the world a thousand years ago—she survived the Tartar invasion and Peter the Great, and still exists today. And let every unbeliever place his hands in the gaping wounds of the Church's body. She stands immutably in the place where she arose, God's witness and God's design" (165). Here the essence of the Church lies in its capacity to heal the wounds of the wayward, exiled soul, and not in the politics to which it succumbs or in the corruption of a secular world by which it is both influenced and rejected. Indeed, Korsakov argues that the Church cannot be rejected, for the Russian cannot "tear either himself out of the Church or the Church out of himself" (165). This inability to escape the hold of the Church is an inability to avoid the call of the Good, just as Jonah could not escape his responsibility to God and to the people of Nineveh; the return from exile is not offered to the penitent as something that he or she may either choose or refuse, but is rather demanded in the demand for repentance. And the path to the repentance that brings me to the Church leads through the ethical relation to my neighbor. "Obedience to the Most High," Levinas explains, "is defined for me by precisely this impossibility of running away; through this my 'self' is unique. To be free is simply to do what nobody else can do in my place. To obey the Most High is to be free" ("Revelation" 202). Nobody can offer in my place the embrace, the kind word and the helping hand, that my neighbor summons from me. And nobody can do my repentance for me. This uniqueness of the individual's position in relation to another, then, is defined by the uniqueness of his position in relation to the transcendent center that the Church symbolizes. In *From under the Rubble* the summons to return to the Church and the summons to an ethical life constitute a single calling.

And the calling, according to Barabanov, is a commandment. "Our life in the Church," he asserts, "is above all a *task* (a commandment)" (192). The wandering that characterizes a condition of exile is a lack of direction that lies in a deafness to commandment. When the prophet Isaiah cries out to God, "Here I am! Send me!" (Isaiah 6:8), this "send me" means "command me," for out of the commandment arises the direction out of exile. "You have to wander so many years," writes Solzhenitsyn in *The Cancer Ward*, "to understand: God sends you" (611). This commandment transforms politics into metaphysics, inasmuch as the voice of the divine is revealed as commandment. Recall in this connection Levinas's insight, where he says, "What you perceive of God is a divine verbal message (*devar elohim*) which is, more often than not, an order. It is commandment rather than narration which marks the first step towards human understanding" ("Revelation" 204). By itself, neither the awareness of sin nor the realization of exile is sufficient to bring about the repentance that leads us homeward. To such a realization must be added the understanding that it is God who commands the movement. Because it is God, the Infinite One, who commands, our repentance itself must assume an aspect of the infinite, as Solzhenitsyn suggests: "Let us behave as people do on the day of forgiveness, and ask forgiveness of all around us. The scope of our repentance must be infinite" ("Repentance" 129). Here, in the infinite aspect of repentance, the human being realizes God's claim to him or her, which, in Russia, is manifested by the inescapable summons of the Church. Thus in *The Cancer Ward* Solzhenitsyn's character Kostoglov declares, "Your blood may still be circulating, but—psychologically—you have gone through the whole preparation for death and endured death itself. You already see everything around you dispassionately, as if from the grave. Though you never called yourself a Christian and sometimes even thought you were the very opposite, you suddenly notice—after all—that you have forgiven all who injured you and harbor no anger toward those who trespassed against you" (37). Like life itself, forgiveness is received to the extent that it is given. The dwelling that is opposed to exile is achieved to the extent that we create a place for our neighbor to dwell.

Thus repentance creates the condition of the soul that might be described as a "despite-me, for-the-other"; that is, in Solzhenitsyn's words, "repentance creates the atmosphere for self-limitation" ("Repentance" 135), which is an effacement of the self for the sake of the other. But in a world where looking out for number one is considered wisdom, where human beings are regarded as higher forms of animals,where increasing the scope and the power of oneself at the expense of another is normal and natural, where what is right is what feels good to me—in such a realm repentance is not couched in shame but is itself the object of shame. Says Solzhenitsyn, "The gift of repentance, which perhaps more than anything else distinguishes man from the animal world, is particularly difficult for modern man to recover. We have, every last one of us, grown ashamed of this feeling; and its effect on *social* life anywhere on earth is less and less easy to discern" ("Repentance" 107). As an egocentric life, social life is life lived in a condition of exile; it is the counterfeit life, the living death, that we have seen in *The Death of Ivan Il'ich*. This, and not just the prospect of nuclear annihilation, is why Solzhenitsyn views repentance as a matter of life and death, declaring, "We have so bedeviled the world, brought it so close to self-destruction, that repentance is now a matter of life and death—not only for the sake of a life beyond the grave (which is thought merely comic nowadays), but for the sake of our life here and now" ("Repentance" 107). Over against this destruction, repentance presents itself as an act of creation, an act of self-creation as Rabbi Joseph Soloveitchik describes it (110), without which the self can have no life, no home, no place to dwell; it lies at the heart of creating a life in the homeland that is opposed to the death of exile. In the opposition between the exile and the kingdom, moreover, the kingdom is not the empyrean kingdom of heaven; rather, it is the kingdom of home. Exile is a problem for those who would dwell on earth. And there is no dwelling on earth without the repentance that establishes a relation to heaven. In the Talmud we are told that repentance was among the seven things that preceded the creation of heaven and earth (*Pesahim* 54a). Why? Because it is among those things without which life on earth cannot be created.

"We cannot convert the kingdom of universal falsehood," Solzhenitsyn insists, "into a kingdom of universal truth by even the cleverest and most skillfully contrived economic and social reforms: these are the wrong building blocks" ("Repentance" 118). These are the wrong building bricks because they are the bricks of politics, and not of morality, responsibility, and repentance. As the political Tower of Babel continues to be constructed, the numbers of the homeless, the refugees, and the wanderers continue to grow. What is required to bring an end to this exile—the lesson that these Russian thinkers would teach us—is that the bricks must themselves be transformed. The exile within that haunts the lives of all can be undone only through the internal transformation that takes us from politics to metaphysics by way of ethics. Only when the moral is tied to the metaphysical, only when our responsibility to our fellow humans is expressive of an accountability to God, only when repentance takes us through the human to the divine—only then can morality, responsibility, and repentance be removed from the confines of cultural curiosity and make it possible for human culture to find a home on earth. The authors of *From under the Rubble* realize this, and they realize it because from under the rubble of Russia and the world they hear the Voice of the Most High that summons our embrace of the most dear. "Were the monsters Behemoth and Leviathan not enough of a revelation for us?" asks Korsakov. "And do we not recognize in today's events the whirlwind, in which the sound of a Voice should be clearly audible to us?" (164). The voices that speak in *From under the Rubble* speak in a hearing of that Voice. And, in the voice from this chorus that we shall attend to next, the Voice of another also reverberates.

8. Fragments of a Broken Silence: Andrei Sinyavsky's *A Voice from the Chorus*

In 1971, when Solzhenitsyn had just started gathering together the essays that he would include in his collection *From under the Rubble*, forty-five-year-old Andrei Sinyavsky (Abram Terts) was released from the Soviet labor camp. He had spent five years there for his violation of Article 70, Section 1, of the criminal code, which states, "Agitation and propaganda carried out with the purpose of subverting or weakening the Soviet regime or in order to commit particularly dangerous crimes against the state, the dissemination or production or harboring for the said purpose of literature of similar content are punishable by imprisonment for a period of from 6 months to 7 years, and with exile from 2 to 5 years" (Dalton 13). Among the "criminal" texts authored by Sinyavsky under the name of Abram Terts are "What Is Socialist Realism? (1956), *The Trial Begins* (1958), *Fantastic Tales* (1955–1961), *Lubimov* (1961–1962), and others. Standing trial for the utterance of a forbidden word, Sinyavsky stood before the authoritative word, which, as Bakhtin notes, "demands that we acknowledge it, that we make it our own; it binds us, quite independently of any power it might have to persuade us internally; we encounter it with its authority already fused to it" (*Dialogic* 342). In the case of Sinyavsky we see that the authoritative word not only demands that the person make it his or her own; more than that, it makes the person its own. As the penalty prescribed in the Soviet criminal code suggests, the authoritative word casts the accused in a state of exile—not just *because* but *before* he has uttered a word of his own, since, as we saw in the last chapter, it is the language of an ideology that insists upon the worship of itself. Prior to his exile to the labor camp near Potma, then, Sinyavsky lived in a condition of exile manufactured by the code—both criminal and ideological—under which he was born. Seeking to break free of the code, he broke free of his name and in 1956 published abroad his essay "What Is Socialist Realism?" under the name of Abram Terts. Thus he attacked one of the -isms of the code from a position outside of it, that is, from abroad.

To assume this new, dialogical voice, Sinyavsky assumed a new name, one that also placed him outside. For the new name in this instance is laden with significance. In order to extricate himself from the exile imposed by the authoritative code, Sinyavsky became other to himself through the appropriation of the name of the other par excellence: the Gentile Andrei Sinyavsky assumed the Jewish name Abram Terts, which he borrowed from the underground ballad "Abrashka Terts from Odessa." To summon a dialogical word that opposes the monological, authoritative word is to engage a question. And "the Jew," Edmond Jabès points out, "has always been at the origin of a double questioning: questioning himself and questioning '*the other*' "(77). This is surely the reason why "Jews hold a certain fascination for Sinyavsky," as Robert Lourie has observed (106). Taking on the Jewish name, Sinyavsky/Terts assumes a position of otherness that shifts the position of exile from which he speaks, so that the exilic function of the authoritative word is exposed. In *A Voice from the Chorus*, for example, he writes, "The very word 'Jew' has a nasty, unsavory ring: Jew is a stranger, an enemy, 'not our kind.' . . . 'But why must I be "one of you?!' " For the simple reason that everyone here is 'our kind,' 'one of us,' and anything 'different' smacks of the outsider: Jew!" (174). And yet he must move into this position of the outsider if he is ever to arrive himself, free of the exile within: he must become the Jew Terts in order to regain the Russian Sinyavsky. The Jew, therefore, figures prominently in several of his works, beginning with Rabinovich in *The Trial Begins*, a novel based on the trial of the doctors accused of conspiring to poison Stalin in 1952–1953. In his later work, *Soviet Civilization*, one recalls further, Sinyavsky takes to task Igor Shafarevich (one of the contributors to Solzhenitsyn's *From under the Rubble*) for his anti-Semitic statements in *Russophobia* (273–74). Thus, like Ernie in Andre Schwarz-Bart's *The Last of the Just*, Sinyavsky joins the victims of inhumanity in order to remain a man.

The chorus of humanity from which the voice speaks in *A Voice from the Chorus* consists of men from every walk of Russian life, with whom Sinyavsky shared the ordeal of the labor camp. This work, then, contains a legion of voices gathered polyphonically into a single text. Sinyavsky's voice is responsive and thus stands in a dialogical relation not only to his chorus but also to the one whom he addresses. And because it is dialogically responsive, the voice on the page serves as his one link to another human being and therefore as the basis of his humanity—that is, of his presence *in* the world, which is a presence *before* another. "The white page," we recall Jabès's insight, "is an imposed absence. It is against this background of silence that the text gets written" (89). To be sure, in the labor camp silence is as much an enemy as the dire conditions are. "They [the inmates] never switch off the radio,"

Sinyavsky relates. "This background of constant noise probably creates the illusion of a life full of meaning and events. Or is it a way of exorcising the emptiness which, like a disease, gnaws at the vitals of people in this kind of plight? With silence all around they would go mad" (*Voice* 127). To go mad here would entail slipping into the absence from life, from relation, from the source of meaning, irrevocably lost to a state of exile. And yet, Sinyavsky teaches us, it is precisely on the edge of exile that the urgency of life, which is essential to dwelling in the world, is to be sought. "Where does one look for a source?" he asks. He replies, "According to the law of contrast (the law of pain) it must be located not in the metropolis, but well away from it, on the periphery—whether of a literature, a city, society, or civilization as a whole—in the same way that monasteries situated beyond the city border, in the desert, at the edge of the world, were in ancient times spiritual and cultural centers" (*Voice* 103). And: "Nowhere is the life of the spirit lived at such a pitch, with such zest, as here, on the edge of the world" (*Voice* 104–5). For it is on the edge, from within this remoteness, that the relation that opposes exile becomes an issue.

In *A Voice from the Chorus* exile is characterized by an absence of relation that renders the self or the soul of the man unreal. Existence in the camp, says Sinyavsky, "has an appearance of unreality, and gives rise to a feeling the reverse of solipsism—namely, that everything around me is more plausible than I am myself. I find it easier to suppose that I do not exist, only this busy other life" (*Voice* 194). This situation is announced by a member of the chorus, who declares, "You, too, were 'I' one time!" (*Voice* 66). The very circumstance, however, that throws the "I" back on itself and locks it within itself in a struggle for survival is just what drains it of itself. Thus in *A Voice from the Chorus* we find a soul seeking to sustain its presence over against an imposed absence and a threatening silence through its relation to another, a relation steeped in love. The "I," explains Sinyavsky, is "the basic reference point by virtue of which everything else provisionally stays in place and remains itself. Love does not believe in this and disturbs the order of the world for the sake of union and mutual interchange. Love is formless and it builds bridges conceiving all things not in my likeness but in yours" (*Voice* 66). The "you" in whose likeness Sinyavsky conceives all things is his wife, to whom this text snatched from letters home is addressed. Sent home, the voice in *A Voice from the Chorus* opens up an avenue out of exile because it established a link to this other, who is at the heart of home and family. Here, in the condition of exile, the family is *outside*, which is to say, the interior of the dwelling place has been moved outside: the relation to the other human being within the family, which is characteristic of dwelling in the home, is a relation to what is remote. The manifestations of the family, then, will be the first point to be considered in this chapter.

Further, it is this relation to the heart of the family, to his wife, that joins Sinyavsky to the basis of human relation, which is the *face*. To break a silence is to mend a relation; speaking to his wife, Sinyavsky takes on a capacity to hear the face of the other speak. And so, after the family, the face will be the second key aspect of *A Voice from the Chorus* that we shall examine. Finally, since for Sinyavsky the word is the medium of his relation to the family and to the face, we shall explore the nature of Sinyavsky's thinking about the artistic word, both as he creates it and as he seeks it. Thus it will be shown that in *A Voice from the Chorus* exile manifests itself not only as a form of punishment for a political "criminal" but also as a remoteness from the family, from the face, and from the word. In short, it is the silence of the absence of human relation, so that this voice that speaks from this chorus has a bearing on the problem of exile as it confronts anyone with a family, anyone who seeks to step before a face, anyone who must generate a word. The silence that Sinyavsky would break is a silence that haunts us all.

Calling Home: Exile from the Family

Suffering an exile within the land, Sinyavsky creates a text by which he struggles to return to the interior, to the home, to the family. And where does the family have its origin? In the woman. "Woman," he says, "is man's support in life because she is closer to nature. Woman is the basis" (*Voice* 286). Closer to nature here means closer to the mystery and the origin of life: life is born into the world through the woman's body, she nourishes the infant with the milk of her body, and in her menstrual cycle she lives out the cycles of life and death. In *Art and Answerability* Bakhtin points out that

the child receives all initial determinations of himself and of his body from his mother's lips and from the lips of those who are close to him. It is from their lips, in the emotional-volitional tones of love, that the child hears and begins to acknowledge his own *proper name.* . . . The words of a loving human being are the first and most authoritative words about him; they are the words that for the first time determine his personality *from outside*, the words that *come to meet* his indistinct inner sensation of himself, giving it a form and a name in which, for the first time, he finds himself and becomes aware of himself as a *something.* [49–50]

Thus the man's first relation to woman, which is a relation to the mother, first establishes his presence and his place in the world. This is what makes woman "the basis," as Sinyavsky refers to her. She signifies the archetypical womb, which in the Russian Church is symbolized by the Virgin's Cloak. "The Russian Church *is* the Virgin's Cloak," declares Sinyavsky. "Inside it we find not infinity of space, not the Cosmos, not the harmony of the spheres, but above all—warmth, protection, coziness" (*Voice* 256). Through woman, the place of dwelling is opposed to the infinity of space; through woman, the finite becomes the vessel of the infinite.

The fundamental relation of man to woman, by which the family comes into being, is a manifestation not just of the infinite but of the Infinite One. The relation that constitutes the family and that creates a place to dwell in the world is expressive of this higher relation. The longing for the mother, then, is a longing for the place where the One known as the Place (*Makom* in Hebrew) is revealed. For Sinyavsky, the longing for the Church is a longing for such a dwelling place, for family and home. The cries of the chorus, of his fellow prisoners, moreover, make it evident that this longing is fundamental not merely to Sinyavsky but to human being as such. "Today I had a dream," says one voice from that chorus, "and saw the place where I was born" (*Voice* 25). On another occasion Sinyavsky overhears someone saying, "His one wish was to get home to his mother. 'Four times,' he said, 'I didn't make it. If only,' he said, 'I could reach my mother. I'll try a fifth time' " (*Voice* 110). This *if only* bespeaks the condition of exile. And it is a *condition*, a state of being—or nonbeing—distinguished by the longing not only for another person or place but for another condition. It is a longing, in other words, for being to be otherwise. Thus when Sinyavsky says that woman is the basis or that the Virgin's Cloak is the Church, he is making a statement about an ontological category in the metaphysical order of things.

This point becomes more clear when we recall Sinyavsky's comment on the maternal image as a landscape rather than a portrait. "A child," he writes, "calls for his mother, however far away she may be, in the certainty that this universal maternal principle animating the world of things will shine out on him, manifesting their inner essence as her presence: he only has to call. . . . In the same way, memories of a beloved person imperceptibly take on the character of a tale, diffuse and spreading out in all directions without end. They amount not so much to a portrait as to a landscape—the geography of a cherished name, dotted about everywhere and waiting for a summons" (*Voice* 242). It is not as though there were nothing but the mother, rather, everything else lives in *her* light (cf. Buber, *I and Thou* 59). Reading Sinyavsky's words, one reads with greater horror his observation that "the landscape is gradually beginning to look like stage scenery to me. I was warned this would happen. Sky and forest are nothing but pasteboard imitations, as I now notice in my fourth year" (*Voice* 178). The loving word of the mother, her loving utterance of the man's name, imparts to him not only a sense that he is someone but a sense that he is *somewhere*, that he has a *place* in the landscape of being. The fundamental presence in life that has its origin in woman is fundamental to the loving aspect of being and to one's relation to the beloved. When the landscape turns to empty stage scenery, the man is turned over to the emptiness—to the loveless-ness—of exile. In the words of Karl Jaspers, "If the power of things to communicate ceases, they sink back into the lovelessness of indifferent uniformity" (*Truth* 39). Sinyavsky's communication with his wife derives its urgency from its power to impart a voice to the things around him, so that the landscape does not sink into the indifference of paste-board imitations, which are imitations *of nothing* and would therefore reduce him to nothing. One realizes, therefore, the significance of Sinyavsky's text as a text addressed to the woman in his life, to his wife.

To see further the extent of this significance, we recall Levinas's statement that "the transcendence of the feminine consists in with-drawing elsewhere, which is a movement opposed to the movement of consciousness. But this does not make it unconscious or subconscious, and I see no other possibility than to call it mystery. . . . [The relation-ship with the feminine] is a relationship with alterity, with mystery—that is to say, with the future, with what (in a world where there is everything) is never there, with what cannot be there when everything else is there—not with a being that is not there, but with the very di-mension of alterity" (*Time* 88). For the man in exile—and where exile is taken to be an existential, phenomenological condition—woman signi-fies not only the mystery but the home, the place of warmth and pro-tection, to which he eternally struggles to return. The dimension of al-terity or difference between woman and man, then, underscores the difference between home and exile. According to the Jewish tradition, to which the name Abram Terts is linked, woman is signified by the House of Jacob because Jacob is associated with a dwelling place. Rabbi Yitzchak Ginsburgh explains, "At the level of Divinity, the house sym-bolizes the ultimate purpose of all reality: to become a dwelling place below for the manifestation of G-d's presence. 'Not as Abraham who called it [the Temple] "a mountain," nor as Isaac who called it "a field," but as Jacob who called it "a house" ' " (46). Since, according to the Talmud, "blessing is found in a man's house on account of his wife" (*Bava Metzia* 59a), the sanctity of the home is determined by woman; hence the women of Israel are known as the House of Jacob. Whereas Sinyavsky declares woman to be closer to nature, Jewish tradition declares that "the souls of women come to this earth from higher worlds than the souls of men" (Langer 136). Whereas Sinyavsky invokes the warmth and protection of the Virgin's Cloak, Levinas reminds us that *Rakhamim*, which in Hebrew means "mercy," "goes back to the word *Rekhem*, which means uterus. *Rakhamim* is the revelation of the uterus as *other*, whose gestation takes place within it. *Rakhamim* is maternity itself. God as merciful is defined by maternity. A feminine element is stirred up in the depth of this mercy" (*Nine* 183). Sinyavsky's accent on woman and the address to his wife, then, contain a deeper parallel between Sinyavsky and Terts than Sinyavsky himself perhaps realized.

When the family enjoys the wholeness of a family, the presence of the mother implies the presence of a father. And so Sinyavsky's father, who also suffered exile during the Stalinist purges of the early 1950s, figures prominently in his struggle for a relation to the family that might sustain his presence in a world of pasteboard scenery. The tenth anniversary of his father's death, for example, comes while Sinyavsky is in the labor camp. Remembering his father's death, he writes, "It was like the crumbling of an epoch: the monument in the dusty little square and the dust behind the truck—his gun carriage—and the sun. And not a soul by my side. And a monologue, a monologue instead of a salute. . . . People talk about 'personality.' I don't really know what they mean. What I most feel in myself is my father and mother, you, Yegor [his son]. . . . It was then, as I followed the coffin, that I realized how much of my father I have in me" (*Voice* 284). The loss announces a presence. The sign of the father that makes his presence felt within manifests itself as a sign of truth; truth and meaning are as essential to dwelling as are love and compassion. Here too one may note a parallel between Sinyavsky and the Jewish tradition implied by the name Terts. The *Sefer Yetzirah*, for example, associates the father with *Chakhmah* or Wisdom (13), and, in regard to the *zachor v'shamor* of Sabbath observance, the *Bahir* teaches that " 'remember' (*zachor*) refers to the male (*Zachar*). 'Keep' refers to the bride" (70). In a word, the object of memory here is the Good, which has been entrusted to the father so that he may offer it to his child as a offering of his whole being. The Good chooses us before we have made any other decisions, just as we are chosen and gripped by the father, who, as a father, shows us the way before we have made any choice.

"What does a child need?" Sinyavsky asks. "To be near his father and mother. Isn't this just what our soul yearns for?" (*Voice* 250). To be near father and mother is to be near the Good and the Love that constitute family and dwelling; it is just the opposite of exile. While Sinyavsky is himself a father, he is also a child, inasmuch as he is overwhelmed by this yearning for a dwelling and for family. While he is in exile his letters home are a link to all of these things; destined for the home, they become the signifiers of the home. In *Totality and Infinity* Levinas writes, "The dwelling is not situated in the objective world, but the objective world is situated by relation to my dwelling" (153). In the text at hand, Sinyavsky's wife signifies all that a dwelling and family signify. As the center of the life and the focus of his address, she is the basis of any meaning and warmth, any *Rakhamim*, that his world might have. Early on he tells her, "When anything of interest happens within or around me I make a mental note to tell you about it, and it is this habit of thinking of things in connection with you that gives them their meaning" (*Voice* 6). As we have seen, the break with the world that occurs in exile is a break with meaning and direction. In Sinyavsky's relation to the events and the people around him, his wife stands in a third position between him and the world, from which the world derives its meaning. His address to her, therefore, is what makes truth an issue in his response to his exile. And only when truth becomes an issue can the prospect of return from exile become viable. Return to where? Return to the family, to home, to wife and child. The path of return, moreover, is charted both symbolically by the word and physically by the paper that bears the word. "I often sit down to write a letter," Sinyavsky tells his wife, "not because I intend to write anything of importance to you, but just to touch a piece of paper which you will be holding in your hand" (*Voice* 41). Putting his hand to the paper, he reaches across a vast distance to touch what forever eludes the touch. "The caress," Levinas expresses it, "consists in seizing upon nothing, in soliciting what slips away as though it *were not yet*. It *searches*" (*Totality* 257–58). What is so striking about Sinyavsky's work is that it sets up a direct link between utterance and caress, between telling and touching.

To touch is to be touched, and to speak is to hear. The soul that cries out for mother and father seeks the voice of the family in its cry; the hand that touches the letter to be sent home seeks the touch of the family. Says Sinyavsky to his wife, "All this idle chatter in my letters is in large measure not so much self-expression on my part as a form of listening to you—turning things over this way and that and seeing what you think about them. It is important for me, when I write, to hear you.

Language thus becomes a scanning or listening device, a means of silent communion" (*Voice* 313). It is for this reason that Sinyavsky asserts, "Words must not shout. Words must keep silence" (*Voice* 82); that is, words must preserve and transmit silence so that they may listen to the voice within the silence. The fragments of the silence broken by Sinyavsky's voice are the fragments of a communion or a relation that is beyond the word because it is the basis of the word. When word and meaning are in place—when meaning finds its place in the word and the word in its meaning—silence speaks and words are unnecessary. Letters home are written in exile; exile is the realm of words torn from their home. Sinyavsky's effort to hear his wife's voice is an effort to return to a place where words and letters open up a vision of what lies beyond them; in short, it is an effort to return to a place of dwelling. There he may meet with the "peaceable welcome," as Levinas expresses it, "produced primordially in the gentleness of the feminine face, in which the separated being can recollect itself, because of which it *inhabits*" (*Totality* 150–51). Sinyavsky's struggle to maintain contact with the family, then, is a struggle to come before the face of the beloved, which speaks without words precisely because it is the origin of the word. Hence the face as such is an important piece of Sinyavsky's broken silence.

Calling to the Other: Exile from the Face

As the origin of the word, the face is the origin of a summons, and the summons is a call to answer to and for what there is to hold dear. While there are many faces, the origin and its summons are one. Hence Sinyavsky declares, "There is really only one face common to us all" (*Voice* 332): one face because there is one truth, one meaning, one God. If, as Rebbe Aharon of Karlin once said, only God can say "I" (see Wiesel, *Somewhere* 39), it is because there is but a single subjectivity, a single living presence, a single ground of significance underlying the responsibility that lays claim to us from the depths of the face. And it manifests itself absolutely, regardless of the contingencies of a given situation. "The face is signification," Levinas states it, "and signification without context. I mean that the Other, in the rectitude of his face, is not a character within a context. Ordinarily one is a 'character': a professor at the Sorbonne, . . . the manner of dressing, of presenting oneself. And all signification in the usual sense of the term is in its relation to another thing. Here, to the contrary, the face is meaning all by itself" (*Ethics* 86–87). When Elie Wiesel, for example, writes, "The hungry child, the thirsty stranger, the frightened old man all ask for me" (*Testament* 38), we do not have to ask, "Which child, which stranger, which old man?" Indeed, we ourselves hear the call. And when Sinyavsky declares, "You must live in such a way as not to eat anyone out of his ration" (*Voice* 47), we do not have to inquire about the context of the statement in order to understand it, for there is a single sanctity inherent in every human being. What we do understand is that without this stepping before the countenance, where we attest to our responsibility to and for the other human being, exile is without egress. What arises through the relation within the family thus extends into the relation with the other person.

Like Levinas, Sinyavsky realizes that "the important question of the meaning of being is not why is there something rather than nothing—the Leibnizian question so much commented upon by Heidegger—but Do I not kill by being?" (*Ethics* 120). For Sinyavsky, as for Levinas, ethics is first philosophy, which is to say: it is through the ethical that we approach the metaphysical, through the human that we draw nigh unto the divine. As the fundamental basis for the sanctity of life in a human community, ethics is opposed to exile. And since, in the words of Levinas, "the face is what forbids us to kill" (*Ethics* 86), the face signifies for Sinyavsky the presence of the holy within the human. "When life," he writes, "is bleak and empty and clothes are drab, the human face acquires the right to greater expressiveness by contrast: its allotted role is to make up for all that is missing and answer for the man as a whole" (*Voice* 4). In his *Mysli vrasplokh* (*Thoughts at Random*) Sinyavsky makes this point by saying, "A man becomes truly close and dear when he loses his official designations—his profession, his name, his age" (69)—that is to say, when all that is expressive of his being is lifted from the contingency of context and concentrated in his face. When the sum of the human being is gathered into the face, "it is the face that has the honor of representing us at the last" (*Voice* 5). Because the face forbids us to kill, the face of a man placed before the firing squad, for example, is often covered, not to spare him from gazing down the bore of a rifle but to spare his executioners from having to look upon his face. Indeed, where there are firing squads there is exile, a condition announced not only by the act of execution but by the obliteration of the face. Recalling an execution by firing squad, Sinyavsky remembers, "One man asked them not to aim at his face when shooting; a shot in the face is final, a death *with no way out*. The face is the soul's only exit" (*Voice* 66). The face is the soul's exit because, again, the face is the origin of the word by which the soul *ex*-presses itself, reaching out to the other and affirming a relation to the Third from Whom the sanctity of the human being is derived. Exile is exile from sanctity; as such, it is exile from the face. And yet within the confines of the labor camp Sinyavsky seeks a passage out of exile through the portal of the face.

"The face is a window," he writes, "a kind of porthole through which you can look or enter, and also out of which a soft light is shed on the earth" (*Voice* 90). As Sinyavsky's statement implies, the light arising from the face and shed on the earth comes from beyond both. Why the metaphor of light? Nissan Mindel explains, "Light is the most subtle and abstruse of all physical phenomena. It is the most immaterial of physical things; it is the borderline between the material and the immaterial. Light is energy; it is the source of existence and life. Light is sensible only when it is reflected in material objects. There is visible and invisible light. Light has a transcending quality; it penetrates all places alike and illuminates all things indiscriminately without itself being affected or soiled. A beam of light can be screened and infracted without affecting its source of radiation" (60). If ethics is first philosophy, it is because the face bears a metaphysical and transcendent aspect opened up by the element of light. Sinyavsky himself makes this point when he says, "If people looked more carefully at each other's faces, they would treat their neighbor with greater caution and respect. . . . The face violates the laws of nature. It seems to serve as a kind of very thin screen which allows the light to pass both ways, back and forth between spirit and matter" (*Voice* 90). Contrary to the laws of nature, the face insists on the survival of the weakest, of the most destitute, of the *other*, who is placed in my charge. For the Good, who is the Most High, has chosen me prior to my freedom of choice, just as the light shines on me before I move into it. The light that emanates from the face, the light of spirit, summons me from a third position to implicate me in my responsibility. Here too it will prove helpful to cite Levinas: "The presence of the face, the infinity of the other, is a destituteness, a presence of the third party (that is, of the whole of humanity which looks at us), and a command that commands commanding. This is why the relation with the Other, discourse, is not only the putting in question of my freedom, the appeal coming from the other to call me to responsibility, is not only the speech by which I divest myself of the possession that encircles me by setting forth an objective and common world, but is also sermon, exhortation, the prophetic word" (*Totality* 213). What is the prophetic word? It is the revelation of spirit, the utterance that arises when the spirit is upon the human being, thus giving rise to the movement between matter and spirit, between the finite and the infinite, between the temporal and the eternal.

If Sinyavsky writes his letters home in order to hear his wife's word, then he speaks in order to behold her face, since her face is the origin of her word. To the extent that the word and the face elude him, time itself is out of joint. On several occasions he complains, "Again this loss of a sense of time, never being sure of where we are in it" (*Voice* 277). And he explains, "The loss of a sense of time also happens because letters travel so slowly that I live simultaneously both a month behind and a month in advance" (*Voice* 284–85). And so the utterance of the word is cast at a distance from the response it summons. Exile in the labor camp, then, is exile from time; exile from time is exile from the other. When the face of the other human being is thus rendered remote, responsibility and the meaning it engenders also recede into the distance; when that happens, time—both past and future, ahead and behind—collapses. "The other is the future," says Levinas. "The very relationship with the other is the relationship with the future" (*Time* 77). For in the relationship with the other the consequences that determine the future of a life are decided. Further, "the dia-chrony of a past that does not gather into re-presentation is at the bottom of the concreteness of the time that is the time of my responsibility for the Other" (*Time* 112). For the past harbors an origin that makes the consequences of my action significant. Responsibility and meaning, moreover, imply direction, and direction entails the anticipation of a time that we approach through the remembrance of a time that has been. The light that emanates from within and from beyond the face, thereby announcing our responsibility, situates us in time and thus draws us out of exile. Sinyavsky's complaint concerning the loss of time, therefore, is a complaint about being lost, removed from the face of the other through which he might resituate and thus recognize himself, not in any hereafter but in the here and now.

If it should be asked how we are to understand the gathering of a past into a face, we need only recall a remark from one of the prisoners in the camp. "My life is written on my face!" he declares, to which Sinyavsky adds, "His whole face was covered with scars and lumps" (*Voice* 40). In the conjunction of these statements we see both how the past appears in the face and in what sense it announces a responsibility. And so this encounter with the scarred face places Sinyavsky at the threshold of at least a momentary exit from exile. Why? Because Sinyavsky's comment on the statement he hears—his voice from that chorus—implies that there must be an accounting for the scarring of the face: hence he speaks, not merely in a description of the face but in an answering to the face. Stepping before the face, he steps before the Good beyond the face, which proclaims that there is something wrong with the suffering of scars and lumps. Into this face is gathered not only a past life of suffering but also the eternal proposition or revelation that it matters, that it is *significant*. "For a face," Levinas explains, "is the unique openness in which the signifyingness of the trans-cendent does not nullify the transcendence and make it enter into an immanent order, here on the contrary transcendence refuses immanence precisely as the ever *bygone* transcendence of the transcendent. . . . The signifyingness of a trace places us in a 'lateral' relationship, . . . answering to an irre-versible past—and this also is perhaps eternity, whose signifyingness obstinately throws one back to the past. Eternity is the very irre-versibility of time, the source and refuge of the past" (*Collected* 103). The transcendent made manifest through the face without becoming imma-nent in the face is just what summons Sinyavsky's response to the face. Something very dear, the life of the holy itself, is at stake in his response and in his art. And Sinyavsky is well aware of this.

Recall, for instance, his remark that "the dominating idea in ancient art was not representation, but the provision of a dwelling place. In later times the graven image conceived as an abode for the soul gave way to the loftier and more 'visible' idea of the icon, where the face is a win-dow" (*Voice* 185). Like the windows of the Holy Temple, the window in this case is intended to allow light not only to penetrate into an interior but to emerge from a height. Perhaps more graphically but less real than in flesh and blood, in the icon the face presents itself as a portal to the transcendent, to the Good, to the holy; hence it posits an avenue of re-turn from exile. In this sense Sinyavsky's art is itself iconographic. His concern with writing in particular and with art in general is not a con-cern for representation or imitation; instead, it is driven by the soul's longing for a place to dwell. The many discussions of art in *A Voice from the Chorus*, then, are not driven by aesthetic curiosity or armchair con-templation, where life is reduced to the appreciation of form and the en-joyment of feelings. Sinyavsky is interested in art rather as an avenue of return from exile, inasmuch as it clears a time and a place in which the soul may dwell. This brings us to the third point to be considered.

Calling Forth the Soul: Art Opposed to Exile

"Art," says Sinyavsky, "does nothing but convert matter into spirit and vice versa" (*Voice* 50). In order to understand what this means, we must address the question of why such a conversion might be an issue for a human being. To convert matter into spirit is to instill matter with a voice; "spirit is word," as Buber has said (*I and Thou* 89). To convert spirit into matter is to give that voice a form, thus transforming an object into a symbol. "The symbol is *communication*," Jaspers states it. "In the contact of the soul with Being it is the enkindling in which Being acquires communicative power" (*Truth* 39–40). In art, as Sinyavsky understands it, what is mute becomes responsive and what is formless acquires a medium. Art, in other words, transforms the object into a symbol through what Jaspers calls the merging of objectivity and subjectivity, of form and voice, into a cipher. "The task of actually taking hold of Being is fulfilled by the symbol (the metaphor of the cypher-status)," he writes. "The cypher is neither object nor subject. It is an objectivity which is permeated by subjectivity and in such a way that Being becomes present in the whole" (*Truth* 35). And being becomes present in the whole when the whole assumes a voice: when art transforms matter into spirit, being speaks. This process cannot be reduced to mere projection or wish fulfillment; rather, it is a question of having been called or chosen before we make any other choices. Life is altered, as it were, before it is lived, so that living a life becomes possible as the result of an assignation or a commandment that comes from beyond life. Here we see that, in religious terms, revelation is not something that happens within the world but something that transforms the world: the conversion of matter into spirit is revelation.

Failing this conversion, the human being is turned over to dead and indifferent matter, to what Levinas calls the "there is." He explains, "This impersonal, anonymous, yet inextinguishable 'consummation' of being, which murmurs in the depths of nothingness itself we shall designate by the term *there is.* The *there is,* inasmuch as it resists a personal form is 'being in general.' . . . There is no longer *this* or *that;* there is not 'something.' But this universal absence is in its turn a presence, an absolutely unavoidable presence. It is not the dialectical counterpart of absence, and we do not grasp it through a thought. It is immediately there. There is no discourse. Nothing responds to us, but this silence" (*Existence* 57–58). We recall once more Sinyavsky's mention of the radio that is in constant conflict with silence: "With silence all around they would go mad" (*Voice* 127). Again, exile is exile of the spirit: the place of exile is the place where matter refuses the transformation into spirit. It is the realm of the "there is," where nothing responds to the human being but the indifferent rumble of an imposed absence. Art, then, would seek or summon a presence where this mute emptiness otherwise reigns. Sinyavsky expresses this idea by saying, " 'And my song—like a bird forlorn— / Is seeking a lost paradise.' This is the definition of art. In its broadest and most general sense" (*Voice* 171). The forlornness of the bird arises from the indifference of the "there is." Nevertheless the bird sings, addressing his song not to the void but to another, so that in the lines cited by Sinyavsky we see art itself at work in a transformation of matter into spirit, in a gathering together of objectivity and subjectivity: bird and song conjoin and congeal into a symbol. The labor camp, in turn, becomes symbolic of the human condition of exile, most distant from the paradise for which the soul yearns. And yet the soul has something for which to yearn precisely because the camp can become a symbol; paradise is at hand in the becoming-symbol of the camp.

What distinguishes paradise, the Garden of Eden? It is the copresence of the human being and the Holy One from whom humanity derives its sanctity. "The God of the prophets and the rabbis," Emil Fackenheim describes it, "is a God capable of *presence*. Having created heaven and earth, He, as it were, *Himself* walks in the garden" (40). What "walks" in the garden, we are told, is the Voice of God (Genesis 3:8), so that the art whose song seeks a lost paradise is seeking a voice—both one that may speak and one that may be heard, just as Sinyavsky writes his letters, we recall, in order to hear the voice of his wife (*Voice* 313). What he seeks in the word sent home is the voice of the beloved. What he seeks in the artistic word is the Voice of the divine that walks in the midst of the garden, even and especially when the garden has been made into a labor camp. Thus art, Sinyavsky declares, is "an act of prayer" (*Voice* 7). We think we pray to God, the Hasidic saying goes, but this is not entirely so, for the prayer is itself divine: "I am the prayer," says the *Shekhinah*, which is the Indwelling Presence of God (see Buber, *Legend* 27). Art, then, transforms life by transforming the human being into a vessel of the divine. What prayer has in common with art is that both take on a divine aspect by taking hold of ordinary words and attempting to instill them with extraordinary meaning, that is, by the speaker's pouring his soul into his artistic word. When the artist is able to achieve this outpouring, he gazes into his work, as Solzhenitsyn said in his Nobel Lecture, and what he sees is not himself or his craft: "Rather, you behold for a moment the Inaccessible." And what is the Inaccessible? It is precisely the "*Heim* [the home]" according to André Neher, "which promises for tomorrow that which yesterday had passed away" (*They* 138). Thus in the moment of its inception art intersects with prayer to create an opening through which the human being may return from exile.

"Prayer," Elie Wiesel maintains, "draws the human being into an eternal dialogue with God. Thanks to prayer, to its intoxicating and overwhelming accents, God becomes present. Better: God becomes presence. Hence everything is possible and meaningful: here the supreme judge, the Father of humanity, has quit His celestial throne to live among His creatures. And, in turn, here the soul transported by prayer quits its dwelling and mounts unto the heavens. The substance of language and the language of silence—that is what prayer is" (*Paroles* 171–72). Wiesel's words about prayer describe very closely what art is to Sinyavsky. Through art, as through prayer, silence turns into eloquence, and the imposed absence distinguishing exile is overtaken by presence. And this presence arises when both the singer and the one to whom he or she addresses the song take leave of where they are. Art's longing for paradise, where God walks in the garden, is reflected in the prayer's longing for God to descend from His celestial throne to dwell among His creatures, who in turn make their ascent toward God. Having said this much, we realize why Sinyavsky says, "Man is a communicating vessel joined up with God" (*Voice* 73). What makes man one who communicates is the dialogical word that characterizes both his life and his art; what joins him up with God is the prayer-like aspect of that word. In the state of exile from which art would liberate the human being, he who might communicate is rendered mute and he who would be a vessel is reduced to an empty shell, remote from the One who imparts holiness to life and thereby creates a place—becomes the Place or *Makom*—where dwelling transpires. The movement out of exile, then, is a double movement that involves both the human and the divine: God descends and the soul ascends. Which means: the dimension of height unfolds.

The immense significance of this point becomes clear with the help once more of Levinas. "Height ordains being," he argues. "Height introduces a sense into being. It is already lived across the experience of the human body. It leads human societies to raise altars. It is not because men, through their bodies, have an experience of the vertical that the human is placed under the sign of height; because being is ordained to height the human body is placed in a space in which the high and the low are distinguished and the sky is discovered" (*Collected* 100). To dwell is to dwell beneath a sky from which dwelling upon the earth derives its meaning; exile, on the other hand, is the absence of height that turns the earth into a wilderness. For Sinyavsky, this is as much to say: exile is the absence of art, whose song, like a bird, seeks a paradise in a movement of ascent. Thus, in Sinyavsky's words, the art that both summons and is summoned by the soul "overcomes the insanity of formlessness and nonbeing and proclaims the actual existence of a world in which beauty and reality eventually converge at some point on a higher level" (*Voice* 169). Beauty descends and reality ascends, not only to converge at a higher level but to establish the dimension of height, the summons from on high, and the realm of the Most High. The insanity of formlessness and nonbeing lies just in the absence of this dimension, this summons, this realm. One realizes, then, what is behind Sinyavsky's words when he says, "Art is not the representation, but the transfiguration of life. An image arises in response to the need for impelling it towards change in another, transfiguring, direction. We notice an 'image' only in so far as it displaces what it is supposed to depict" (*Voice* 225). When the image displaces what it is supposed to depict the object is transformed into symbol; something else, something more, something past depiction gets depicted. The point here is not that one signifier leads to another within a chain of signifiers; rather, there is a breaking of that chain and the emergence of the "sign" of the giving of signs, which is the basis of signification itself.

The transfiguration that Sinyavsky describes is much like the transformation that Jaspers comments on when he writes, "The transformation of the world into a mediation between us and God is its transformation into *being-a-cypher*" (*Truth* 74). This is the transformation that turns the place of exile into a place of dwelling, the fireplace into a hearth, the house into a home, the table into an altar. As prayer transforms language and silence, so art transforms life and its images. Here, once again, lies the link between art and prayer: both enable us to hear the Voice walking in the garden and to behold the presence that makes even the wilderness into a garden. Art is a Tent of Meeting , where we are transformed by our encounter with the Countenance; where death had lurked, life is made manifest. Thus, Sinyavsky declares, art works its ultimate transformation in an overcoming of death. "Art is created," he asserts, "in order to overcome death" (*Voice* 35)—not by gaining a counterfeit immortality for the artist but by affirming what is most dear and therefore most threatened in life, what there is to die for. "Man lives in order to die," Sinyavsky maintains in *Thoughts at Random*. "Death imparts to life a thematic direction, a unity and a certainty" (128–29). To be sure, Sinyavsky describes the whole point of his *Thoughts at Random* as an exploration of the problem of "how to fulfill the most important task in life: death" (131). In the condition of exile death is a release; dwelling is made possible where death is made into a task. And it is made into a task inasmuch as it constitutes a testimony to what is dear in life. "When one man dies on his feet," Wiesel states it, "another is saved" (*Town* 26). To die on one's feet is to die standing for something and making one's death into a sign of what there is to love and hold dear—what there is that brings us out of exile. The act of creation in the face of death—and it is always in the face of death—transforms life by transforming death. When death is no longer the negation of life but is rather the occasion for affirming life, the silence of exile is broken and the word leading homeward is heard.

The last pages of Sinyavsky's *Voice from the Chorus* consist of his thoughts on his return home; even after his return, he continues to seek the Voice. For example, he writes, "The most interesting thing I have experienced during these first days and weeks after my release has been the feeling of a dead man appearing at life's feast" (343). And: "Coming out of prison is like making a posthumous appearance in the world. It is not like being born again, because one is old and weak" (345). The ordeal of exile makes the movement of return into an ordeal. Now in the place to which his letters were sent, he has no place to send his letters: he has caught up with his words only to slip behind his time, old and weak. Confronted now with a new task, he meets with a new silence that must be broken so that a new life might be forged from the fragments of a broken silence. For the source of all our dwelling and all our days recedes as we approach it. No sooner do we land on one shore than another looms on the horizon—or one the other side of the horizon: the earth is indeed a sphere.

Perhaps, then, Sinyavsky's homelessness, with his effort to find a place at life's feast, teaches him what Walker Percy's castaway learns: "The worst of all despairs is to imagine one is at home when one is really homeless. But what is it to be a castaway? To be a castaway is to search for news from across the seas" (144). And so, as Sinyavsky struggles to find a place at the table laid for life's feast, we hear him cry out in an echo of the chorus from which he emerges, "You don't have to feed me, but give me my letter!" (*Voice* 285). And yet letters are received only by those who write them. Thus even upon the man's return to his household, the exile within makes itself felt. Return is characterized not by a change of place but by a continual movement toward the source and center of life through the repeated affirmation and embrace of all there is to hold dear, which in *A Voice from the Chorus* is exemplified by the family, the face, and the ascent of art. Exile is stasis. Though he now sits in familiar surroundings, Sinyavsky is still faced with writing his letters home in an effort to come before the Face. Like his daily prayers—like his wife and child—his art summons him to a daily repetition. Home is just this process of repeating the movement homeward.

Because the movement homeward entails a movement of the word, the condition of exile is the exile of the word. And since, to quote Emerson, "the poet is the Namer, or the Language-Maker" (314), the word that goes into exile soon becomes the focus of the poetic word. It should not be surprising, then, to find that those Russian poets who live in exile are often concerned, in their poetry, with the exile of the word. For the exile of the word is a tearing of the word from its meaning and therefore a tearing of meaning from life. As the language maker, the poet is the meaning maker, who pens his or her poems from the midst of the breakdown of meaning. The poetic word thus becomes the response to the exile of the word, an attempt to return from exile and thus restore meaning to the word through an articulation of the rupture. And so we come to Part Five.

PART FIVE
The Word in Exile

9. Exile in the Diaspora: The Poetry of Joseph Brodsky

Valentina Polukhina has pointed out that "indirectly, and sometimes directly, Brodsky's thought lies in the orbit of the ideas of Kierkegaard and Shestov" (263). This is the orbit of the ultimate, where the word takes up its search for meaning and the person sets out in search of a home. Indeed, home is precisely the place where word and meaning join to make life hale, whole, and holy. The home and the holy are of a piece. As a poet of ultimate concern and therefore of spiritual concern, Brodsky is attuned to the function of the word in its capacity to open up a place where the sacred may enter life. In an interview with Nataliya Gorbanevskaya he says, "If I were to begin to create some form of theology, I think it would be a theology of language. In this sense, the word is really something sacred for me" (9, trans. Polukhina). The sacred, however, manifests itself as something that is at a distance from us. Thus the notion of making sacred includes the idea of drawing nigh unto the sacred, so that the poet engages in his effort to join word and meaning not in the midst of the sacred but in a movement toward it. The poet *in* exile, then, becomes the poet *of* exile by undertaking this movement of return. He is the one who, in his homelessness, announces the homelessness of the human condition as it is defined by its distance from the sacred. Perhaps this is why Franz Rosenzweig insists, "Every complete human being must have a taste for poetry; indeed he really has to be an amateur poet himself. At the very least he must have once written poetry. Even if, at a pinch, one can be human without composing poetry, one cannot become human without having once done so for a time" (246). In a word: the poet's condition is essentially the human condition as a condition of exile.

One understands, then, why Polukhina asserts that "poetry itself is its own kind of alienation, for it is the exteriorization of one's own 'I,' the objectification of the poet's emotions and thoughts. In this sense any work of art, once finished, is alienated from the creator" (244). Operating in a state of exile, the poet of exile finds that the completion of the poem precedes the condition it addresses. Both the time and the space that frame it are out of joint; this is what makes Brodsky's poetry not only a poetry about exile but the site where exile reveals itself. Like the sense of home, the notions of time and place are felt only in their elusiveness. Cut off from both, the poet of exile is continually struggling in a time that is too late and a place that is elsewhere. "Perhaps exile is the natural condition of the poet," Brodsky comments in an interview with Giovanni Buttafava. "I feel a kind of great privilege in the coincidence of my existential condition and my occupation" (156, trans. George Kline). One will notice that Brodsky regards his exile not as a political condition but as an existential condition, one that is characteristic of his condition as a human being; before he was invited to leave his homeland, his homeland had already abandoned him. Further, the occupation he undertakes is not simply a livelihood but a means by which he may occupy or endure the condition of exile and thus establish a place for himself within that condition. Yet Brodsky's occupation with his existential condition is not so much an occupation or even a preoccupation as it is a *post*-occupation; the man becomes a poet after the fact. What George Kline says of Brodsky is true: "Few poets have expressed the sense of loss, separation, and estrangement more powerfully than Brodsky" (78). And since what we find in Brodsky is indeed an *expression* of separation, the separation is sensed precisely in its expression; that is, the expression is itself a separation. It is the separation of word from meaning, of the soul from itself, of the exile from his or her home. The ring of hopelessness as a word already uttered echoes the poet's homelessness. Meaning lies in the word yet to be voiced. And home is the place to which we have yet to return.

In the coincidence of his existential condition and his existential occupation Brodsky exemplifies the Wandering Jew. And, as the Wandering Jew, he signifies a wandering humanity. Hence much of his poetry, as Efim Etkind points out, deals with a humanity "wandering about the planet without any goal or meaning, realizing that nothing changes anywhere and that all the notions of an earthly paradise are merely illusions" (13). It must be noted that the primary threat to the poet in his own humanity—the chief danger of exile—lies not in illusion but in the indifference that may arise in the collision with changelessness. For here arises the temptation to slip into the deadly sleep of "it's all the same" and thus be swallowed up by the law of identity that Florensky describes as "the spirit of death, emptiness, and nothingness" (*Stolp* 27). In the process of undoing the illusion the poet not only posits a difference between reality and illusion or truth and lie; through the utterance of the poem he transforms that difference into a nonindifference. This transformation makes a poetry of exile into a poetry of return. One example that may demonstrate this point can be found in just a few lines from Brodsky's "Kolybel'naya treskovogo mysa" ("Lullaby of

Cape Cod"): "In genuine tragedy / it's not the fine hero that finally dies, it seems, / but, from constant wear and tear, night after night, / the old stage itself, giving way at the seams" (*Part* 112). Here we see that the undoing of an illusion is the collapse of a ground: the wandering that distinguishes the state of exile is a condition of groundlessness, a distance from the ground or the soil itself; to be sure, the Russian word for "groundlessness," *bespochvennost,'* literally means "being without the soil," without *pochva*. That the breakdown of the illusion implies a need for return is more clearly seen in the original Russian verse. There the word translated as "stage" is *kulisa* (*Chast'* 103), which may be used in the singular to refer to the flat scenery that projects out from the side of the stage. Once the scenery is exposed as flat, the homeland loses its dimension of depth. And this loss parallels the loss of the word gone flat, drained of its meaning and sanctity. It is a loss, therefore, that bears implication for anyone who makes use of words.

When the word manifests itself as something drained of meaning, it opens up a future—and a silence—in which the poet seeks to restore its meaning. Through the word that he holds sacred Brodsky becomes the messenger of the word forever yet to be uttered, the bearer of the silence of the yet-to-be. "The radiations of the future," André Neher observes in *The Exile of the Word*, "are totally silent. Indeed, of the three dimensions of time—present, past, and future—the future alone is completely identified with silence, in its plenitude but also in its remarkable ambivalence" (168–69). As the messenger of silence the poet bears the memory of the future, which is the opposite not of the past but of the absence of the past. In spatial terms this silence suggests that exile is opposed not to a place called home but to the absence of a home made present precisely by its absence. In this condition of exile, then, Brodsky affirms the dearness of a home that is forever elsewhere. Thus, as we shall see, the sacred, the silent, and the elsewhere are the terms that shape the notion of exile in Brodsky's poetry. Let us turn now to that poetry in an effort to hear the voice that issues from the core of this rupture—and perhaps to hear the cry of our own souls.

The Sacramental Sign

"The powerful revelations invoked by the religions," writes Martin Buber, "are essentially the same as the quiet one that occurs everywhere and at all times" (*I and Thou* 165–66). One task of the poet in his endeavor to make felt the dearness of what is lost is to make visible the sanctity of what is unseen. This ability is just what distinguishes Brodsky as a poet.

W.H. Auden expresses it in his introduction to Brodsky's *Selected Poems* by noting the poet's unusual "capacity to envision material objects as sacramental signs, messengers from the unseen" (10). This envisioning, of course, is a mode of hearing. Making visible the sacramental sign, Brodsky draws on the word in an act of hearing and making heard. Through the said we behold the unseen; through the seen we hear the unheard. A good illustration of Auden's statement appears in an untitled verse from the *Selected Poems:*

> In villages God does not live only
> in icon corners, as the scoffers claim,
> but plainly, everywhere. He sanctifies
> each roof and pan, divides each double door.
> In villages God acts abundantly—
> cooks lentils in iron pots on Saturdays,
> dances a lazy jig in flickering flames,
> and winks at me, witness to all of this. [81]

Where God sanctifies, man dwells. The sacramental sign is the site of human dwelling, where each fixture has its place—roof, pan, and door—and each action has its time: on Saturdays. The illusion here unveiled as a lie is the illusion of the scoffers, who are deaf and blind to the sign and therefore to the holiness of the preparation of "lentils in iron pots." Like the word itself—like the word *pots*—such pots are the vessels of the sacred, preparing, as they do, the foodstuff that joins creature to creation and thus to the Creator. The dance underscores the harmony in this joining of word and thing, of the human and the divine. And the truth of this harmony, the truth as harmony, issues from the light of the flickering flame, calling to mind the light brought forth upon the first utterance of the Creator in His act of creation. Calling forth a world, the poet himself imitates the Creator in his response to creation. He looks on, and God looks back, ever so subtly, with a wink from between the lines, and thus transforms the man into a witness. A witness to what? To the dwelling in villages that occurs upon the hidden but abundant action of God. When God acts, man dwells.

And yet the poet does not belong to the village. He looks on to become a link between the villagers and those of us who, like himself, live on the outside, in exile. One begins to see why exile is a necessary feature of the poet's existential situation: the one who sings of the sacramental sign is placed outside of it as soon as he consigns his song to the page. The villagers dwell in the village, while his consciousness, or the inscription of that consciousness, places the poet before the village. And as he who thus reads the sacramental signs makes us into readers of the signs, he takes us with him into the realm of exile, making strange the familiar. Consider, for instance, the closing lines to an untitled poem from *A Part of Speech:*

> A morning milkman, seeing the milk that's soured,
> will be the first to guess that you have died here.
> Here you can live, ignoring calendars,
> gulp Bromo, never leave the house; just settle
> and stare at your reflection in the glass,
> as streetlamps stare at theirs in shrinking puddles. [62]

Here the milkman is made into a reader of signs, and death is presented as that form of living that is void of dwelling. Never leaving the house, the man is never at home; staring only at his reflection, he never sees himself. In these lines we have an inversion of the sign made visible in the lentils and iron pots above. Here the sacred is revealed under the inverted sign of sickness: the milk sours as the man guzzles Bromo, medicating himself to death. The light that would illuminate the road into a community, through which the man may seek a return home, is swallowed up in a shrinking puddle that sullies the path. Once again, however, there is an "and yet" underlying the poem: the reflection of the light that catches the poet's eye rises upward, and in this rising upward the sanctity of the word manifests itself. The reflection is in the puddle, but the light comes from above. Poetry, says Brodsky in *Less than One,* "is language negating its own mass and the laws of gravity; it is language's striving upward—or sideways—to that beginning where the Word was" (186). That beginning is where the poem both begins and seeks its end. What is it that negates the laws of gravity and the mass of language, levitating even iron pots? It is the sacramental sign.

Brodsky illustrates this point very effectively in the last few lines of his "Ekloga 4-ya: Zimnyaya" ("Eclogue IV: Winter"), where we read,

> That's the birth of an eclogue. Instead of the shepherd's signal,
> a lamp's flaring up. Cyrillic, while running witless
> on the pad as though to escape the captor,
> knows more of the future than the famous sybil:
> of how to darken against the whiteness,
> as long as the whiteness lasts. [*To Urania* 81]

In this poem the sacramental sign that flares up is not simply the iron pot or the streetlamp but is the poem itself, which is made of the imposition of black on white, as if the flame that burned were a dark one.

Nonetheless, it is the dark letter carved into the wilderness of white that makes the wilderness visible, transforming it from an expanse of emptiness into a *page*. The pastoral presence is eclipsed by the Cyrillic scrawl that signifies an absence; it is as if the very letters of which the word is made get in the way of its contact with meaning. The word thus struggles to escape the letters that confine it, struggles, in a sense, to escape itself in the poet's effort to capture it. The scrawl takes on the significance of sacramental sign, however, not so much in its making visible a lack or an absence as in its opening up the yet-to-be: it knows more of the future—that is, it bears a deeper memory of the future, of the *afterward*—than the sybil. Like the Word that was in the beginning, the end of the poem about to be written precedes it. Here one may recall Brodsky's statement in *Less than One* that "words, even their letters—vowels especially—are almost palpable vessels of time" (125). For the time they contain is not just the past or present but, above all, the future. The capacity of the word to contain this time is its capacity to convey meaning. Meaning, then, happens in transit, eternally on the way to a place where it has yet to be fulfilled. The poet in exile, however, has no star to guide him as his word carries him along this path. The flaring up of the poem takes the place of a star, as we see upon an examination of the Russian version of these lines. There the lamp replaces not the shepherd's signal but the *svetilo*, which means "light" or "star"; taking the place of this light, the poem takes on the sacred. What the Cyrillic knows, moreover, it knows through a *greshnym delom* or through a "sinful affair" (*Uraniya* 123), because it usurps the signal or sign that is forever yet to be revealed. The prospect of redemption arises from the realization of this usurpation; the light is perceived as a presence displaced; and the return homeward that always comes *afterward* happens from within a condition of exile.

     What is perhaps most striking about these lines from Brodsky's "Eclogue IV: Winter" is that the Cyrillic stuff of writing has a certain life of its own. The word is sacred for Brodsky because it is alive; it speaks and is not merely a tool used by the speaker. Brodsky makes this explicit in *Less than One*, where he declares, "Writing is literally an existential process; it uses thinking for its own ends, it consumes notions, themes, and the like, not vice versa. What dictates a poem is the language, and this is the voice of the language, which we know under the nickname of Muse or Inspiration" (124–25). It is the voice of language that sanctifies the sign, not the other way around, and in its sanctification the sign signifies the living presence of another—the Muse or the Spirit—who renders the poet other to himself. The sacramental sign, therefore, not only reveals to me the sacred but also tells me where I am not . "There is always a word living secretly under the word," Edmond Jabès expresses it. And, he adds, "to be attentive to language is to be attentive to one-self" (91). Why? Because there is always a self—or another—living secretly under oneself. Announcing his distance from the sacred, the voice of the other in the midst of language proclaims the poet's distance from a world in which he might dwell. Thus in "Venetsianskie strofy 2" (Venetian Stanzas II) the exiled poet writes,

> I am writing these lines sitting outdoors, in winter,
> on a white iron chair, in my shirtsleeves, a little drunk;
> the lips move slowly enough to hinder
> the vowels of the mother tongue,
> and the coffee grows cold. And the blinding lagoon is lapping
> at the shore as the dim human pupil's bright penalty
> for its wish to arrest a landscape quite happy
> here without me. [*To Urania* 94–95]

The poet's distance from himself, from the sacred, and from a dwelling place is proclaimed in images of disjuncture: shirtsleeves in winter, cold coffee, a landscape there without him. The time is out of joint, and the man is out of place, drunk enough so that the vowels that might be the vessels of time, and therefore of the sacred, elude him. Like the eye that would arrest the landscape, the word would capture meaning, the written the vocable, but both rush ahead without the man. To be in the presence of the sacred—to be present—is to be in a state of motion, a point indicated by the use of the present tense. Yet the verb is no sooner off the tongue and onto the page than the man has slipped behind.

While Brodsky may have the ability to perceive the sacramental sign, as Auden says, and thus to make it speak, the sacred itself eternally and necessarily escapes him. The poet in exile, the poet of exile, is forever adrift. Commenting on the poet in the *Phaedrus*, Plato asserts that there is a "form of possession or madness of which the Muses are the source" (492). In this case the poet, indeed, has much in common with the madman, especially as Michel Foucault describes him when he writes, "Confined to the ship, from which there is no escape, the madman is delivered to the river with its thousand arms, the sea with its thousand roads, to that great uncertainty external to everything. He is a prisoner in the midst of what is the freest, the openest of routes: bound fast at the infinite crossroads. He is the Passenger *par excellence*: that is, the prisoner of the passage" (*Madness* 11). What Foucault articulates Brodsky illustrates in these lines from "Lullaby of Cape Cod":

> Preserve these words. The paradise men seek
> is a dead end, a worn-out, battered cape
> bent into crooked shape,
> a cone, a finial cap, a steel ship's bow
> from which the lookout never shouts, "Land ho!" [*Part* 116]

The poet sketches the symbol, but the thing it symbolizes remains beyond the horizon of his vision; the homeland, like the word beneath the word, remains forever hidden in silence. Hence it is sacred. In the Russian text the term rendered as "Land ho" is the single word *Zemlya* (*Chast'* 108), which means "earth," as well as "land." As the Passenger par excellence, the poet is continually in search of this center, or this origin and organ of life, of the mother and the mystery: the earth. That is where he seeks his dwelling place. That is what the signifiers of exile struggle to signify. And that is what abides in the silence of the "other" language, the silence of all tongues, to which the poet strives to give voice and which gives it voice to the poet. "Poetry, in essence," says Brodsky, "is itself a certain *other* language—or a translation from such" (*Less* 234). In order to become the translator of the other language, of the silent language, the poet must draw on the word to carry over what the word cannot convey. The bearer of the sacramental sign thus bears something more than the sign can bear: he is the messenger of silence.

The Messenger of Silence

We have seen that the sacramental sign signifies not only the sacred but a distance from the sacred, and that the sign positions the sacred beyond the horizon of the yet-to-be. This beyond is the realm of silence, where the voice of language no longer speaks—or rather speaks in the mode of silence, in the mode of nonspeaking: in the mode of death, for death is the one certainty situated in the yet-to-be. Death defines and delineates the realm of exile. In his article "Variations on the Theme of Exile" Kline comments on Brodsky's poetry, saying, "The increasing deafness of the old is a rehearsal for the non-speaking which is death, the silence which is eternity" (69). If words are the vessels of time, then silence is, indeed, the vessel of eternity, the path to which leads through death. In *The Exile of the Word* Neher offers a helpful insight in this connection. "It is not we," he writes, "who cast the veil of silence over death as we put upon it the veil of darkness. Death is silence. . . . The moment of death is silence overtaking life. The duration of death is silence, becoming infinitely removed from life" (37). Brodsky, of course, is aware of this element not only in his own poetry but in any art that might bespeak this absence of speech. "Art," he asserts, " 'imitates' death rather than life; i.e. it imitates that realm of which life supplies no notion: realizing its own brevity, art tries to domesticate the longest possible version of time" (*Less* 104). That realm of which a life steeped in language supplies no notion is not only the realm of death but also the realm of silence. Here lies the ineffable that the poet translates into a poem and in which he seeks the image of himself and through which we catch a glimpse of ourselves.

"Death as a theme," Brodsky notes, "always produces a self-portrait" (*Less* 100). In the condition of exile, moreover, the portrait of the self is sketched along the lines of separation from the other; home is made not only of familiar places but of familiar faces. The separation from those human relations determines a certain relation of the poet to his poetry. The messenger of silence is the messenger of separation and thus of infinite longing for the other, for silence is the stuff of which separation and exile are made. A poem about the end of love, for example, may have its links to a deeper existential concern, especially when it appears not only in the context of two lovers but in the context of exile. As a lover, the man separates; as a poet, he writes of the deeper implications of the separation to reveal what lurks in every farewell. As an illustration of this, it is worth citing at length a poem titled "Stanzas" from Brodsky's *Selected Poems:*

> Let our farewells be silent.
> Turn the phonograph down.
> Separations in this world
> hint at partings beyond.
> It's not just in this lifetime
> that we must sleep apart.
> Death won't bring us together
> or wipe out our love's hurt.
> . . . .
> As our union was perfect,
> so our break is complete.
> Neither panning nor zooming
> can postpone the fade-out.
> There's no point in our claiming
> that our fusion's still real.
> But a talented fragment
> can pretend to be whole.
>
> Swoon, then, to o'erflowing,
> drain yourself till you're dry.
> We two halves share the volume,
> but not the strength, of the wine.

But my world will not end if
in future we share
only those jagged edges
where we've broken apart.

No man stands as a stranger.
But the threshold of shame
is defined by our feelings
at the "Never again."
Thus, we mourn, yet we bury,
and resume our concerns,
cutting death at its center
like two clear synonyms.
. . . .
Let our farewell be silent. [67–69]

The parting from the other is a tearing away of the self from its soul and a rending of meaning from the word. The wholeness of the heart, of the very core of life, is torn asunder, and the messenger here conveys what he has retrieved from the bleeding silence of that gaping wound. Separation hints at a parting beyond because the volume constituted by self and other contains a world, a time yet to come, and therefore a home. The separation is silent because it is a form of death, and, as Brodsky says, this death culminates in a portrait of the self left to the frayed edges of itself. The poet of exile moves along this jagged edge that traces the silhouette of death. The difficulty confronting him is to fetch the word from that grave without tumbling into it.

The struggle of life with death, of exile with homeland, is a struggle of the word with silence. One poem in which this struggle unfolds most explicitly and most thoroughly is "Gorbunov and Gorchakov," which is an extended dialogue between two patients in a psychiatric hospital outside of Leningrad. In this poem the messenger of silence joins his voice to the voice of the madman to make silence itself speak. Listen:

"And nothing can be more impenetrable
than veils of words that have devoured their things;
nothing is more tormenting than men's language."
"But if we view things more objectively
it may be that we'll come to the conclusion
that words are also things. And thus we're saved!"
"But that is the beginning of vast silence.
And silence is the future of all days
that roll toward speech; yes, silence is the presence
of farewells in our greetings as we touch.
Indeed, the future of our words is silence—

> those words which have devoured the stuff of things
> with hungry vowels, for things abhor sharp corners.
> Silence: a wave that cloaks eternity.
> Silence: the future fate of all our loving—
> a space, not a dead barrier, but space
> that robs the false voice in the blood-stream throbbing
> of every echoed answer to its love.
> And silence is the present fate of those who
> have lived before us; it's a matchmaker
> that manages to bring all men together
> into the speaking presence of today.
> Life is but talk hurled in the face of silence." [*Poems* 146–47]

It bears repeating: silence is not a barrier but a space, the place of exile, the poet's point of departure and return. And in silence we are gathered together with him, confronted with our own exile. If poetry is an exploration of the word, then silence is its subject matter; and, just as the theme of death ends in a self-portrait, the pursuit of silence leads to a collision with the self. And yet, once again, the thing that posits the separation also implies a union: silence is a matchmaker that brings us together in a speaking presence, and the poetic word enables us to hear it. Like the death that accentuates life, silence calls forth the spoken part of the human being, as part of speech, that vibrates on the breath of life. Human presence is a speaking presence that harbors a nonspeaking, and the human task is to become present as a human being before another human being in an offering up of oneself joined with one's word. In this task the poet is our teacher.

But, like all teachers, the poet learns by hard lessons, for he takes up the way of response from within an absence of response. "The absence of response," says Brodsky, "has done in many a poet, and in so many ways, the net result of which is that infamous equilibrium—or tautology—between cause and effect: silence" (*Less* 173). The silence that threatens the poet is not the silence that gathers human being unto human being but the blank silence born of the collapse of difference into indifference. The one who is faced with the translation of silence into utterance is faced with the transformation of this emptiness into eloquence. This he accomplishes through a return to a difference that is nonindifference, and that return is effected by assuming responsibility for the absence of response. Only in this way can the poet overcome the death that stalks him as a poet. Recall in this connection the words of Emmanuel Levinas: "The self is nonindifference to the others, a sign given to the others" (*Otherwise* 171). And: "Subjectivity is the other in the same" (*Otherwise* 16). Brodsky offers a poetic expression of Levinas's philosophical remarks in "Pen'e bez muzyki" ("A Song to No Music"):

> the embrace's stifling blindness
> was in itself a pledge of an
> invisibility that binds us
> in separations: hid within
> each other, we dodged space [*Part* 28–29]

Seeking the word hidden beneath the word, the silence beneath the vocable, the poet seeks the other within the self, the one who is drawn into the self in the act of embrace. This movement, this response of nonindifference, creates the proximity that might, if only for a moment, dodge space and span the distance that constitutes exile. The point is perhaps better made in the Russian line, *my skryvalis' ot prostranstva*, or "we were hiding from space" (*Konets* 78), suggesting a hiddenness in a place beneath the word or beyond the word where meaning happens—silently. In that place beyond space the silence of emptiness is transformed into the silence of eloquence. From the place beyond space the messenger of silence bears his message of embrace.

And yet, in his exile, the poet is invariably thrown back to the message of what has been lost to exile, of what is felt only as pain. One passage in which the pain of isolation is most strongly felt appears in the last two lines of "I Sit by the Window": "I sit in the dark. And it would be hard to figure out / which is worse: the dark inside, or the darkness out." [*Part* 42] For "dark" and "darkness" we may read "silence." This is the darkness that the flaring up of the lamp of poetry endeavors to illuminate; this is the silence, the nonspeaking, that drives the poet to speak or die, or to die in the speaking. What is left of the messenger's message? Brodsky tells us in "Chast' rechi" ("A Part of Speech"):

> and when "the future" is uttered, swarms of mice
> rush out of the Russian language and gnaw a piece
> of ripened memory which is twice
> as hole-ridden as real cheese.
> . . . .
> What gets left of a man amounts
> to a part. To his spoken part. To a part of speech. [Part 105]

In the Russian text the penultimate line contains an important word left out of the English translation; it is the second-person pronoun *vam* (*Chast'* 95): what is left of a man *for you* is a part of speech, that part that remains of the soul that the poet offers to you, his reader. And it is not *his* spoken part, exactly, but *chast' rechi voobshche,* "a part of speech in general," of speech as such. The messenger of silence is one who, in the end, cannot deliver his message, for he cannot convey the full word or speech that contains the silence of a meaningful future. All we have are fragments of the message and pieces of the messenger, the eternal passenger, he is thus the eternal messenger. Brodsky reiterates this lament, this message, in "Dekabr' vo Florentsii" ("December in Florence"), where he writes, "A man gets reduced to pen's rustle on paper, to / wedges, ringlets of letters, and also, due / to the slippery surface, to commas and full stops" (*Part* 120). Hence we see the poet addressing in his poetry the very thing that threatens it. The message is that the word is inadequate to the message, that the You who is addressed must find some way not to stop at the full stop, some way to dodge space and step through the ringlets of letters that occlude the word.

These, then, are the signposts of exile: wedges and ringlets of letters, commas and periods of punctuation. But, just as the word that comprises a poem bespeaks the silence from which it is born, so do the signposts pointing in one direction posit another. Brodsky etched such a sign for himself on 4 June 1977, the fifth anniversary of his exile from his homeland, when he wrote, "I don't know anymore what earth will nurse my carcass. / Scratch on, my pen: let's mark the white the way it marks us" (*To Urania* 35). The poet is marked by the white in his marking of it; the sign he imposes on the emptiness is imposed on him, making him into who he is: a poet. Like the exile Cain he is marked, but without the crime. Or with a different crime: marking the white and thus groping for meaning in the void, the messenger of silence has breached the silence. Instead of building cities, as Cain did, he erects words, ringlets and wedges, in an effort to construct a place to dwell, only to have the construct underscore his distance from home. Recall in this connection the lines from his "Litovskii noktyurn" ("Lithuanian Nocturne"):

> nobody stands to inhabit
> air! It is our "homeward!" That town
> which all syllables long
> to return to. . . .
> . . . .
> That is why it is pure!
> In this world, there is nothing that bleaches
> paper better (except
> for one's dying) than air.

> And the whiter, the emptier, which is
> homelike. Muse, may I set
> out homeward? [*To Urania* 15–16]

The very thing that the poet would convey on his page places it under erasure, "bleaches" it back into silence. Here we see that the shore from which the messenger sets out is precisely the place he seeks: it is a certain elsewhere hidden in the emptiness of the air, for even the emptiness has its secret side. It is home. Looking at the Russian text, we notice that in both of these stanzas the word *domoi*, "homeward," is immediately followed by the word *vosvoyasi*, which is translated as "town" but means "home" or "go home" (*Uraniya* 63–64). Home takes on its sense through the movement toward it, and yet it recedes as it is approached, "bleached" into a distant elsewhere. It should also be noted that the word rendered as "emptier" is *beschelovechnei*, which in usage means "more ruthless" but literally means "without human beings": the emptiness is the signifier of exile, while home is where humaneness and humanity dwell.

The exile's absence from home must come to signify and thus affirm the presence of a home in a place that is eternally elsewhere, forever under erasure. Brodsky himself makes this point when he writes, "Absence, in the final analysis, is a crude version of detachment: psychologically it is synonymous with presence in some other place and, in this way, expands the notion of being. In turn, the more significant the absent object, the more signs there are of its existence" (*Less* 261). Let us consider more closely now the significance of the absent home and the poet's affirmation of the elsewhere that harbors it.

The Affirmation of the Elsewhere

In her book on Brodsky, Valentina Polukhina points out that "as the material means and goal of poetry, the word becomes the bearer of the spiritual content of human life" (177), and, in the words of Jacques Lacan, "the spirit is always somewhere else" (*Language* 34). Why? Because the material means of capturing the spiritual invariably ends by displacing it. For the material traces the spatial, and the spatial is the opposite of the spiritual. Where dwelling happens, space is transformed into spirit, just as the breaking and sharing of bread constitutes a spiritual union of human beings. That is why, in the human realm, it is the body that brings the spirit to bear: a spiritual dimension of life can be an issue only for a creature of flesh and blood, only for one who eats. The absence of the body that Brodsky proclaims in "K Uranii" ("To Urania"), then, is a spiritual absence; that is, the poem uses a material means to declare that the spirit is elsewhere, particularly where we read, "And what is space anyway if not the / body's absence at every given / point? That's why Urania's older than sister Clio!" (*To Urania* 70). Urania is the Muse of the heavens and the contemplation of the heavens, while Clio is the Muse of history. Urania is older because it is the longing for the heavens—which is the abode of the gods and where one may become as the gods—that gives rise to history. History is the tale of the human effort to reach the heavens in the vain construction of one Tower of Babel after another. The heavens comprise the realm of the Great Elsewhere that reveals to us where we are *not*, and the voice of their Muse reverberates in the voice of the poet in exile.

Venturing into the voice, the poet may catch a glimpse of himself from the standpoint of that nowhere that defines his condition of exile and his endeavor as a poet. In a poem titled "Meksikanskii romansero" ("Mexican Romancero") Brodsky affirms the elsewhere of home by way of this "nowhere" when he writes,

> Something inside of me went slightly
> wrong, so to speak—off course.
> Muttering "God Almighty,"
> I hear my own voice.
>
> Thus you dirty the pages
> to stop an instant that's fair,
> automatically gazing
> at yourself from nowhere. [*Part* 83]

While the English phrases "slightly wrong" and "off course" imply a loss of direction, the corresponding Russian words in the original are much stronger. They are *sorvalos'* and *raskololos'*, meaning "torn apart" and "broken to pieces" (*Chast'* 68). The soul has not just gone off course; it has lost the wholeness of what it is. It has lost itself and therefore is broken off from the divine: in the outcry "God Almighty" that would make heard the voice of God, the person hears only his or her own voice. And there is no deeper, more dreadful isolation. To be nowhere is to hear only your own voice; that is what defines the condition of exile. And yet the self upon whom the person gazes from nowhere is . . . elsewhere. Although the soul has lost its home, something of the home remains in the soul, *radi melkogo chuda*, "for the sake of a small miracle," as the Russian line reads; in the English text it is rendered by the much weaker "to stop an instant that's fair." The invocation of the small miracle entails an affirmation of the elsewhere from which the miracle stems; it amounts to the declaration that even though I am nowhere, there is a place of presence somewhere, a place where God dwells in lentils and iron pots. There is a place somewhere, or the remnant of a place within the soul, in which the person can claim to be native.

For the poet, however, that place remains elsewhere as long as he is a poet. Exile is his essential condition, as Brodsky has said, because there is always a distance between word and place, which is precisely the distance between word and meaning; the exile of the man is an exile of the word. As a poet, all he has is the word, the native tongue, that strands him in a strange place from which he affirms the elsewhere. Recall, for example, the lines from Brodsky's "1972," the year in which he was sent into exile:

> Listen, my boon and brethren and my enemies!
> What I've done, I've done not for fame or memories
> in this era of radio waves and cinemas,
> but for the sake of my native tongue and letters.
> For which sort of devotion, of a zealous bent
> ("Heal thyself, doctor," as the saying went),
> denied a chalice at the feast of the fatherland,
> now I stand in a strange place. The name hardly matters. [*Part* 65]

In this poem it is not so much the fatherland as the feast that designates the elsewhere. To be at home, on one's native and natal soil, is to sit at the table and consume the bread born from that soil, the bread that joins the man to the native land. The poet in exile and of exile is hungry. Hunger makes the place strange, casting it in that irreality Brodsky speaks of when he says, "Usually it is not reality but precisely irreality that gives occasion for a poem" (*Less* 241). This hunger, this internal emptiness, is the absence of what Levinas refers to above as "the other in the same." It is a hunger that derives, moreover, not only from what might be received but from what might be offered to the other. The distance from home is a distance from the other, from one's brother. Reaching for the chalice forever out of reach, the poet extends a hand to his fellow human being, seeking that proximity to the human reality that is the opposite of irreality. For the bread we break and share at the feast of the fatherland joins us not only with the native soil but with our brethren, those with whom we share our native tongue, for whom whom we answer.

Again, the affirmation of the elsewhere lies not just in the articulation of emptiness but in the stretching forth of the hand. The hand that descends to the page to grope for the word reaches up for the elsewhere and for the other. Consider how these images work in "Iork" ("York"), a poem written in memory of W.H. Auden: "The emptiness, swallowing sunlight—something in common with / the hawthorn—grows steadily more palpable / in the outstretched hand's direction, and / the world merges into a long street where others live" (*Part* 127). A human element is here added to the landscape that is there without the man in "Venetian Stanzas II." The distance from home lies in the distance from others; home is constituted by this human presence, and to be at home is to be in the midst of a human community. The emptiness described in these lines is the emptiness of the outside, of exteriority, of being left to a place that has no proximity to the human other. To be sure, the word translated as "emptiness," *pustota* (*Uraniya* 79), also means "wilderness." The wilderness is that place that is external to the human community where others live. The affirmation of the elsewhere, then, is the affirmation of an interior, the kind Levinas refers to when he says, "Isn't . . . the alienation of man primarily the fact of having no home? Not to have a place of one's own, not to have an interior, is not truly to communicate with another, and thus to be a stranger to oneself and to the other" (*Nine* 109). And: "There is no salvation except in the reentry into oneself. One must have an interiority where one can seek refuge. . . . And even if 'at home'—in the refuge or in the interiority—there is 'terror,' it is better to have a country, a home, or an 'inwardness' with terror than to be outside" (*Nine* 190). This is the interior that the poet seeks through his affirmation, through his reaching out, which is a reaching in, through his scrawl on the page. Inwardness, therefore, lies not in the isolation with oneself, where all a person hears is his or her own voice. The path to the interior leads through the other. Interiority is to be found in the space *between* self and other.

Brodsky provides us with a poem about the poetry's affirmation of an interior elsewhere in his "Lullaby of Cape Cod." In connection with the matter at hand we note particularly those lines where he writes,

> Preserve these words against a time of cold,
> a day of fear: man survives like a fish,
> stranded, beached, but intent
> on adapting itself to some deep, cellular wish,
> wriggling toward bushes, forming hinged leg-struts, then
> to depart (leaving a track like the scrawl of a pen)
> for the interior, the heart of the continent. [*Part* 114]

It is worth noting that in his simile Brodsky does not use the Russian word *ryba* for "fish" but rather the English word *fish* spelled with Cyrillic letters (*Chast'* 106). Like the creature undergoing its own metamorphosis to form leg-struts, the word itself takes on an alien form that signifies the man's transformation. We acquire, then, a better sense of the terror of the interior. In order to initiate a movement of return toward the elsewhere, toward this other place, the man himself must become other than who he is. This process of becoming, of course, links the elsewhere to the yet-to-be that was discussed above. And the two are linked by silence. As Brodsky puts it in his "Strofy" ("Strophes"), "You won't receive an answer / if "Where to?" swells your voice" (*Part* 141). If there is an answer or, better, a response to this question, it is "elsewhere." Since the approach toward, and affirmation of, the elsewhere entails taking on a new being, the terror that lurks in the interior is the terror of nonbeing, of the loss of what I am in order to become other and thus to become my own answer to the question of "Where to?" A point made in earlier chapters applies here as well: the truth is not what I know but what I am, or rather what I am in the process of becoming. And in order to sustain that process of becoming, I must overcome the fear of no longer being who I am. The elsewhere is not only *where* but *what* I am yet to be.

Brodsky demonstrates his insight into this aspect of the condition of exile in the closing lines of "Na vystavke Karla Veilinka" ("At Karl Weilink's Exhibition"), where we read, "This, then, is 'mastery': ability / to not take fright at the procedure of / nonbeing—as another form of one's / own absence, having drawn it straight from life" (*To Urania* 121). From the depths of these lines, the abyss into which the man gazes peers back into the man. For here he discovers that not only is he *in* exile, but he *is* exile: not only is his home elsewhere, but he is himself elsewhere, clutching at mere traces of himself along the jagged edges of his art. The poet struggles to regain his soul by offering it up to the other, both human and divine, through his song, but the song ends by eclipsing the offering. The word uttered is more than just the dead flesh of meaning: it is the dead flesh of the soul. Thus the poet no sooner speaks than he is thrown back to that position of absence from which he must once again listen for the voice that comes both from within and from beyond. In this eternal repetition, this repeated affirmation of the elsewhere, we catch a glimpse of the infinite at work in poetry. In *Less than One* Brodsky explains: "Love is essentially an attitude maintained by the infinite toward the finite. The reversal constitutes either faith or poetry" (44). A poem, like the home that the exile seeks, is a finite vessel of the infinite; home, like a poem, is the place where iron pots can contain the Infinite One. The realm of exile is that place where the law of

identity equates the finite with the finite and the infinite with the infinite; where love is not at work in life—in the realm of exile—life gets reduced to such equations. But love undoes the equation to open up the
path to the elsewhere that is home, where the life of the soul unfolds in
the affirming embrace of the other.

Perhaps now we may have a better sense of that life that silently abides
in the sanctity of the elsewhere. The sacramental signs that go into the
making of Brodsky's poetry silently convey a message that is otherwise
left to mere silence. And even if the message tells us that we have no answers to the question of "Where to?" it nonetheless affirms the urgency
of the question and the dearness of what is at stake. "When it comes
down to it," Brodsky raises the question for himself, "where am I
from?" (*Less* 443). This is the question that points to a place where he has
yet to arrive; it is the question that guides not only his poetry but the
journey homeward undertaken by those who step before his poetry.
And this is the question for which the poet expresses his defiant gratitude in a poem written on his fortieth birthday titled "May 24, 1980":

> I've admitted the sentries' third eye into my wet and foul
> dreams. Munched the bread of exile: it's stale and warty.
> Granted my lungs all sounds except the howl;
> switched to a whisper. Now I am forty.
> What should I say about life? That it's long and abhors transparence.
> Broken eggs make me grieve; the omelette, though, makes me vomit.
> Yet until brown clay has been crammed down my larynx,
> only gratitude will be gushing from it. [*To Urania* 3]

This, then, is mastery: to give thanks for the thing that wounds the soul.
For the soul is animated and known by its wounds, by the questions that
emerge, like life, from broken eggs, and not by answers that, in this
poem, are omelettes. The soul is punctuated not by full stops but by
question marks and speaks through the howl it holds back. Thus it
transforms the howl into words and silences that breathe words like a
whisper. Here we see poetry's link to faith and gratitude's link to poetry: I shall sing my song even—or especially—when, by every right, it
should not be there. I shall affirm the sanctity of the silent elsewhere
even from within the confines of this noisy, alien nowhere.
    No poem can take the place of the sacred; no poem can impart the
silence; no poem can bring us to the elsewhere that is home. But the
poem can invoke the star that sheds its light on the place of exile as well
as the homeland from a sky that spans both. And so by the light of the

poem we perceive that light of the star, like the one in "24 Dekabrya 1971 goda" (December 24, 1971"):

> But when drafts through the doorway disperse
> the thick mist of the hours of darkness
> and a shape in a shawl stands revealed,
> both a newborn and Spirit that's Holy
> in your self you discover; you stare
> skyward, and it's right there:
>
> a star. [*Part* 48]

The power of this invocation is the power to take us toward a place where Within and Above are synonyms. It is not only the land that the poet, or any human being, is in need of but a sky that harbors a star and a word that holds a sky. Thus it may happen that a poet returns to a homeland, to the Promised Land, only to find that his quest for the Above that is Within has only begun. Here too the concern with a poet provides the occasion for a much larger concern with exile. It is just such a concern that characterizes the poetry of Mikhail Gendelev.

10. Exile in the Promised Land: The Poetry of Mikhail Gendelev

Born in Leningrad in 1950, Mikhail Gendelev emigrated to Israel in 1977. He served as a doctor in the Israeli army during the war in Lebanon from 1982 to 1985 and has been considered a professional writer since 1983. His poems have appeared in numerous periodicals, including *Vremya*, as well as in anthologies such as *Scopus* (1979) and *Russian Poets in the West* (1986). The three volumes of his poetry with which we are here concerned are *V"ezd v Ierusalim* (*Journey to Jerusalem*, 1979), *Poslaniya Lemuram* (*Messages to the Lemures*, 1981), and *Stikhotvoreniya Mikhaila Gendeleva* (*The Poems of Mikhail Gendelev*, 1984). The poems in the first volume were written while the poet still lived in the Soviet Union, and they bear the formal features that distinguish the "literary principles of the Diaspora in the West," as Gendelev describes them (conversation with the author, July 1989). In the second and third volumes Gendelev struggles to leave behind Western conventions "to find new forms adequate to a new, Israeli reality" (conversation with the author, July 1989). For Gendelev, this shift entails both an aesthetic and an existential transition from his endeavors as a Russian poet to an endeavor as an Israeli poet: the change in the poetic word brought about by this geographic shift brings with it a change in consciousness, as well as a disjuncture at the heart of the man's being. What he is lies to a large degree in where he is, and where he is lies in the poetic word to which he would give utterance. And that is where the difficulty arises. Although he draws on images peculiar to an Israeli existence, Gendelev nonetheless writes and therefore thinks in Russian. The linguistic difficulty, moreover, is amplified by the existential condition of exile that begins in the place of his birth and follows him to the birthplace of his fathers. In his poetry, then, we find a confluence of the exile of the word and the word of the exile that reveals much not only about this poet but about language and meaning as such. Exile, human homelessness itself, lies in the violent divorce between word and meaning, between sign and substance. And the poet's struggle to rejoin the two is the struggle of a soul to return to itself and thus to life. Poetry is the place of human dwelling. As such, the poetry of one who occupies Gendelev's unusual position can provide us with unusual insight into the general problem of exile within the general human condition.

As we have seen in our concern with Brodsky, the poetic word, despite all its depth, is never quite deep enough to take on the meaning it seeks, the meaning that would return the man to his home. Expressing this thought in poetic fashion, Gendelev speaks of the flesh, or the body, which is never quite enough for the soul it would regain. In a poem from *Journey to Jerusalem* he writes, "The flesh was not enough, / on the whole planet it was not enough, / to span, to complete, to close up / the clamp between cosmos and being" (108). Here the failing of the flesh is a failing of the word, so that poetry is forever haunted by the breach between the physical and the metaphysical. For the Jew it is a breach created *by* a certain metaphysical outlook when that outlook takes the form of a myth imposed upon the Chosen from the outside. In his poem "Vitebsk," for instance, Gendelev cries out,

> We were always stepchildren of the earth,
> always we appeared in the shadows of ailing
> capitals,
> we longed for the strange, made ready
> for our memories by others. We have passed by,
> we are a myth! [*V"ezd* 131]

Gendelev here addresses the mythologizing power of the stereotype imposed on the Jew and, by implication, on anyone in such a way that it robs the human being of the ability to summon a word of his or her own. Yet in the Diaspora—particularly in the Soviet Union—it is the only means left to the man for defining even a pseudo-place for oneself. The myth of which Gendelev speaks, therefore, is itself the place of Jewish exile. Caught "in the shadows of ailing capitals," the Jew is trapped in the darkness of static images and fixed formulas. And when the word is locked into such formulas, meaning flees. For meaning abides only in the dynamic interchange of summons and response, through which the image lives in its transformations. The myth, on the other hand, is as deaf as an idol of stone.

The problem of speaking the word, then, is a problem of hearing the word. This difficulty surrounding language also finds its way into Gendelev's poetry. Consider, for example, these lines from *Journey to Jerusalem*: "Grown deaf, we listen to our howl, / Jews, Russians—do not go off to home— / there is no home for us, and can it be that / my voice alone is homeless in the world?" (135). These words amount to a translation of the howl they invoke, and they suggest a link between deafness and homelessness. For Gendelev, the return homeward lies in an effort to draw the word out of the howl. Hence his poetry is itself the journey homeward, the journey to Jerusalem. He arrives there, however, only to find that his journey has just begun. Even Jerusalem, the home of the Jews, lies in the shadow of ailing capitals. One senses this in a poem from Gendelev's third book that ends with "look upon Babylon / from the walls of Jerusalem / look upon Babylon!" (*Stikhotvoreniya* 48). The site of the confusion of tongues and of the exile of the Jews, Babylon signifies the link between the loss of the word and the loss of a dwelling place for the soul. Its Tower casts its shadow over the Jew's would-be home, just as language casts its shadow over the word, drawing the word into its own shadow.

Reflecting on the foregoing, we call to mind Brodsky's statement in *Less than One* that may apply to Gendelev as well: "At best, I'm a traveler, a victim of geography. Not of history, be it noted, but of geography" (443–44). When the self or the soul of the man is here, the word is elsewhere; and when the word is here, the soul is elsewhere. And meaning is forever floating somewhere in between. The project before us, then, is to examine this poet's endeavor to retrieve the word from the shadow of meaninglessness. For this darkness is precisely the darkness of homelessness that threatens anyone who would dwell upon the earth. As we shall see, Gendelev reveals not only a condition peculiar to a Jewish, Israeli reality but the problematic condition of human reality as it struggles to find a dwelling place in an inhospitable world and to unearth meaning from a language hostile to meaning. Going to Israel, Gendelev thus goes to the core of the existential problem that haunts all humanity, a point that Levinas helps us to grasp when he says,

There is no longer any difference between day and night, between outside and inside. Do we not smell here, more strongly than a while back, beyond all violence which still submits to will and reason, the odor of the camps? Violence is no longer a political phenomenon of war and peace, beyond all morality. It is the abyss of Auschwitz or the world at war. A world which has lost its "very worldliness." It is the twentieth century. One must go back inside, even if there is terror inside. Is the fact of Israel not unique? Does it not have its full meaning because it applies to all humanity? All men are on the verge of being in the situation of the State of Israel. The State of Israel is a category. [*Nine* 190–91]

Gendelev relentlessly explores this category, this signifier of the "ontological event," as he describes it (conversation with the author, July 1989), of the familiar grown strange, of the light turning dark, and of the word falling silent. Let us proceed, then, into his movement of return to see whether the poet might overturn the exile of the word.

Homelessness in the Homeland

Journey to Jerusalem, the volume of poems that Gendelev wrote in his native Russia, contains a section of verses titled "Dom" ("Home"). The third poem in that section opens with the lines, "And no one lives in this house. / Only the shadows quietly creak into the parquets. / There is just nothing in it of the living or the once alive except / unwatered, withered plants" (44). The time is out of joint, the space displaced. In the one place where life should be there is no life but only the mute traces of a life deprived of its sustenance. But there are traces; even thirst is a sign of life, inasmuch as it is a sign of what is needful for life. As in many of Gendelev's poems the shadow appears as an indicator of something of substance that may cast a shadow, something elsewhere, visible only as a shadow, audible only as an echo. Water is present by its absence. It is worth noting in this connection that water is a symbol of the Torah in talmudic and prophetic texts; consisting both of the written word and of the oral response to the word, the Torah is the truth that sustains life in a joining of word and meaning, of summons and response. The house void of living presence is an image of the word void of truth and meaning; the only sound that remains is the silent groan of the shadow or trace of meaning. The poem ends with the lines, "And when your heart grows weary from the white light, / and, frozen from the wind, for the first time you cannot soothe the bitterness— / look—this is your house, no one lives in this house, / only the shadows of the day quietly passed creak into the parquets" (44–45). Ending as it begins, the poem conveys a sense of imprisonment in a place that is no place, a nonplace. The structure is there, but the soul or substance is gone, trapped in an elsewhere inaccessible to words. And the self inaccessible to words is a self inaccessible to itself.

This absence that distinguishes homelessness is an absence of self not only from home but from any relation to others. A sense of home is rooted not just in the structure but in a life harbored by the structure created through a dialogical relation to another human being. Gendelev makes this point in a poem from *Messages to the Lemures*, where he writes,

> And
> the guests in my house do not listen to my words.
> Or do they not understand me?
> and then
> where are we?
> where are we
> and what will become of us next? [14]

The distance that creates a state of exile is comprised of the deafness that Gendelev here describes, a deafness characterized by the absence of response. The word, and with it the self, is exiled from its meaning when it no longer connects one human being to another; the exile of the word is the exile of the self from the other and therefore from itself. "The life of the word," as Bakhtin has said, "is contained in its transfer from one mouth to another" (*Problems* 202), and in the life of the word lies the life of the soul, with both abiding in a space *between* two. This *between* space of relation stands over against the *elsewhere* of isolation. Thus, losing the word that constitutes the between, the poet asks "Where are we?" from the elsewhere of his isolation, which is as much temporal as it is spatial: what will become of us next? The future is lost to this future tense, and to be without a future is to be without a home.

From the time of the Exodus out of Egypt, in Jewish consciousness one spatial symbol of the elsewhere has been the wilderness that separates the exiled soul from its homeland. Gendelev invokes this wilderness indirectly when in the poem just cited he writes,

> Moshe Rabbenu—
> I shall say—
> Moshe Rabbenu, is it not time for us to go home?
> . . . be we have been distracted,
> my soul! [15]

Moshe Rabbenu, or Moses, is the one who leads the Israelites from their exile homeward, not because he has the right road map to a geographical location but because he receives the Torah and thus the truth from the Holy One. For the Jew, this holy Presence is what signifies home; the Presence is itself signified on the door of the Jewish home by the *mezuzah*, which is attached to the door post and contains the Word. As the conveyor of the Torah—of the Word that is the vessel of life, truth, and meaning that constitute a home—Moses anticipates a deliverance that is forever yet to come and that is thus beyond temporal sequence. "Moses was considered the father of the prophets," Adin Steinsaltz points out, "of those who preceded him and those who came after him" (*Biblical* 74). He is not only a giver of signs but is himself a sign—both of the exile and of the homeland. Calling upon this prophet in a moment of distraction, the poet takes a step out of the exile from which he longs to be delivered. Indeed, the poem is itself a word born in a moment of distraction from the wordlessness of exile. If only for an instant, the poem itself provides a place where the homeless one may dwell, just as

the word of Moses promises a dwelling place, one at which he himself
never arrives.

But, as we have noted, even the arrival in the homeland promised
by Moses does not solve the problem of homelessness. Gendelev makes
this point repeatedly in the volume *Poems*, which was written in Erets
Yisrael. Note, for example, the poem that begins,

> I have
> no one in my home
> we shall notice only a trace
> they are not
> but not because
> they are not
> they are not at all. [59]

The confusion in these lines might be clarified if we consider certain an-
tecedents for the pronouns. One "they," for instance, may refer to people, while the other might indicate words: people, other living souls, are
absent not because they are not there, filling the space, but because their
words are not there. "The form alone in which Language is expressed
defines subjectivity," Lacan has said, and yet "as Language becomes
more functional, it becomes improper for the Word, and as it becomes
too particular to us, it loses its function as Language" (*Language* 61–62).
This conflict between language and the word, between what is said and
the act of saying, creates a problem of presence for the poet himself: I
have no one in my home, no one at all, not even myself. The reason for
this homelessness even within the homeland may be found in the allusion to the trace, or the *vsled* in Russian. In order for the homeland to be
the homeland, it must retain a trace of the exile, as if the Jew who is not
wandering were not a Jew. The poem endeavors to capture this trace, or
this wandering, to make it visible or heard, but it is no sooner voiced
than lost, rendering both the self and the other alien.

The poem is made of a language that would make heard a silence
that fades into mere noiselessness. Language itself, then, returns the
man to the zero point; from the midst of the homeland he is ever again
turned over to exile. Thus the Russian poem born in Israel harbors the
trace of the poem voiced in Russia, where we read, "And no light
dawned in my home. / My home grew empty, alien, unfamiliar. /
And I realized that I was no longer at home, / and I was not the
guardian of my home" (*V"ezd* 14). Where there is no light that comes
from beyond, there can be no light that arises from within. The man is

a guardian in his own home only to the extent that he serves a higher guardian, the source of a higher light. And so the poem ends, "And it became impossible for me to go on living, / but in my home, there— my soul slept" (*V"ezd* 15). The poem sets up the absence that hollows language as a dormant presence, that is, as the shadow or trace of presence. And yet the utterance is itself an awakening of the sleeping soul; the utterance of the poem itself brings into play the movement of return, the journey to Jerusalem. The home, then, is a tomb that the poem endeavors to transform into a womb in its effort to create a place for the word in the midst of language, a place where the word may find its meaning. To be sure, this association between tomb and womb—between the said as the dead flesh of meaning and the act of saying that brings the soul to life—is just what links home with the poem. Again, homelessness is wordlessness, a silence envisioned as darkness, as in the verse from *Poems* that begins, "Silence / in my home / darkness and silence" (56). In the original, Russian text the hushed sound of the word *tish'* (silence) stands in contrast to the sharp sound of *mrak* (darkness) to create a tension and therefore a tie between the two. Poetry generally strives to join sound and vision, word and image, but in the case of Gendelev the sound he attempts to capture is soundless, and the vision is void of light.

Voices of Silence, Visions of Darkness

In Gendelev's first volume of poems we find the lines, "Thus I summoned life and grew afraid of silence, / for I did not know who would be its interpreter for me!" (*V"ezd* 102). Looking once again to the Russian version of the poem, we note Gendelev's selection of *molchanie*, rather than *tishina*, for "silence," and we recall Bakhtin's distinction between the two: "In stillness [*tishina*] there is no sound (or nothing makes a sound); in silence [*molchanie*] no one says anything (or no one speaks). Silence is possible only in the human realm" (*Estetika* 338). The silence Gendelev invokes is not the absence of a sound but the absence of a voice that might be made to speak through the proper interpreter. Or better: he hears the voice, but he does not understand it. And his fear is that there may be no interpreter and that therefore nothing may be made to speak. It is through his poetry that the poet summons life, yet he calls out only to meet with silence. Thus it is through the word that silence manifests itself, and underlying its manifestation is the conviction that it harbors a message: who, he asks, will be its interpreter? This question implicates the poet in his own task to become the interpreter or translator of silence, which is an impossible task. Yet the maddening dilemma is that he must see it through if he is to take on the life he struggles to summon through the poetic word. With the word comes the life, and the return of the word from exile is a return to life.

"The eternal silence of these infinite spaces," Pascal once wrote, "fills me with dread" (95). In the case of Gendelev, however, the dread is stirred not so much by the silence itself as by its voicelessness; it is *molchanie* rather than *tishina* that haunts him. Hence the silent space is not only the space making up the cosmos but the silence of the space between words—this is the silence that must speak if the word is to come out of exile. In the poem "Lunnaya noch' v Ierusalime" (Moon-Lit Night in Jerusalem) Gendelev addresses the silence of that space when he writes,

> The silence of between-speech is such,
> that if it were a paradisiacal brook
> flowing near this page—
> we,
> having grown used to the sound of the waters,
> we would suddenly find:
> it has dried up. [*Poslaniya* 52]

If, as Emerson has said, "the poet is the Namer, or Language Maker" (316), he is in this instance the Silence Maker as well. For here Gendelev creates a word—*mezhdurechie* or "between-speech"—to bespeak a silence that haunts and inhabits language. Not within the word but there, between the words, he seeks the meaning that eludes the word. As Elie Wiesel has pointed out, "when God gave the Torah He gave not only the words but also the blanks between the words" (*Against*, II, 82). The sound of the water flowing near the page is the sound of this truth of the Torah, or the Word of life, flowing over, under, and through the poetic word. Lending ordinary words an extraordinary sense, the poem attempts to exhaust the possibilities of language and thus make heard the silence within and beyond language. Only in this way can language assume the new possibilities that would return meaning to the word and the exile to his homeland.

Gendelev's notion of between-speech suggests that a given word, line, or poem serves to impart a certain eloquence to the silence that separates it from the next word, line, or poem. Taken out of this context of silence, the poem miscarries in its effort to convey meaning, as Gendelev implies when he writes, "It is sad: sound and sense are incompatible, / like singing and acting in trousers, / like a combination of something—the abyss, / me—with love, muteness and—silence"

(*Poslaniya* 87). In the between-speech that separates sound from sense lies the abyss of the self, which, as the poem's structure suggests, is not a spatial notion but an aural one, a soundless gap signified by the dash that fills it: the abyss of the self is the silence between sound and sense, between word and meaning. Yet this silent between-space, or between-speech, is precisely where love and therefore life transpire. Thus, Buber notes, "there is in reality no I except the I of a tension: in which it brings itself together. No pole, no force, no thing—only polarity, only stream, only unification can become I" (*Daniel* 142). In this polarity abides the silence that Gendelev is after. The absence of meaning from the word, then, creates an emptiness that inserts itself into a gap between two human beings, as well as into the heart of the single human being.

Since light is often a metaphor for life, truth, and meaning, we are not surprised at Gendelev's use of darkness as an image of the absence that silence may signify. Consider, for example, the poem from *Journey to Jerusalem* that reads,

> who will take not of my flight over the waters when not
> a word is left,
> not even a single word!
> and the darkness is a light unuttered as a light—
> whose blind face will the wind from the wings touch, and again
> who will take note of the trace dying away? [102]

An insight from Lacan's *Language of the Self* once again comes to mind: "What I seek in the Word is the response of the other. What constitutes me as subject is my question" (63). Indeed, nearly all of Gendelev's poetry is punctuated by a question mark to two questions that are in fact one: Where are you? and Who am I? In this poem the poet's consciousness of the other, his reader, mirrors the reader's consciousness of the poetic word. The poetic word—unlike the words, words, words of idle talk—struggles to take flight over the abysmal waters of the between-speech that isolate self from other, poet from reader. The wind from the wings is the passion that fuels this endeavor; to the extent that the reader feels that wind, the dark space of the between-speech takes on light; for the poet has enabled us to "see" that space, that darkness. Yet, in its proclamation to the reader, the poem is a dissimulation of the poet: we have the words on the page, but only the trace of the aesthetic event that brought them there remains—that event that posits the between space and that the poet strives to convey. This, of course, is precisely what he cannot convey. "All is night," he writes, "and again the darkness is presaged" (*V"ezd* 162). For Gendelev, the rhythm of poetry is not just a matter of repeated intonation but of this pulsation of light, dark, light—of word, silence, word.

In *Poems* this repetition that distinguishes Gendelev's poetry is tied to the repetition that distinguishes life and death. In that book, to take one example, is a poem that begins, "First there is darkness / then of course childhood then / direct speech" (53). Completing a cycle of repetition that sets up another repetition, the poem ends, "first there is darkness / then melancholy and memory / and / again darkness" (54). Structured in such a manner, the poem implies a link between direct speech—which is opposed to the poetic word of between-speech—and darkness; the darkness that the poet would overcome is the darkness, the muteness and emptiness, of language itself. And in the relation of childhood to melancholy and memory we see what is present by its absence, discovered in its loss, present only as a trace or a shadow. It may be helpful to recall here Lacan's insight that "through the word—already a presence made of absence—absence itself comes to giving itself a name in that moment of origin whose perpetual recreation Freud's genius detected in the play of the child" (*Language* 39). As the Namer, the poet names this absence, this darkness, not through any single word but through that concern with the word that engenders the aesthetic event. Through the aesthetic event he pursues the relation not only between the word and language but between word and meaning, where absence—the voice of silence and the vision of darkness—poses itself as the divorce emblematic of exile.

The Divorce of Word and Meaning

Early on it was pointed out that Gendelev operates from the midst of a disjunction or divorce: he attempts to bespeak a Jewish, Israeli reality in a language that cannot accommodate that reality. The poem that serves as a preface to his *Poems*, for example, is

> In the Russian language definitive for me
> I think
> what
> in and of themselves are
> love war and death
> are somehow
> a pretext for simple-minded descriptions
> in a narrative about darkness and silence. [6]

It is revealing to note that the root of the Russian word here translated as "definitive," *poslednii* (which also means "final" or "last"), is *sled*, which means "track" or "trace": the poet's trace, as it were, is the language of his poetry. And the word for "pretext," *predlog*, literally means "pre-logos," that is, something prior not just to a text but to the word itself. Writing from such a pre-text and defined by such a language, the poet works from the heart of the silence and darkness we have discussed. And that silence and darkness comprise the mute space that arises in the divorce of word from meaning. It is the site of the exile, from which he seeks his soul and his soil.

Gendelev, however, addresses this tearing, this exile, of the word from its meaning long before his immersion in an Israeli reality, since the pre-text for that reality is a Russian reality, or rather a Russian irreality. In *Journey to Jerusalem*, for instance, we read,

> Speech is concluded with a dying sound.
> The brook flows. The well holds water.
> Where to draw it up?—speech is ended, it
> is like a drink—not a water pipe
> . . . .
> But the meaning of a word is sucked
> from the withered clays of a waterless well.
>
> And if there was no quenching of the thirst,
> and knowledge drained into the sand—
> a dry, empty palm is raised
> to the lips by the trembling hands of a proselyte! [29]

A proselyte is one who would embrace a new word and meaning in a deliverance from meaninglessness. The land of exile is a land of waterless wells and meaningless words; the Patriarch Abraham, therefore, establishes a home in the land of promise by digging a well, thus tapping the earth for the stuff of life. Bearing in mind once more that in the Jewish tradition water means Torah and Torah means truth, the proselyte— he who would become *other*— abandons a dried-up well in search of another (the first Jew, Abraham himself, was a proselyte). In this respect the poet too is a proselyte who longs to draw forth meaning from dried-up words. The poem's imagery of water and well harbors a theory of language and meaning, suggesting a view of the word as a vessel. Yet, like the life of human relation, the life of the word is born in an act of response: the hand raised to the mouth is the hand that pens the poem, receiving meaning through an offering up of meaning, transmitting the word not from mouth to ear but from mouth to mouth. That is what poetry is: mouth-to-mouth resuscitation. Meaning, then, occurs in the bridging of word and word.

In the Talmud we read, "And when are men examined?—Said Resh Lakish: When they pass over a bridge" (*Shabbat* 32a). Bearing this in mind, we realize the importance of the image of the bridge in these lines from *Journey to Jerusalem*:

> . . . but only on the bridge,
> suddenly seeing the reflection,
> did I realize that the dialogue is recorded.
> Most agonizingly an undisclosed syllable,
> like a butterfly, took wing
>   and flew up,
> fell to my feet—but
>   it reverberated in speech!
> itself like a butterfly.
>   And somewhere near,
>   right
> there—
> was a bridge across the flow of the river.
> I waited for the boat. But the ferryman slept. [80]

Many things are at work on various levels in this poem. One notes first of all the interplay of words in the poet's effort to bridge the chasm between word and meaning. In the Russian text the words *rech'* ("speech") and *rechka* ("river"), for example, reverberate off one another, coupling an image with a concept of language. And the word for "ferryman," *perevozchik,* is just a letter away from the word for "translator," *perevodchik.* The poet on the bridge is himself a bridge; the one who seeks a ferryman or a translator is himself the translator of silence into sense. He who seeks a ferryman, moreover, is one who longs to be elsewhere, and his longing announces the presence of the elsewhere. Thus the poem is itself an image or illustration of the idea that the elsewhere inhabits the utterance at hand, that the other flows through the same. Meaning is returned to the word not through the elimination of alterity or difference but through its accentuation, making it into a nonindifference. In Gendelev's poetry, then, we have a view of language much like the one described by Gary Saul Morson when he says, "The idea that language is a system, so dear to the Saussurians and their Formalist-structuralist heirs, is a fiction: language is a constant struggle *among* systems and between systematic and unsystematic elements" ("Who" 229). And where does that struggle transpire? Between the poet and the page: again, it is he who must become the bridge between word and meaning. He is the ferryman. Why does the Talmud teach that we are examined on a bridge? Because each person, like this poet, must become a bridge to another.

Meaning, therefore, is something we take on through our relation to another. Offering up my word to the other, I take on meaning within myself. And so in *Journey to Jerusalem* we read, " . . . the flame flickers / on the edge, like a word whose utterance has died, / and somehow it must burn in this world, / and the word takes on meaning between us" (162–63). The flame suggests a meeting of word and meaning, of self and other, as a conjoining of fuel and heat that bears light. The edge here is the between, the realm where word and meaning are joined in an act of touching and being touched. "The purpose of relation," Buber expresses it, "is the relation itself—touching the You. For as soon as we touch a You, we are touched by a breath of eternal life" (*I and Thou* 112–13). Gendelev himself invokes a similar image of the depth of the touch in *Messages to the Lemures*, saying, "when you make out the word by touch— / it—by God—will answer (60). The root of the Russian verb translated as "will answer," *otzvetsya*, is *zvat'*, which means "to call" or "to summon"; the implication is that the poet seeks to bring meaning to the word through an act of response to a summons that is yet to be heard. Or better: the summons is heard precisely through the act of response. Feeling his way, the poet makes out the word by touch; thus he provides the word with a *text*ure by which it may be read. The divorce of word and meaning not only renders us mute—it strikes us blind. Enabling us to hear, the poet enables us to touch and thus to see what eludes the eye—by touching us. What is meaningful is moving, and to be moved is to be touched as we touch.

There is one more important point in Buber's remark just cited that remains to be tied to Gendelev: the breath of eternal life. First it will be useful to recall Aryeh Kaplan's commentary on the Hebrew word for "breath," *ruah*, from the *Sefer Yetzirah*. "In general," he explains, "the word *ruah* indicates motion and communication. It is related to the words *O-rach*, meaning a path, and *O-reah*, meaning a guest. The spirit *(ruah)* of life in an animal is the power that causes it to move. . . . The spiritual continuum is undetectable, except when it moves. It is then experienced as spirit *(ruah)*. Hence, *ruah* is the word for wind, breath, and spirit" (69). The movement and communication that characterize breath and spirit *(ruah)* are couched in the Hebrew concept of *teshuvah*, which means "return," "redemption," and "response": return to God, redemption through God, response seeking God. Thus the movement of the breath of eternal life is a movement toward God. We find, therefore, that the divorce of word and meaning is a divorce from God; that the exile of the word is an exile from God; and that the effort to return meaning to the word is a struggle to return to God, to make a movement of *teshuvah*.

For Gendelev, the condition of homelessness, silence, and darkness is a condition characterized by the absence of—or distance from—God. "God has forgotten us," he writes in "Vitebsk," a poem about the Jewish Holocaust. "We forget ourselves" (*V"ezd* 129). Absence of God? Not exactly. Rather: absence of self from God. For the poet Gendelev, this is what distinguishes the exile of the word, as well as the exile of the person. Hence, as an effort to return word to meaning and self to God, the problem of poetry is a problem of prayer: the two intersect at the heart of the language of the God relationship. And so Gendelev laments that prayers are drawn from "decrepit representations of words" (*Poslaniya* 51). The difficulty of articulating a Jewish, Israeli reality in the Russian tongue, then, pertains not only to an existential condition but to a theological relation, as we see in Gendelev's *Poems* when he cries out, "our Lord does not know Russian / and does not remember Russian names" (83). Thus Gendelev provides us with a variation of Miguel de Unamuno's statement that "Tell me thy name! is essentially the same as Save my soul!" (181). It is: Remember my name! If memory lies at the root of redemption, for Gendelev it is not only man's memory of God that is at issue but God's memory of man. "Let Him remember," Wiesel therefore insists, "for He alone can make us remember" (*Against*, I, 114). But the word does not lend itself to memory, and that is the difficulty. For it approaches meaning only to be distanced from it. And so the poet goes on to his next utterance, giving voice to a poem about his attempt to bridge the between space, the between-speech, that isolates one human being from another.

We end this glimpse of Gendelev not so much with an "and so" as with an "and yet." The homelessness of the human being is intractable, and yet, through the poetic word, he struggles to fashion a home. The silence with which he collides is ineluctable, and yet, through the poetic word, he seeks a voice, both from within and from beyond. And the loss of meaning is insuperable, and yet, through the poetic word, it finds a presence even in its absence. The thing sought is revealed in the seeking, and what is needful is announced in the need. Gendelev reveals to us that, like prayer, poetry imparts to ordinary words an extraordinary sense by joining the language of human relation to a higher relation. And yet—and this is the most crucial "and yet"—the truth, the meaning, and the life sought in the higher relation lie forever beyond the horizon of poetry. " 'Bent thus over the awe-inspiring abyss,' " as Nikos Kazantzakis's character puts it, " 'we tremble with terror. From that moment begins . . . ' I stopped. I wanted to say 'from that moment begins poetry,' but Zorba would not have understood. I stopped. 'What begins?' asked Zorba's anxious voice. ' . . . begins the great danger, Zorba. Some grow dizzy and delirious, others are afraid' " (301). And Gendelev? He speaks not so much from the dizzying heights as from the dizzying depths of exile.

In the Jewish tradition the preservation of human life takes precedence over all 613 of the commandments; indeed, the Talmud tells us that saving a single human life is comparable to saving the entire world (*Sanhedrin* 4:5). Mikhail Gendelev, the physician turned poet, chooses life in the midst of a reality constantly threatened by death, and he makes his choice by imparting his own life to his poetry. As long as King David was engaged in his song, legend tells us, the Angel of Death had no power over him. Although his tongue is foreign to his ancestral tradition, Gendelev pursues this ancestral tradition in an eternal movement of return homeward.

Concluding Remarks

"In addition to being primary and natural," Adin Steinsaltz has pointed out, "the question of identity is also threatening, and not only stirs a vast number of possible answers but offers a glimpse into an abyss of yet further, and unanswerable, questions" (*Thirteen* 140). The problem of exile is above all a problem of identity, one that concerns not only the object of investigation but the subject who undertakes it as well. What we glean from the tribulations here encountered is much more than information and observations about a motif in modern Russian letters. It is also more than an analysis of the social, political, or even metaphysical circumstances that give rise to these letters. Beyond all that, what we conclude—or collide with— is something that goes to the heart of our own being, where our own essence is decided. "Every man must have some place to go," cries Marmeladov in Dostoevsky's *Prestuplenie i nakazanie* (*Crime and Punishment* 14). And the determination of our relation to that place determines our relation to every other aspect of life.

Like the superfluous man, like the persona who speaks from the pages of Dostoevsky's *Winter Notes*, a human being enters the world a stranger in the midst of other human beings. There he seeks a word of his own within the the the realm of human relation and human speech. But he soon discovers a breach between life and the word that would engender it, for the language in which he would say who he is comes to him as something ready-made, as something already said: a person's very name precedes him. "Identity is the name," Jabès puts it. "Four letters were enough for God—*Dieu*—to be God. Man—*l'homme*—needed five, one of which is double. What does that mean? Well, it means simply that language deprives us of identity by offering us an identity that is but an assemblage of letters belonging only to it and that we find again dispersed all over. . . . The first manifestation of my existence was an absence which bore my name" (4–5). The condition of being already named initiates a movement toward a primary Word that issues from the Nameless. Thus in the between space of the relation of myself to another soul I seek a third presence that is both immanent and transcendent. In our examination of these Russians we have seen some examples of the forms that this seeking may take. Here the discourse of the one in exile takes on a religious aspect in an effort to transcend and then return to a universal discourse. If religiosity or spirituality inheres in life's attachment to life, the life of the soul is engendered by its relation to the life of another by way of a relation to a third, living presence. Or, to state it differently, the I-saying of the I who would emerge from exile lies in a saying of Thou that is a manifestation of the Eternal Thou. Remember Bakhtin's insight: "I must be for the other what God is for me" (*Estetika* 52). The rupture in life that characterizes exile is a rupture in these two forms of being, in these two realms of relation, which, again, constitute a single relation, a single presence, a single place of dwelling.

Because the relation to the other and to God is dialogically determined—determined, that is, by the word—the exile of the human being is an exile of the word. And because the place of exile is language, the human being takes up a way of response that would bespeak more than language can say. Hence we have thinkers such as Florensky and Shestov; novelists such as Dostoevsky, Tolstoy, Solzhenitsyn, and Sinyavsky; and poets such as Brodsky and Gendelev. "Poetry," we recall Brodsky's comment, "seems to be the only weapon able to beat language, using language's own means" (*Less* 56). What is the poet trying to "beat" in his effort to beat language? It is this: the inscription and the circumscription of the fixed formula and ready answer that renders the human being deaf to the needful question. The word, and with it the human being, begins its return from exile not just in an act of speaking or even in an act of asking but in an act of hearing that is at the same time a movement of response. And response, we recall, is one meaning of *teshuvah*, of return and redemption.

We have found that underlying the movement of return, redemption, and response is responsibility: this is the key to presence, to the place of dwelling that is opposed to the nonplace of exile. "What can guarantee the inner bonding of the elements of the personality?" Bakhtin raises the key question. "Only the wholeness of responsibility. With my life I must answer for what I have experienced and understood in art. . . . Art and life are not one and the same, but they must become one within me through the wholeness of my responsibility" (*Estetika* 5-6). And the wholeness of responsibility happens when the soul becomes whole, in a healing of the rupture of identity that distinguishes exile. This healing, in turn, can happen only in a saying of "Here I am" in the face of the other. What we have before us, then, in these selections from modern Russian letters are not only philosophical and literary tracts but human testimony in perhaps its most profound form. For it is a testimony that transforms the very process of analytical investigation into a process of bearing witness. In the words of Levinas, "The witness testifies to what was said by himself. For he has said 'Here I am!' before the Other; and from the fact that before the Other he recognizes the responsibility which is incumbent on himself, he has manifested what the face of the Other signified for him. The glory of the Infinite reveals itself through what it is capable of doing in the witness" (*Ethics* 109). This revelation of the Holy One is a revelation of the *Makom*, of the Place, that alone may be called home.

Thus, coming to the end of this exploration, we come to no conclusion, if by conclusion we mean something settled or finalized. Having met the task of critical inquiry, we meet with a new task: to undertake a movement of return from our own exile, to go to the core of our own rupture and make that absence into a presence. This, of course, is the most difficult, the most fearsome, task of all. "When I shall face the celestial tribunal," Rebbe Zusia once said, "I shall not be asked why I was not Abraham, Jacob, or Moses. I shall be asked why I was not Zusia" (see Wiesel, *Souls* 120). And yet home is just that place where we meet with this question. For this is the question that sets into motion the movement of return from exile in its declaration of the condition of exile. Thus we end where we started, with the question that generated this investigation, the first question put to the first man, the question forever put to every human being: Where are you? As long as we remain deaf to it, we languish in the throes of exile. But as soon as we struggle to respond, we undertake the movement of return—to ourselves, to others, and to God.

Works Cited

A.B. "The Direction of Change." *From under the Rubble*. Ed. Alexander Solzhen-
itsyn. Trans. A.M. Brock, et al. Chicago: Regnery Gateway, 1981. Pp. 144–50.
Augustine. *Confessions*. Trans. R.S. Pine-Coffin. New York: Penguin, 1961.
The Bahir. Trans. with commentary by Aryeh Kaplan. York Beach, Maine:
Samuel Weiser, 1979.
Bakhtin, Mikhail. *Art and Answerability*. Trans. Vadim Liapunov. Ed. Michael
Holquist and Vadim Liapunov. Austin: U of Texas P, 1990.
———. *The Dialogic Imagination*. Trans. Caryl Emerson and Michael Holquist.
Austin: U of Texas P, 1981.
———. *Estetika slovesnogo tvorchestva* (Aesthetics of Verbal Art). Moscow:
Art, 1979.
———. *Problems of Dostoevsky's Poetics*. Trans. Caryl Emerson. Minneapolis:
U of Minnesota P, 1984.
Barabanov, Evgeny. "The Schism between the Church and the World." *From
under the Rubble*. Ed. Alexander Solzhenitsyn. Trans. A.M. Brock et al.
Chicago: Regnery Gateway, 1981. Pp. 172–93.
Bayley, John. *Tolstoy and the Novel*. London: Chatto and Windus, 1966.
Berdyaev, Nicolas. *The Destiny of Man*. Trans. Natalie Duddington. New York:
Harper, 1960.
Bergson, Henri. *The Two Sources of Morality and Religion*. Trans. R. Ashley Audra
and Cloudsley Brereton. Garden City, N.Y.: Doubleday, 1954.
Borisov, Vadim. "Personality and National Awareness." *From under the Rubble*.
Ed. Alexander Solzhenitsyn. Trans. A.M. Brock et al. Chicago: Regnery Gate-
way, 1981. Pp. 194–228.
Bourmeyster, Alexandre. "Les hommes de trop, les types littéraires et la lutte
avec les types." *Canadian-American Slavonic Studies* 14 (1980): 257–72.
Brodsky, Iosef. *Chast' rechi*. Ann Arbor, Mich.: Ardis, 1977.
———. *Konets prekrasnoi epokhi* (The End of a Beautiful Epoch). Ann Arbor,
Mich.: Ardis, 1977.
———. *Less than One: Selected Essays*. New York: Farrar, 1986.
———. *A Part of Speech*. Trans. Anthony Hecht et al. New York: Farrar, 1980.
———. *Selected Poems*. Trans. George Kline. New York: Harper, 1973.
———. *To Urania*. Trans. Joseph Brodsky et al. New York: Farrar, 1984.
———. *Uraniya*. Ann Arbor, Mich.: Ardis, 1987.
Brusov, B. "Lishnie slova o 'lishnikh lyudyakh.' " *Voprosy literatury* (April 1960):
107–18.
Buber, Martin. *Between Man and Man*. Trans. Ronald G. Smith. New York:
Macmillan, 1965.

————. *Daniel: Dialogues on Realization.* Trans. Maurice Friedman. New York: Holt, 1964.

————. *I and Thou.* Trans. Walter Kaufmann. New York: Scribner's, 1970.

————. *The Legend of the Baal-Shem.* Trans. Maurice Friedman. New York: Schocken, 1969.

Budanova, N.F. " 'Podpol'nyi chelovek' v ryadu 'lishnikh lyudei,' " *Russkaya literatura* 3 (1976): 109–21.

Buttafava, Giovanni. "Interview with Joseph Brodsky." *L'Espresso* 6 (December 1987): 156–57.

Cain, T.G.S. *Tolstoy.* New York: Barnes, 1977.

Cate, Hollis L. "On Death and Dying in Tolstoy's 'The Death of Ivan Ilych.' " *Housman Society Journal* 7 (1974): 195–205.

Chances, Ellen B. *Conformity's Children: An Approach to the Superfluous Man in Russian Literature.* Columbus, Ohio: Slavica, 1978.

Chekhov, A.P. *Duel'. Sochineniya.* Moscow, 1977.

Christian, R.F. *Tolstoy: A Critical Introduction.* Cambridge: Cambridge UP, 1969.

Clardy, Jesse V., and Betty S. Clardy. *The Superfluous Man in Russian Letters.* Washington: UP of America, 1980.

Clark, Katerina, and Michael Holquist. *Mikhail Bakhtin.* Cambridge, Mass: Harvard UP, 1984.

Dalton, Margaret. *Andrei Siniavskii and Julii Daniel': Two Soviet "Heretical" Writers.* Wuerzburg: Jal-Verlag, 1973.

Descartes, René. *Meditations on First Philosophy.* Trans. Donald A. Cress. Indianapolis: Hackett, 1979.

Dobrolyubov, N.A. "Chto kakoe oblomovshchina?" *Izbrannye filosofskie proizvedeniya.* Vol. 1. Leningrad, 1948.

Donnelly, John. "Death and Ivan Ilych." *Language, Metaphysics, and Death.* Ed. John Donnelly. New York: Fordham UP, 1978. Pp. 116–30.

Dostoevsky, F.M. *Brat'ya Karamazovy* (The Brothers Karamazov). Petrozavodsk, 1970.

————. *Dvoinik* (The Double). *Polnoe sobranie sochinenii.* Vol. 1. Leningrad, 1972.

————. *Idiot.* Moscow, 1981.

————. *Neizdannyi Dostoevsky: Zapisnye knizhki i tetradi 1860–1881 gg. Literaturnoe nasledstvo.* Vol. 30. Ed. V.R. Shcherbina et al. Moscow, 1970.

————. *The Possessed.* Trans. Andrew R. MacAndrew. New York: NAL, 1962.

————. *Prestuplenie i nakazanie* (Crime and Punishment). Moscow: Prosveshchenie, 1982.

————. *Winter Notes on Summer Impressions.* Trans. David Patterson. Evanston, Ill: Northwestern UP, 1988.

————. *Zapiski iz podpol'ya* (Notes from Underground). *Polnoe sobranie sochinenii.* Vol. 5. Leningrad, 1973. Pp. 99–179.

Edgerton, William B. "Tolstoy, Immortality, and Twentieth-Century Physics." *Canadian Slavonic Papers* 21 (1979): 289–300.

Emerson, Ralph Waldo. *Selected Writings.* Ed. William H. Gilman. New York: NAL, 1965.

Etkind, Efim. *Protsess Iosifa Brodskogo.* London: Overseas, 1988.

Fackenheim, Emil. *God's Presence in History: Jewish Affirmations and Philosophical Reflections*. New York: Harper, 1970.

Feuerbach, Ludwig. *The Essence of Christianity*. Trans. George Eliot. New York: Harper, 1957.

Florensky, Pavel. "O literature." *Voprosy literatury* 1 (1988): 146–76.

———. *Stolp i utverzhdenie istiny: Opyt pravoslavnoi feoditsei v dvenadtsati pis'-makh* (The Pillar and Foundation of Truth). Westmead, Eng.: Gregg International, 1970.

Foucault, Michel. *The Archaeology of Knowledge and The Discourse on Language*. Trans. A.M. Sheridan Smith. New York: Pantheon, 1972.

———. *Madness and Civilization*. Trans. Richard Howard. New York: Pantheon, 1965.

Frank, Joseph. *Dostoevsky: The Stir of Liberation, 1860–1865*. Princeton, N.J.: Princeton UP, 1986.

Gei, N.K. 'Kommentari." *Povesti i rasskazy*, by L.N. Tolstoy. Moscow, 1982. Pp. 361–62.

Gendelev, Mikhail. *Poslaniya Lemuram* (Messages to the Lemures). Jerusalem: Lexicon, 1981.

———. *Stikhotvoreniya Mikhaila Gendeleva* (The Poems of Mikhail Gendelev). Jerusalem: Lexicon, 1984.

———. *V"ezd v Ierusalim: 1972–1976* (Journey to Jerusalem). Jerusalem: Knigotovarishchestvo "Moskva-Ierusalim," 1979.

Ginsburgh, Yitzchak. *The Alef-Beit: Jewish Thought Revealed through the Hebrew Letters*. Northvale, N.J.: Jason Aronson, 1991.

Goethe, J.W. *Faust: Part One*. Trans. C.F. MacIntyre. New York: New Directions, 1949.

Goncharov, I.A. *Oblomov. Sobranie sochinenii*. Vol. 2. Moscow, 1952.

Gorbanevskaya, Nataliya. "Interview with Joseph Brodsky." *Russkaya mysl'* 3 (February 1983): 8–9.

Gustafson, Richard F. *Leo Tolstoy: Resident and Stranger—A Study in Fiction and Theology*. Princeton, N.J.: Princeton UP, 1986.

Harkins, William. *Dictionary of Russian Literature*. London: Allen, 1957.

Husserl, Edmund. *Phenomenology and the Crisis of Philosophy*. Trans. Quentin Lauer. New York: Harper, 1965.

Jabès, Edmond. *From the Desert to the Book*. New York: Station Hill, 1990.

Jahn, Gary R. "The Role of the Ending in Lev Tolstoi's *The Death of Ivan Il'ich*." *Canadian-Slavonic Papers* 24 (1982): 229–38.

Jaspers, Karl. *Der philosophische Glaube*. Munich: R. Piper, 1948.

———. *Truth and Symbol*. Trans. Jean T. Wilde, William Kluback, and William Kimmel. New Haven, Conn.: College and University, 1959.

———. *Vernunft und Existenz*. Bremen: Johannes Storm, 1949.

Jung, Carl. *Psychology and Religion*. New Haven, Conn.: Yale UP, 1938.

Kazantzakis, Nikos. *Zorba the Greek*. Trans. Carl Wildman. New York: Ballantine, 1952.

Kierkegaard, Soren. *Attack upon "Christendom"*. Trans. Walter Lowrie. Princeton, N.J.: Princeton UP, 1944.

———. *The Concept of Dread.* Trans. Walter Lowrie. Princeton, N.J.: Princeton UP, 1944.

———. *The Concluding Unscientific Postscript.* Trans. David F. Swenson and Walter Lowrie. Princeton, N.J.: Princeton UP, 1941.

———. *Edifying Discourses—A Selection.* Trans. David F. and Lillian Marvin Swenson. New York: Harper, 1958.

———. *Fear and Trembling and The Sickness unto Death.* Trans. Walter Lowrie. Princeton, N.J.: Princeton UP, 1968.

———. *Training in Christianity.* Trans. Walter Lowrie. Princeton, N.J.: Princeton UP, 1944.

Kline, George L. "Variations on the Theme of Exile." *Brodsky's Poetics and Aesthetics.* Ed. Lev Loseff and Valentina Polukhina. New York: St. Martin's, 1990. Pp. 56–88.

Korsakov, F. "Russian Destinies." *From under the Rubble.* Ed. Alexander Solzhenitsyn. Trans. A.M. Brock et al. Chicago: Regnery Gateway, 1981. Pp. 151–70.

Kratkaya literaturnaya entsiklopediya (Short Literary Encyclopedia). Vol. 4. Moscow, 1967.

Lacan, Jacques. *Écrits.* Trans. Alan Sheridan. New York: Norton, 1977.

———. *The Language of the Self.* Trans. with commentary by Anthony Wilden. Baltimore: Johns Hopkins UP, 1968.

Langer, Jiri. *Nine Gates to the Chassidic Mysteries.* Trans. Stephen Jolly. New York: Behrman, 1976.

Lermontov, M. Yu. *Geroi nashego vremeni* (A Hero of Our Time). *Sobranie sochinenii.* Vol. 4. Moscow, 1958.

Levi, Primo. *The Drowned and the Saved.* Trans. Raymond Rosenthal. New York: Vintage, 1989.

Levinas, Emmanuel. *Collected Philosophical Papers.* Trans. Alphonso Lingis. The Hague: Martinus Nijhoff, 1987.

———. *Difficult Freedom: Essays on Judaism.* Trans. Sean Hand. Baltimore: Johns Hopkins UP, 1990.

———. *Ethics and Infinity.* Trans. Richard A. Cohen. Pittsburgh: Duquesne UP, 1985.

———. "Ethics as First Philosophy." Trans. Sean Hand and Richard Temple. *The Levinas Reader.* Ed. Sean Hand. Oxford: Basil Blackwell, 1989, Pp. 75–87.

———. *Existence and Existents.* Trans. Alphonso Lingis. The Hague: Martinus Nijhoff, 1978.

———. *Nine Talmudic Readings.* Trans. Annette Aronowicz. Bloomington: Indiana UP, 1990.

———. *Otherwise than Being or Beyond Essence.* Trans. Alphonso Lingis. The Hague: Martinus Nijhoff, 1981.

———. "Revelation in the Jewish Tradition." Trans. Sarah Richmond. *The Levinas Reader* Ed. Sean Hand Oxford: Basil Blackwell, 1989, : Pp. 190–210.

———. *Time and the Other.* Trans. Richard A. Cohen. Pittsburgh: Duquesne UP, 1987.

———. *Totality and Infinity.* Trans. Alphonso Lingis. Pittsburgh: Duquesne UP. 1969.

Levinas, Emmanuel, and Richard Kearney. "Dialogue with Emmanuel Levinas." *Face to Face with Levinas*. Ed. Richard A. Cohen. Albany: State U of New York P, 1986. Pp. 13–33.

Literaturnaya entsiklopediya (Literary Encyclopedia). Vol. 6. Moscow, 1932.

Loseff, Lev, and Valentina Polukhina, eds. *Brodsky's Poetics and Aesthetics*. New York: St. Martin's, 1990.

Lourie, Richard. *Letters to the Future: An Approach to Sinyavsky-Tertz*. Ithaca, N.Y.: Cornell UP, 1975.

Marlowe, Christopher. *The Tragedy of Doctor Faustus*. Ed. Louis B. Wright and Virginia H. LaMar. New York: Washington Square, 1969.

Mathewson, Rufus W. *The Positive Hero in Russian Literature*. 2nd ed. Stanford, Calif.: Stanford UP, 1975.

Mekilta de-Rabbi Ishmael. Trans. Jacob Z. Lauterbach. Philadelphia: Jewish Publication Society, 1961.

Midrash on Psalms. Vol. 2. Trans. William G. Brande. New Haven, Conn.: Yale UP, 1959.

Midrash Rabbah. Vol. 8. Trans. J. Rabbinowitz. London: Soncino, 1961.

Mindel, Nissan. *The Philosophy of Chabad*. Brooklyn: Kehot, 1973.

Morson, Gary Saul. *The Boundaries of Genre: Dostoevsky's Diary of a Writer and the Tradition of Literary Utopia*. Austin: U of Texas P, 1981.

———. "Who Speaks for Bakhtin?: A Dialogic Introduction." *Critical Inquiry* 10 (1983): 225–43.

Napier, James J. "The Stages of Dying in *The Death of Ivan Ilych*." *College Literature* (Spring 1983): 147–57.

Neher, André. *The Exile of the Word: From the Silence of the Bible to the Silence of Auschwitz*. Trans. David Maisel. Philadelphia: Jewish Publication Society, 1981.

———. *They Made Their Souls Anew*. Trans. David Maisel. Albany: State U of New York P, 1990.

Pascal, Blaise. *Pensées*. Paris: Club des Libraires de France, 1961.

Percy, Walker. *The Message in the Bottle*. New York: Farrar, 1982.

Plato. *The Collected Dialogues*. Ed. Edith Hamilton and Huntington Cairns. Trans. R. Hackforth et al. Princeton, N.J.: Princeton UP, 1961.

Polukhina, Valentina. *Joseph Brodsky: A Poet for Our Time*. Cambridge: Cambridge UP, 1989.

Pushkin, A.S. *Evgeny Onegin. Sobranie sochinenii*. Vol. 5. Moscow, 1969.

Rogers, Thomas F. *"Superfluous Men" and the Post-Stalin Thaw*. The Hague: Mouton, 1972.

Rosenzweig, Franz. *The Star of Redemption*. Trans. William Hallo. Boston: Beacon, 1971.

Russell, Robert. "From Individual to Universal: Tolstoy's 'Smert' Ivana Il'icha.' " *Modern Language Review* 76 (1981): 631–42.

Sandmel, Samuel. *Philo's Place in Judaism*. New York: Ktav, 1971.

Sartre, Jean-Paul. *Being and Nothingness*. Trans. Hazel E. Barnes. New York: Pocket, 1978.

Salys, Rima. "Sings on the Road to Life: 'The Death of Ivan Il'ic'. " *Slavic and East European Journal.* 30 (1986): 18–28.

Seeley, Frank F. "The Heyday of the 'Superfluous Man' in Russia." *The Slavonic and East European Review* 31 (1952): 85–99.

Sefer Yetzirah: The Book of Creation. Trans. with commentary by Aryeh Kaplan. York Beach, Maine: Samuel Weiser, 1990.

Shafarevich, Igor. "Does Russia Have a Future?" *From under the Rubble.* Ed. Alexander Solzhenitsyn. Trans. A.M. Brock, et al. Chicago: Regnery Gateway, 1981. Pp. 26–66.

———. "Socialism in Our Past and Future." *From under the Rubble.* Pp. 279–294.

Shakespeare, William. "The Phoenix and the Turtle." *The Complete Works of William Shakespeare.* New York: Avenel, 1975. P. 1229.

Shestov, Lev. *Afiny i Ierusalim* (Athens and Jerusalem). Paris: YMCA Press, 1951.

———. "Dnevnik Myslei" (Diary of Thoughts). *Kontinent* 8 (1976): 250–64.

———. *Kierkegaard and the Existential Philosophy.* Trans. Elinor Hewitt. Athens: Ohio UP, 1969.

———. *Na vesakh Iova* (In Job's Balances). Paris: La Société d'Éditions Franco-Slaves, 1929.

———. *Speculation and Revelation.* Trans. Bernard Martin. Athens: Ohio UP, 1982.

Sinyavsky, Andrei (Abram Terts). *Mysli vrasplokh* (Thoughts at Random). New York: Rausen, 1966.

———. *Soviet Civilization: A Cultural History.* Trans. Joanne Turnbull. New York: Arcade, 1990.

———. *A Voice from the Chorus.* Trans. Kyril Fitzlyon and Max Hayward. New York: Bantam, 1978.

Slesinski, Robert. *Pavel Florensky: A Metaphysics of Love.* Crestwood, N.Y.: St. Vladimir's Seminary Press, 1984.

Smyrniw, Walter. "Tolstoy's Depiction of Death in the Context of Recent Studies of the 'Experience of Dying.' " *Canadian Slavonic Papers* 21 (1979): 367–79.

Soloveitchik, Joseph B. *Halakhic Man.* Trans. Lawrence Kaplan. Philadelphia: Jewish Publication Society, 1983.

Solzhenitsyn, Alexander. "As Breathing and Consciousness Return." *From under the Rubble.* Ed. Alexander Solzhentisyn, Trans. A.M. Brock, et al. Chicago: Regnery Gateway, 1981. Pp. 3–25.

———. *August 1914.* Trans. Michael Glenny. New York: Bantam, 1974.

———. *The Cancer Ward.* Trans. Rebecca Frank. New York: Dial, 1968.

———. *The First Circle.* Trans. Thomas P. Whitney. New York: Harper, 1968.

———. *The Gulag Archipelago.* Trans. Thomas P. Whitney. New York: Harper, 1973.

———. *One Day in the Life of Ivan Denisovich.* Trans. Max Hayward and Ronald Hingley. New York: Bantam, 1963.

———. "Repentance and Self-Limitation in the Life of Nations." *From under the Rubble.* Pp. 105–43.

———. "The Smatterers." *From under the Rubble.* Pp. 229–78.

Sorokin, Boris. "Ivan Il'ich as Jonah: A Cruel Joke." *Canadian Slavic Studies* 5 (1971): 487–507.

Spinoza, Benedict de. *Tractatus Politicus. Opera.* Vol. 2. 3rd ed. The Hague: Martinus Nijhoff, 1914.

Steinsaltz, Adin. *Biblical Images: Men and Women of the Book.* Trans. Yehuda Hanegbi and Yehudit Keshet. New York: Basic, 1984.

———. *Teshuvah: A Guide for the Newly Observant Jew.* Trans. Michael Swirsky. New York: Free, 1987.

———. *The Thirteen Petalled Rose: A Discourse on the Essence of Jewish Existence and Belief.* Trans. Yehuda Hanegbi. New York: Basic, 1980.

Tarasov, B. "Analiz burzhuaznogo soznaniya v povesti L.N. Tolstogo *Smert' Ivana Il'icha.*" *Voprosy literatury* 3 (1982): 156–76.

Tillich, Paul. *Dynamics of Faith.* New York: Harper, 1957.

———. *The New Being.* New York: Scribner's, 1955.

Tolstoy, L.N. *Anna Karenina.* Moscow, 1947.

———. *Confession.* Trans. David Patterson. New York: Norton, 1983.

———. *Kazaki* (The Cossacks). *Sobranie sochinenii.* Vol. 3. Moscow, 1951.

———. *Kritika dogmaticheskogo bogosloviya* (Critique of Dogmatic Theology). *Polnoe sobranie sochinenii zapreshchennykh v Rossii.* Vol. 2. Christchurch, Eng.: Izdanie "Svobodnago Slova," 1903.

———. *Mysli o Boge* (Thoughts on God). 2nd ed. Berlin: Izdanie Hugo Steinits, 1901.

———. *O razume, vere i molitve* (On Reason, Faith, and Prayer). Christchurch, Eng.: Izdanie "Svobodnago Slova," 1901.

———. *Ponyatie o Boge* (The Concept of God). Geneva: M. Elpidine, 1897.

———. *Smert' Ivana Il'icha* (The Death of Ivan Il'ich). *Povesti i rasskazy.* Moscow, 1982. Pp. 176–230.

———. *Soedinenie, perevod i izsledovanie chetyrekh Evangelii* (Harmony, Translation, and Investigation of the Four Gospels). *Polnoe sobranie sochinenii zapreshchennykh v Rossii.* Vol. 3. Christchurch, Eng.: Izdanie "Svobodnago Slova," 1906.

———. *Tolstoy's Diaries.* Ed. and Trans. R.F. Christian. 2 Vols. London: Athlone, 1985.

———. *Tolstoy's Letters.* Ed. and Trans. R.F. Christian. 2 Vols. New York: Scribner's, 1978.

———. *Tsarstvo Bozhie vnutri vas* (The Kingdom of God Is within You). Geneva: M. Elpidine, 1895.

———. *Voskresenie* (Resurrection). *Sobranie sochinenii.* Vol. 13. Moscow, 1983.

Turgenev, Ivan. *Diary of a Superfluous Man.* Trans. David Patterson. New York: Norton, 1984.

———. *Rudin. Sochineniya.* Vol. 6. Moscow, 1963.

Unamuno, Miguel de. *Tragic Sense of Life.* Trans. J. E. Crawford Flitch. New York: Dover, 1954.

Vinge, Louise. *The Narcissus Theme.* Trans. Robert Dewsnap et al. Lund, Sweden: Gleerups, 1967.

Voloshinov, V.N. *Marksizm i filosofiya yazyka* (Marxism and the Philosophy of Language). 2nd ed. Leningrad, 1930.

Vorovsky, V.V. "Lishnie lyudi." *Literaturno-kriticheskie stat'i.* Moscow, 1956. Pp. 98–118.

Wasiolek, Edward. *Tolstoy's Major Fiction.* Chicago: U of Chicago, 1978.

Wiesel, Elie. *Against Silence: The Voice and Vision of Elie Wiesel.* Ed. Irving Abrahamson. 3 Vols. New York: Holocaust Library, 1985.

———. *From the Kingdom of Memory: Reminiscences.* New York: Summit, 1990.

———. *The Gates of the Forest.* Trans. Frances Frenaye. New York: Holt, 1966.

———. *Paroles d'étranger.* Paris: Éditions du Seuil, 1982.

———. *Somewhere a Master.* Trans. Marion Wiesel. New York: Summit, 1981.

———. *Souls on Fire.* Trans. Marion Wiesel. New York: Vintage, 1973.

———. *The Testament.* Trans. Marion Wiesel. New York: Summit, 1981.

———. *The Town beyond the Wall.* Trans. Stephen Becker. New York: Schocken, 1982.

Wiesel, Elie, and Phillipe de Saint-Cheron. *Evil and Exile.* Trans. Jon Rothschild. Notre Dame, Ind.: U of Notre Dame P, 1990.

Wilden, Anthony. "Lacan and the Discourse of the Other." *The Language of the Self,* by Jacques Lacan. Trans. Anthony Wilden. Baltimore: Johns Hopkins UP, 1968.

Williams, Michael V. "Tolstoy's 'The Death of Ivan Il'ich': After the Fall." *Studies in Short Fiction* 21 (1984): 229–34.

Index

www.ingramcontent.com/pod-product-compliance
Lightning Source LLC
Chambersburg PA
CBHW030529100426
42813CB00001B/192